KU-481-012

# THE WORLD'S NAVIES

**An illustrated review of the navies of the world**

# THE WORLD'S NAVIES

## An illustrated review of the navies of the world

CRESCENT BOOKS
New York

# A Salamander Book

©Salamander Books Ltd 1992

All rights reserved. No part of this book may be reproduced, stored in a retrieval system or transmitted in any form or by any means electronic, mechanical, recording or otherwise, without the prior permission of Salamander Books Ltd.

This 1992 edition published by Crescent Books, distributed by Outlet Book Company, Inc., a Random House Company, 225 Park Avenue South, New York, New York 10003.

Filmset by The Old Mill, London

Edited by Chris Westhorp

Designed by Studio Gossett and Paul Johnson

Colour Reproduction by Scantrans PTE Ltd, Singapore

Printed and bound in Spain

ISBN 0-517-05241-5

8 7 6 5 4 3 2 1

**Photo Credits**

The publishers would like to thank Virginia Ezell and all the embassies, defence attaches, and manufacturers who assisted with photographs and information.

**Jacket:** (front) US DoD, (back, clockwise from top left) US DoD, Audio Visuele Dienst KM, Westland Helicopters Ltd, US DoD, **Endpapers:** Audio Visuele Dienst KM, **Page 1:** Audio Visuele Dienst KM, **2/3:** US Navy, **4/5:** US DoD, **6/7:** US DoD, **8:** US DoD, **10/11:** Canadian Forces, **12:** (top) US Navy, (bottom) US DoD, **13:** US DoD, **14:** US DoD, **15:** (bottom, left) US Navy, (rest) US DoD, **16:** (top) US Navy, (bottom) US DoD, **17:** US DoD, **18:** (top, right) US Navy, (rest) US DoD, **19:** US DoD, **20/21:** US DoD, **22:** (top) Ingalls Shipbuilding Ltd, (bottom) US DoD, **23:** US DoD, **24/25:** US Navy, **26:** (top) USMC, (bottom, left) General Motors Canada, (bottom, right) US Navy, **27:** (top) US DoD, (bottom) US Navy, **28:** Argentinian MoD, **30:** Argentinian MoD, **31:** (top) Dassault-Breguet Aviation, (bottom) Bahaman Defence Office, **32/33:** Servico de Relacoes Publicas da Marinha, **34:** (top) US DoD, (centre) Chilean Embassy, (bottom) Bell Textron Helicopters, **35:** HDW, **36:** (top) US DoD, (bottom) Leo Van Ginderen, **37:** US DoD, **38:** Leo Van Ginderen, **39:** Jamaica Defence Force, **40:** (top) MBB, (centre) US DoD, (bottom) Mexican Embassy, **41:** Cessna, **42:** (top, left) HDW, (top right) US DoD, (bottom, left) Salamander Books Ltd, **43:** Souter Shipyard Ltd, **44:** US DoD, **45:** (top) Agusta, (bottom) HDW, **46:** HDW, **48:** High Commission for the People's Republic of Bangladesh, **49:** Leo Van Ginderen, **50:** Salamander Books Ltd, **51:** (left) US DoD, (right) RN Submarine Museum, **52:** (top) Salamander Books Ltd, (bottom) US DoD, **53:** (top) Salamander Books Ltd, (bottom) Royal Hong Kong Marine Police, **54:** Leo [illegible], **55:** Indian High [illegible], Leo Van Ginderen, **57:** [illegible] US DoD, **59:** Leo Van [illegible] High Commission for [illegible] US DoD, **62:** Leo Van [illegible] (top) Leo Van Ginderen, [illegible] Fijenoord BV, **64:** (top) [illegible] Leo Van Ginderen, **65:** [illegible] Navy, **66:** Bell Textron [illegible] **68:** (top) Australian Defence [illegible] Van Ginderen, **69:** [illegible] Submarine Museum, (rest) Leo Van Ginderen, **70:** (top) HQ Fiji Military Forces, (bottom) New Zealand MoD, **71:** Australian Shipbuilding Industries (WA) Ltd, **72:** ©British Crown Copyright/MoD, **74:** (top) Heeresbild und Funkinformationstelle, (rest) Leo Van Ginderen, **75:** Leo Van Ginderen, **76:** Royal Danish Embassy, **77:** Leo Van Ginderen, **78:** (left) ECPA, (right) US DoD, **79:** (top) Salamander Books Ltd, (centre) ECPA, (bottom, left and right) DCN/Jean Biaugeaud, **80:** (top) DCN/Jean Biaugeaud, (bottom) Leo Van Ginderen, **81:** (top) Dassault/Katsuhiko Tokunaga, (centre) Dassault-Breguet Aviation, (bottom) Leo Van Ginderen, **82:** (top right) US DoD, (rest) Leo Van Ginderen, **83:** Leo Van Ginderen, **84:** Koninklijke Maatschappij de Schelde, **85:** (bottom, left) Icelandic Coastguard, (rest) Patrick Walsh, **86/87:** Italian Embassy, **88:** Italian Embassy, **89:** (top) Italian Embassy, (bottom) Leo Van Ginderen, **90/91:** Audio Visuele Dienst KM, **92:** Norwegian MoD, **93:** Polish Embassy, **94:** (top and bottom) Leo Van Ginderen, (rest) Ministerio da Defensa Nacional Marinha, **95:** Ministerio da Defensa Nacional Marinha, **96:** Spanish Embassy, **97:** (top, right) McDonnell Douglas, (rest) Spanish Embassy, **98:** Kockums, **99:** (top, left) Saab/Scania, (top, left) Swedish MoD, (bottom) Swiss Armeefotodienst, **100/101:** Turkish Embassy, **102/103:** US DoD, **104:** (top) TASS, (rest) US DoD, **105:** (centre) Leo Van Ginderen, (rest) US DoD, **106:** (top) US DoD, (bottom) Leo Van Ginderen, **107:** (top) US DoD, (bottom) TASS, **108:** US DoD, **109:** (bottom) RN Submarine Museum, (rest) US DoD, **110/111:** Salamander Books Ltd, **112:** (top) RN Fleet Photographic, (rest) Right Stuff Productions, **113:** (top) RN Fleet Photographic, (bottom) US DoD, **114:** (top) Leo Van Ginderen, (centre) RN Fleet Photographic, (bottom) Rolls-Royce Limited, **115:** (left) US DoD, (right) VSEL, **116:** (top) RN Fleet Photographic, (bottom) British Aerospace, **117:** Westland Helicopters Ltd, **118:** Vosper Thornycroft (UK) Ltd, **120:** Leo Van Ginderen, **121:** (top) Vosper Thornycroft (UK) Ltd, (bottom, left) Leo Van Ginderen, (bottom, right) US Navy, **122:** (top) US DoD, (rest) Leo Van Ginderen, **123:** Nikolaus Sifferlinger, **124/125:** IDF Spokesman, **126:** (top) Vosper Thornycroft (UK) Ltd, (bottom) US DoD, **127:** Mike Louagie, [illegible]

(top) Sultanate of Oman MoD, (bottom) US DoD, **129:** (top) DCAN, (bottom) Mike Louagie, **130:** (top) Mike Louagie, (bottom) Leo Van Ginderen, **131:** Mike Louagie, **132:** Seychelles People's Defence Forces, **134:** Leo Van Ginderen, **135:** US Navy, **136:** Leo Van Ginderen, **137:** Vosper Thornycroft (UK) Ltd, **138:** (top) Blohm und Voss, (bottom) Vosper Thornycroft (UK) Ltd, **139:** (top) Westland Helicopters Ltd, (bottom) Seychelles People's Defence Forces, **140:** (top) Leo Van Ginderen, (bottom) Gilbert Gysells, **141:** Leo Van Ginderen.
**Jacket:** (front) Iowa class battleship, (back) USS *Saratoga*, Walrus class of RNethN, RN Leander class and Lynx HAS.3, German Navy's Bremen class.

**Endpapers:** Dutch Marines
**Page 1:** RNethN's Tromp class
**2/3:** USN SH-60B Seahawk from USS *Deyo*
**4/5:** USN Virginia class cruiser in the Gulf
**6/7:** Soviet Kiev class carrier (background) with a Sovremenny class destroyer
**8:** USS *America* in the Suez Canal
**28:** Argentine Etendards aboard *Veinticinco de Mayo*
**46:** Malaysian Kasturi class
**66:** Australian Bell.206 aboard an Adelaide class frigate
**72:** RN Lynx HAS.3
**118:** *Hettein*, Egyptian Ramadan class FAC
**132:** Seychelles' FPB42 *Andromanche*

# Contents

# INTRODUCTION

The early-1990s has seen a possible end to the Cold War, momentous changes in central and eastern Europe, and hopes of peace in many of the world's war-torn regions. The pace of these events has left the participating nations and their armed forces trying to come to terms with a new strategic situation. In the maritime sphere, it is becoming apparent that not only are there new navies emerging to challenge the balance of naval power — at least within their geographical areas — but new technology is appearing too which could well change the nature of naval warfare.

The techniques of land and air warfare have been tested repeatedly in small wars since 1945. For the navies, however, modern warfare has been tested only on a very small scale in the Falklands War of 1982. There have been no fleet engagements since World War II and therefore the way a group of ships would cope with a massive air and missile attack has not been tested in reality. There have only been skirmishes, and then usually one-sided ones, such as those between Indian and Pakistani units or HMS *Conqueror* and the *General Belgrano*. Computer modelling has had to suffice, but even the best such models cannot allow for all the factors arising when real people become involved in warfare.

A survey of the world's navies suggests that there are a number of levels of effectiveness, although not every navy fits neatly into any one category. At the top comes the "bluewater" navy which is capable of distant and sustained operations on a global scale against a strong enemy. This requires carrier-borne air power, a good ASW and anti-ship capability, sound defences against missile and air attack, the ability to replenish the force at sea, and prepositioned stocks to sustain naval and amphibious forces. The only navy in this league is the US Navy and even it has weaknesses, since it cannot be strong everywhere and has neglected some capabilities, such as mine counter-measures.

It did at one time appear that the Soviet Navy was seeking the same status; but today, despite a number of carriers, it is clear that they will not be able to afford more than they already have. Their carrier battle groups are unlikely to operate outside the range of land-based air power except against a weak opponent. Their navy, however, remains the world's second strongest and has considerable abilities, notably in its very large submarine fleet.

At what might be classed as the third-level are a series of fleets with distant-water capabilities for a limited period against weaker enemies. They have some carrier-borne air power, good ASW defences and adequate replenishment strength. Only France, India and the United Kingdom meet these requirements, with the two European powers having SSBNs to boost their armouries. China fails to attain such status because, despite its size, it lacks carrier air power, has poor replenishment capability and poor shipboard technology; so too does another Far Eastern power, Japan, which has the technological know-how but is constrained by a constitution and hostile public opinion.

China and Japan are in the fourth category of short-range navies that do not have or do not need distant-water power. They share this status with a range of smaller but technologically advanced fleets such as those of Italy, Spain and Turkey.

The fifth-level consists of coastal navies equipped with patrol boats and possibly several frigates or corvettes. These forces would be unlikely to involve themselves in a naval war but do use their ships to dominate economic zones and demonstrate their "strength" to neighbours.

Finally, there are the inshore patrol navies possessing boats armed with small cannon and machine-guns whose tasks preclude anything but occasional forays to the edge of the 200nm economic zone. Some use elderly vessels for this purpose, but many others have purchased small, fast and reasonably well armed craft for their navy to operate.

Standardizing ship designations has long been desirable. It is generally agreed that the very large carriers displacing over 50,000tons merit the title "super-carrier", while those between 20-50,000 are "medium carriers" and those under 20,000tons are classified "light-carriers".

The problems begin with other surface warships. It used to be an unwritten convention that ships were designated according to a descending order of size: battleships, cruisers, destroyers, frigates and corvettes. This is now somewhat confused. The US Navy's Ticonderoga class has an air-defence role, displaces 9,500tons and is listed as a cruiser, while the Arleigh Burke class has the same role, displaces 8,315tons and is designated a destroyer. Furthermore, the West recognizes the Soviet Udaloy class (8,100tons) as destroyers and the much smaller Kynda class (5,500tons) as cruisers. The British used to operate a system which differentiated between frigates, which were said to specialize in anti-submarine warfare, and destroyers, which were for air-defence or general-purpose escort; today, however, the Duke class (4,200tons) are of similar size to the Manchester class destroyers (4,775tons) but are seen as general-purpose frigates.

*The World's Navies* often outlines a class's armament, but this is only a rough guide to assessing its capability in comparison to others. Of almost equal importance today are the array of ships sensors which enable detection, tracking and attacking of a hostile ship; also, much depends on how ships are handled by their crews. Thus care must be taken when making relative power assessments between ships or fleets.

A convenient way of showing the relative size of a ship is by stating its displacement, and there are a variety of categories for each ship. The figures given here for surface ships are for full load, and for submarines the submerged displacement.

Other important factors have to be borne in mind when making comparisons. The first is a fleet's disposition and its ability to concentrate. The US Navy, for instance, has its fleet split on a global basis, but by using the Panama and Suez Canals they have relative freedom of movement between their various theatres. The USSR, however, has to make time consuming journeys through potentially hostile waters — which now include the Baltic Sea — and major choke-points in order to move between its theatres.

A further factor is maintenance which keeps ships in fighting shape and abreast of the latest technology. Short refits may take up to three months and be carried out every three years to maintain the hull, engines, living spaces and defective equipment — although submarines require much more frequent attention than this. Modernizations are, inevitably, much more time consuming, often involving major structural work in a shipyard and nearly always meaning equipment replacement which takes the ship out of service for some time. This can be accommodated when a navy has enough vessels of a type to enable a rotation system to operate, but it means trouble for a navy — such as Spain's or Italy's — which has only one of a major type, such as a carrier.

The future in naval warship design is not easily predicted. The collapse of the NATO Frigate (NFR-90) project appeared to show that a common hull is not as crucial as a common weapon system, and that the frigate escort would appear to be the principal surface combatant vessel in the future. The apparent end of the Warsaw Pact threat does not end the need to think about the future; indeed, the Gulf War shows the need for "out-of-area" capabilities and that the naval power of small countries will only increase as time goes by. Increasingly, as budgets tighten, this may mean modifying and modernizing existing vessels rather than building new designs.

Modern designs that are appearing often revolve around the multi-purpose, common hull, module concept, as put into practice by Germany's MEKO and Denmark's StanFlex designs. Smaller, better-trained crews on more operationally flexible vessels seems to be one view of the future; another is the increased power and importance of missiles and defences against them. With most of the earth covered in water navies, with us for hundreds of years, are definitely here to stay.

# NORTH AMERICA

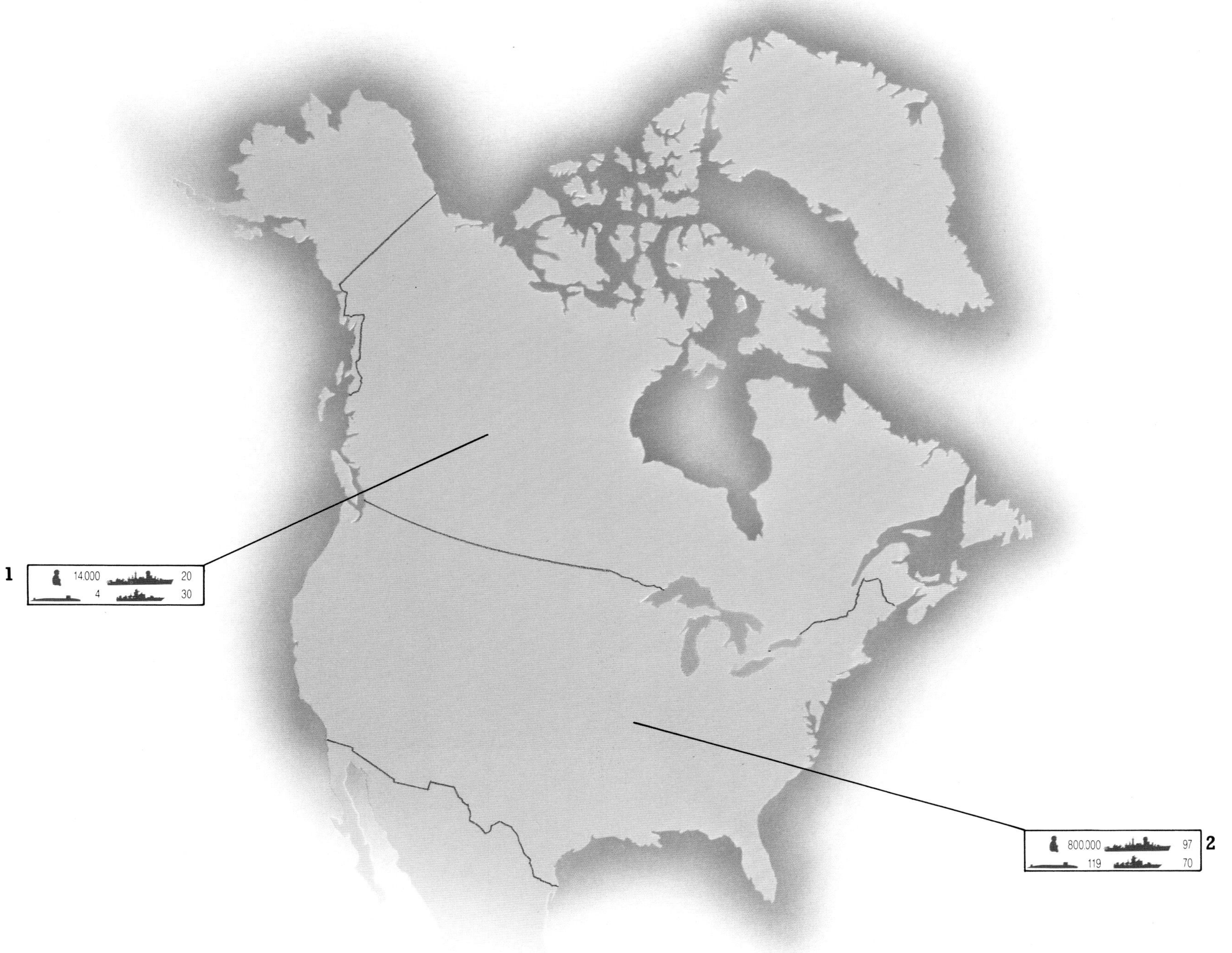
1
14,000
20
4
30
2
800,000
97
119
70

Men
FFs
Subs
FACs

## CANADA

**Above:** A Protecteur class replenishment ship leads a group of three Iroquois class destroyers and two St Laurent class frigates. Aboard HMCS *Iroquois* (nearest the camera) a crewman hitches the Beartrap hauldown system to a Sea King.

**Left:** One of the three Ojibwa class (British Oberon) submarines built for the RCN in the mid-1960s. They were joined in 1989 by a fourth ex-RN boat which is used as a dockside trainer. A project to replace them with SSNs was cancelled.

THE Royal Canadian Navy (RCN) was raised in 1910, but for many years was virtually a part of the Royal Navy, operating only British ships and using British tactics and procedures. It gradually asserted its own identity, fought most courageously in WWII, and in the 1960s became the Maritime Command of the unified Canadian Armed Forces.

During the Cold War the Maritime Command's primary responsibility was for the provision of ASW forces in the North Atlantic, although nationally it was also responsible for patrol forces on the Canadian west coast, as well as patrolling Canada's vast Arctic seas.

Canada acquired three diesel-electric submarines from Britain and during the 1980s it embarked on an expensive programme to replace these with up to 12 nuclear submarines. This then dragged on for years until it was cancelled in 1989; the repercussions of this apparent fiasco are still being felt within the Maritime Command.

Today's Maritime Command is some 17,000 men and women strong and is, inevitably, split between two oceans. In the Atlantic — the major commitment — are 12 destroyers and frigates in two squadrons, plus all three submarines and two underway replenishment ships; the Pacific force consists of eight destroyers and one underway replenishment ship, again in two squadrons. The Maritime Command is also responsible for patrolling the huge areas to the north and there is a strong feeling in Canada that these waters have been open for too long to unauthorized incursions by ships of other nations, particularly the USSR. However, there is also an underlying awareness that their United States allies may also make over-frequent and unannounced use of these waters too; indeed, it was just such considerations which led to the abortive SSN programme.

The largest ships in the fleet are four Iroquois class (5,100tons) destroyers based on the British Tribal class. They were constructed in Canada during the early 1970s and are currently undergoing a major modernization programme which will take a minimum of 18 months per ship. On completion of this refit each ship will be armed with the US Mk 41 Vertical Launch System (VLS) on the foredeck for 32 Standard SAMs, with an OTO Melara 3in (76mm) gun before and one deck-level below the bridge. A Mk 15 Vulcan Phalanx 0.8in (20mm) Closed-In Weapons System (CIWS) is mounted atop the large hangar which, in turn, accommodates two Sikorsky Sea King Anti-Submarine Warfare (ASW) helicopters. Shipboard ASW armament comprises six 12.7in (324mm) torpedo tubes. The gas-turbine engines have all been changed in the refit and the characteristic split engine uptakes have been replaced by one larger, but more conventional, single stack. When this completes, and HMCS *Algonquin* is already modernized, these four ships will be ready to serve on until 2004 at the very least.

Between 1951 and 1964 the RCN built a series of 20 frigates of unusual appearance which divided into four sub-types, each an improvement on its predecessor. The original design was based on that of the British Type 12 (Rothesay class), but modified to take account of the RCN's extensive experience of operations in the inhospitable waters of the North Atlantic. The first in the series was the St Laurent class (2,920tons), of which four remain in service after updates in the early-1980s. They have now reached the end of their economic lives and are being decommissioned. Equally old are the remaining four Restigouche class (2,900tons) ships, improved in the mid-1980s, and armed with two 3in (76mm) guns, an eight-cell ASROC launcher, a Mk 10 Limbo ASW mortar and six 12.7in (324mm) torpedo tubes, but lacking helicopter facilities. They serve on the Pacific coast and, despite their age, will be kept in service until 1994-96.

Next in the series, and only slighly younger, are the four Mackenzie class (2,890tons) frigates which make up the balance of the Pacific force. They are virtually repeats of the Restigouche class, but with better accommodation and improved cold-weather protection. Last in this interesting series came the two ships of the Annapolis class (3,063tons) which had the same hull but radically different armament, the ability to accommodate a large helicopter and a redesigned superstructure. There is a single twin-turret 3in (76mm) gun on the foredeck and six 12.7in (324mm) torpedo tubes beneath the flight-deck. The large hangar and very long flight-deck enable a Sea King ASW helicopter to be operated. These two ships are due to be kept in service until 1994-96.

Some of these 20 frigates were stricken in the 1970s, but the majority have served on. The problem of their replacement has been exacerbated by political indecision and the financial problems stemming from the great costs of the abortive nuclear submarine programme. Those are now, however, in the past and the Halifax class (4,750tons) are now under construction, although even this programme has been subject to delays and indecision. Numerous decisions over armament and accommodation standards have been made and then reversed, and the final numbers have yet to be fully agreed, although 12 is likely. The first units HMCS *Halifax* and HMCS *Vancouver*, are now in service. Armament comprises eight Harpoon SSMs, a VLS for NATO Sea Sparrow, a single Bofors 2.25in (57mm) gun, a Mk 15 0.8in (20mm) CIWS and six 12.7in (324mm) ASW torpedo tubes. One Sea King ASW helicopter will be operated from each.

A force of 1950s-built coastal minesweepers was transferred to the naval reserve for use as general-purpose training ships in 1972, leaving a major gap in the mine countermeasures capability. This was recognized but it took many years before a new class of minesweeper was ordered. These 900ton Maritime Coastal Defence Vessels will enter service from mid-1993 onwards. The patrol boat fleet is almost as light with a dozen or so 1950's boats serving which are now very aged indeed: one Fort class, six Bay class and five Porte class.

Maritime Command is also responsible for the operation of all ship-based helicopters, as well as those land-based aircraft which operate in direct support of the fleet. There is just one helicopter type, the Sikorsky Sea King which operates under the Canadian designation of CH-124A. Most are used in the ASW role, but some are employed in the transport and logistics roles aboard the three replenishment ships. The main types of fixed-wing aircraft in use are the Lockheed CP-140 Aurora, with 18 purchased in 1980-81 for use in the ASW role, and Lockheed CP-140A Arcturus (being delivered 1992-93) for Arctic patrol. All use the same airframe as the US Navy's P-3 Orion, but the CP-140 has a slightly different sensor fit, while the CP-140A has the ASW equipment removed.

**Above:** *Quest* (AGOR-172) is a civilian-crewed, oceanographic research ship with a specially reinforced hull for operations in ice-fields. Canada's government is worried about patrolling its vast Arctic waters.

**EQUIPMENT**

**Submarines:**
Ojibwa (British Oberon) class
**Destroyers:**
Iroquois class
**Frigates:**
St Laurent class
Modified Restigouche class
Mackenzie class
Annapolis class
Halifax class
**Patrol Boats:**
Bay class
Fort class
Porte class
**Naval Aircraft:**
Lockheed CP-140 Aurora
Lockheed CP-140A Arcturus
Sikorsky CH-124A Sea King

**Below:** HMCS *Qu'Appelle*, one of four Mackenzie class frigates which joined the fleet in 1962/63. Stationed on the Pacific coast, all four are due to be replaced shortly.

**Below:** HMCS *Halifax*, nameship of the new, sophisticated class of frigates. Note the 2.25in (57mm) DP gun on the foredeck, Sea Sparrow vertical launchers amidships and the large flight-deck aft.

## UNITED STATES

THE United States Navy is the mightiest maritime force the world has ever known. The many hundreds of ships, over 600,000 personnel, some 1,500 naval aircraft and the 200,000 men and women in the Marine Corps (USMC) collectively form one of the most potent means by which the United States can exercise its post-Cold War power. Indeed, as was shown in the 1990/91 Gulf War, the navy and marines have an inherent flexibility and a speed of response not available to any other service.

During WWII the US Navy overtook the Royal Navy as the most powerful in the world and since that time the margin of strength between those two forces has increased inexorably. In the 1970s, however, the Soviet Navy began to grow stronger and is now, without a doubt, the second most powerful navy in the world. Great as has been the expansion of the Soviet Navy, however, it never reached — nor even approached — parity of numbers, let alone of quality, with the US Navy during the Cold War, and it is now highly unlikely that it will ever do so.

The basis of US naval power is its sheer size combined with a breadth of capability which ranges from aircraft carriers to frigates and from battleships to replenishment oilers. This strength does not only lie in surface warships but also in submarines and naval aviation. Then, of course, the US Marine Corps adds a capability for amphibious warfare which is without parallel.

**Above:** Grumman F-14 Tomcat fighters stand on ready alert, prepared for any Iraqi attack, aboard USS *John F. Kennedy* in the Red Sea during Operation Desert Storm.

All of this is also *sustainable* power, which requires an enormous (and very expensive) infrasructure of forward bases, support ships and prepositioned stocks.

The most important naval mission is to establish control of the sea; a three-dimensional task involving superiority on the surface, in the skies above it and in the oceanic depths beneath it. Such sea control is not, however, an end in itself, but is a vital prerequisite to projecting forces ashore into disputed areas and to sending reinforcements and supplies to bolster any threatened allies.

Not instruments of sea control in themselves are the two most important weapons systems available to the US Navy: submarine-launched ballistic missiles (SLBM) and ship/submarine-launched cruise missiles (SLCM). Both these systems give the navy a strategic capability against targets deep inland which it has never had before. For 30 years the SSBN/SLBM combination has given the United States a guaranteed survivable, second-strike force which has been a vital component of the deterrent strategy. However, these weapons are only usable with nuclear warheads and it is the precision of the conventional warhead on the recently-operational SLCMs that has introduced a new dimension to warfare. In the 1990/91 Gulf War, submerged submarines in the Red Sea and surface ships in the Persian Gulf itself were able to launch conventionally-armed cruise missiles against targets deep inside Iraq, including Baghdad, with some success.

For the 40 years of the Cold War the identity of the major potential enemy — the USSR — was clear; today, however, the Cold War is over and the US Navy has now to consider other possibilities. One factor having to be treated with increased seriousness is the expansion of Third World submarine fleets. One or two modern submarines can pose a very serious threat to a task force and thus the US Navy is currently re-examining its capability in this area to ensure that it can continue to operate in any ocean, despite such developments.

**Below:** Naval might unmatched by any other power: a US Navy aircraft carrier sails across the Pacific Ocean for the Persian Gulf flanked by no less than 17 escorts.

**Above:** During NATO Exercise Distant Drum in the Mediterranean in 1982, a US carrier is being followed by USS *California* (CGN-36) and an Italian Navy Andrea Doria class cruiser.

The United States armed forces come under a complicated network of unified and integrated commands, so that virtually all field commanders are responsible to two superiors: one in the unified (joint-service) chain and the other in the single-service (ie, navy, army, air force, or marine) chain.

The professional head of the navy and the officer responsible for supervising the execution of its duties is the Chief of Naval Operations (CNO), a four-star admiral whose headquarters are in the Pentagon. Reporting to him are numerous departmental heads, located across the United States, who are responsible for the infrastructure of the navy. The actual fighting elements of the USN are divided into three major geographical commands, each under its own commander-in-chief.

The United States Marine Corps (USMC) is a very large force in its own right and, accordingly, has the status of one of the four US services. The USMC, however, occupies an unusual position in the defence hierarchy since, despite its size and commitments, it remains totally within the Navy Department, although its commandant has the same rank and status as the CNO.

The navy has two main organizational commands, Pacific and Atlantic, which contain a number of fleets and from which units are seconded to compose various task forces. Between them these fleets utilize hundreds of ships dispersed all around the world. In addition there is a large reserve; an auxiliary fleet, composed principally of support tenders; a coastguard which would come under navy control in wartime and is very strong with some 200 ships, aircraft and nearly 40,000 regular personnel; and a large force known as Military Sealift Command which operates surveillance ships and a host of other specialist vessels.

There are two further units, the Middle East Force and the Indian Ocean Task Force, which operate in areas nominally under the control of fleets belonging to the Pacific or Atlantic Fleet Commands. These units contain ships from fleets within both commands.

The Commander-in-Chief Pacific Fleet has his headquarters at Pearl Harbor in Hawaii and is responsible for an area stretching in length from the west coast of the USA half-way across the world to the Indian Ocean and in breadth from the Antarctic to the Arctic. This vast command is sub-divided between two fleets: Third Fleet (HQ Pearl Harbor) which covers the eastern and central Pacific, the Aleutian islands and the Bering Sea; and Seventh Fleet (HQ Yokosuka, Japan) which covers the western Pacific, Japan, the Philippines, Australasia and the Indian Ocean.

A typical Third Fleet composition might be five carrier battle groups (CVBG), a battleship surface action group (SAG), four underway replenishment groups (URGs) and an amphibious group. Whereas Seventh Fleet might dispose of two carrier battle groups, a battleship surface action group, an underway replenishment group and an amphibious group with a Marine Expeditionary Unit (MEU) embarked.

Pacific Fleet also includes part of the strategic nuclear deterrent force, with eight SSBNs operating out of their base at Bangor in Washington State. At least one attack submarine (SSN) task force would also operate under Pacific Fleet Command. Other, large Pacific Fleet bases include San Diego and Long Beach, in California, USA; Subic Bay in the Philippines; and the vital base of Diego Garcia in the Indian Ocean.

The Atlantic Fleet is based at Norfolk, Virginia, and is responsible for the Atlantic from the Arctic to the Antarctic, and from the US east coast to the western shores of Africa and Europe. It has bases at Groton, Charleston, Kings Bay and Mayport along the eastern seaboard; Guantanamo Bay in Cuba; Reykjavik in Iceland and Holy Loch in Scotland (which is shortly to close).

Atlantic Fleet is composed of two fleets, but one of these, Sixth Fleet, exists as an almost separate entity forming the basis of US Naval Forces Europe. The other is Second Fleet based at Norfolk which has a huge area of the Atlantic Ocean to cover. At the northern end is the Arctic Ocean and the Norwegian Sea, which would have been the Soviet Navy's route out into the Atlantic in the event of a general war. Also in the northern area are the main operating areas of the Soviet Navy's strategic missile submarines. The older Soviet SSBNs with shorter range missiles still patrol off the United States' Atlantic seaboard, while the newer boats with the longer range missiles patrol in the Barents Sea and under the Arctic ice-cap — the so-called SSBN "bastions". If a war was to break out in Europe Second Fleet's responsibilities would include containing the enemy fleet, delivering the US Marine Corps Marine Expeditionary Force (MEF) to Norway, taking American reinforcements across the Atlantic to Europe, and keeping the sea lines of communication open. In this, the Second Fleet would, of course, be assisted by the navies of its NATO allies, but the primary responsibility would rest in Norfolk, Virginia.

Sixth Fleet's responsibilities extend from the Pillars of Hercules at the entrance to the Mediterranean to the troubled Middle East and the Black Sea. The Commander Sixth Fleet does, of course, have the additional help of his NATO allies. A typical peacetime Sixth Fleet deployment would be one carrier battle group, one underway replenishment group, an amphibious group and a submarine task force.

As with the other arms of service the US Navy makes a significant contribution to the Special Operations Forces and there are two naval special warfare groups. Within these groups are seven Sea-Air-Land (SEAL) teams, two SEAL delivery teams, three Special Boat units and four Special Warfare units. The navy has also converted two surplus SSBNs (USS *Houston and USS Marshall*) into underwater transports for these forces. Some 1,400 reservists form further navy special forces units, trained for SEAL and other special warfare duties, and they also provide two special duties helicopter squadrons. This capability, above and beyond that offered by the USMC, has received much investment from the navy and has been used frequently in recent years.

Another often overlooked element of the US Navy is the Naval Reserve Force (NRF). According to recent figures, ships in the NRF include 27 frigates, 19 ocean-going minesweeprs, two LCTs and three salvage ships, but more are being transferred to the NRF as the navy's active manpower figures are cut. The NRF also augments regular cadres in other units such as special boat

**Below:** Like the other US armed forces, the US Navy has a major commitment to special operations forces, contributing elements such as these SEALs (SEa Air Land).

units, undersea warfare units and mobile construction battalions (the "Sea-Bees").

The central feature of the US Navy's strategic capability — short of nuclear war — is its aircraft carriers, which give it a global power unparalleled in history. These huge carriers, which operate either singly or in pairs accompanied by escorts in a Carrier Battle Group (CVBG), can reach almost any spot on the oceans within days and their air power can bring US influence to bear in a very immediate fashion.

There are currently 15 aircraft carriers in-service, with three more Nimitz class due to join the fleet during the 1990s. With at least two ships in refit at any one time, there are normally 13 carriers in operational status. Of the 15 carriers, nine are powered by conventional means, the remainder are nuclear-powered.

One of the great survivors is the USS *Midway* dating from WWII. Displacing 67,500 tons and modernized extensively over the years, she will decommission shortly and her role is likely to be taken by USS *Independence*. (Another WWII veteran still serving, although only as a trainer, is USS *Lexington* modernized in the 1950s from an Essex class design.)

The oldest carriers now in front-line service are the four ships of the Forrestal class: USS *Forrestal* (CV-59), USS *Saratoga* (CV-60), USS *Ranger* (CV-61) and USS *Independence* (CV-62).

These carriers have a full load displacement (which varies slightly between ships) of 79,250-80,643tons. The complement comprises 6,180 officers and ratings, of whom 2,790 are responsible for operating the ship and 3,390 man the air wing.

As with all US carriers, the armament carried for the defence of the ship is very light. It consists of two or three Mk 29 launchers for Sea Sparrow SAM and three 0.8in (20mm) Mk 15 Vulcan Phalanx CIWS, which makes an interesting comparison with the heavy armament of Soviet carriers. The difference, of course, lies in the tactical concept whereby the US carriers rely on their aircraft and the surface escort ships for their protection.

Despite their many innovations and years of distinguished front-line service, the Forrestal class suffer a number of limitations, perhaps the most important of which is that launching and landing aircraft simultaneously is difficult. USS *Forrestal* and *Saratoga* serve with the Atlantic Fleet, USS *Ranger* and USS *Independence* with the Pacific Fleet. They will continue until early in the next century.

The Kitty Hawk class consists of four carriers. The first two, USS *Kitty Hawk* (CV-63) and USS *Constellation* (CV-64), displace 81,000tons and were ordered as improved versions of the Forrestals, but incorporating some signficant advances. The flight-deck area was increased and the layout of the lifts altered in order to improve aircraft handling, the port-side lift was moved aft so that it could continue to operate while aircraft were landing-on, and the centre lift was moved forward of the island so that two lifts could be used to support the forward catapults. All lifts had an amended shape to enable larger aircraft to be carried.

The third ship, USS *America* (CV-66), was not laid down until four years after USS *Constellation* and as a result she was able to incorporate further improvements. These included a newer sonar system and the first integrated Combat Information Center (CIC) and airborne ASW control centre. Her displacement is marginally more at 81,773tons.

The fourth is a modified Kitty Hawk design. This carrier, USS *John F. Kennedy* (CV-67), has dimensions and displacement

**Above:** On Gulf duty in 1990, a Grumman F-14 Tomcat flies over its parent ship USS *John F. Kennedy*, the most recent of the US Navy's conventionally powered carriers.

(80,940tons) virtually identical to those of USS *America*, and she is normally grouped as a member of the Kitty Hawk class. Visually she can be distinguished by a canted stack, intended to carry corrosive exhaust gasses clear of the flight-deck, and by the shape of the forward part of the angled deck.

The armament of all four carriers is identical with the Forrestal class. USS *John F. Kennedy* and USS *America* normally serve in the Atlantic Fleet, with frequent forays into the Mediterranean, and the other two in the Pacific Fleet. All four will serve well into the next century.

The US Navy's first nuclear-powered surface warship was the cruiser USS *Long Beach* (CGN-9). The first nuclear-propelled carrier, USS *Enterprise* (CGN-65) (92,200tons), was laid down shortly afterwards, launched just 31 months later and commissioned 14 months after that — a remarkably short time in which to construct and fit-out such a large and revolutionary ship. The overall cost, however, was over 450 million US Dollars, an astronomical sum at that time; it was estimated to be twice that of an oil-fuelled aircraft carrier of the same displacement and capability, and actually led to the cancellation of five other ships. Nevertheless, her virtually limitless range and increased aviation fuel capacity make her relatively cheap to run; indeed, she can sustain no less than 12 days of intensive air operations before she needs to replenish from a tanker and even has bunkers for fuel-oil to replenish conventional ships.

The USS *Enterprise* is similar in layout and general size to the Kitty Hawk class, but her island structure is significantly different since there is no need for exhaust stacks. Prior to her first refit she had four large planar arrays on a box structure for her main radar, but this was replaced by the more usual rotating arrays in 1979. Her self-

**Left:** A Nimitz class aircraft carrier with the greater part of its 86 strong air wing lined up on the flight-deck — more airpower than in most national air forces around the world.

**Above:** The weight of aircraft, air ordnance, aviation spares and fuel carried by USS *Theodore Roosevelt* is nearly 15,000tons — equivalent to three complete destroyers.

**Above:** An F-14 roars down the catapult of a US Navy carrier. Naval flying is inherently dangerous and by September 1988 no less than 101 F-14s alone had been lost in accidents.

defence armament, originally non-existent, is similar to the previous classes and she serves in the Atlantic with a life expectancy to the year 2011.

When the time came to replace the Midway class carriers there was no doubt that the USS *Enterprise*'s success showed that nuclear-propulsion was the most effective answer, despite the capital costs. Indeed, there had been many technological advances since the construction of the USS *Enterprise* and the eight A2W reactors used in the earlier ship could now be replaced by just two A4W reactors which gave the same power. Congress therefore agreed to a new class of CVNs — the Nimitz class.

The dimensions and layout of the flight-deck on the Nimitz class are virtually identical with those on USS *John F. Kennedy* but the reduction in the number of reactors permitted major improvements in the internal arrangements below hangar-deck level. The propulsion machinery is divided between two engine-rooms with some of the magazines in the space between them, and there is a 20 per cent increase in the volume of aviation fuel, munitions and stores that can be carried. Armament is similar and the five ships in the class range in size from 72,915tons for USS *Nimitz* (CVN-68) to 102,000tons for USS *Abraham Lincoln* (CVN-72).

There are two distinct types within the class, the later builds being improved designs. The first three consist of USS *Nimitz* herself, USS *Dwight D. Eisenhower* (CVN-69) and *Carl Vinson* (CVN-70); all were commissioned between 1975 and 1982. The combat power concentrated in these hulls is enormous and this requires a large amount of equipment and manpower. There are 86 aircraft and 6,286 men — a major concentration of resources and a very attractive target in a major conflict! The USS *Nimitz* is scheduled to last until at least 2020, the other two ships even longer.

There are currently two carriers of an improved Nimitz class design in service, USS *Theodore Roosevelt* (CVN-71) and USS *Abraham Lincoln* (CVN-72). These are the most powerful warships every built and there are a further two under construction, with one more planned. The design has low-pressure catapults and better protection, including Kevlar armour over vital spaces. The total aviation payload carried amounts to some 14,909tons, while the armament is the same as USS *Carl Vinson*.

Carriers exist to deploy air power and the US Navy is the only one in the world to operate all the types of aircraft necessary for a fully balanced carrier air wing. For the fixed-wing crews every flight is operational, involving the hazards of catapult take-off and an arrestor landing on a heaving flight-deck. In 1991 there were a total of 5,036 aircraft operational, of which 3,659 belonged to the US Navy and 1,377 to the US Marine Corps. (USMC aircraft are described separately below.) In 1991 the US Navy operated 13 active attack air wings, with another two carrier air wings in the NRF. There are four types of carrier air wing currently in use (Kennedy, Conventional, Transitional and Roosevelt) which incorporate nine types of aircraft.

Of these four wing types, the Conventional is the normal arrangement. The Kennedy Wing exists only on USS *Ranger* and consists of 24 F-14s, 24 A-6Es, four KA-6Ds, four EA-6Bs, four E-2Cs, 10 S-3A/Bs and six ASW helicopters. The idea is for the navy to move to the Roosevelt Wing arrangement from the Conventional one via the Traditional Wing. The Conventional Wing has 10 more aircraft, making a total of 86. It has mostly the same make-up, the difference is due to the fact it has added 24 F/A-18s and retained only 10 of 24 A-6Es. The Transitional Wing has 80 aircraft, with 20 each of the F-14 and F/A-18, 16 of the A-6E, five each of the EA-6B and E-2C,plus eight S-3A/Bs and six ASW helicopters. The 86 strong Roosevelt Wing exists only on USS *Roosevelt* at the moment but should operate on all carriers within a decade; its composition is as per the Traditional with the addition of four A-6Es and two S-3A/Bs.

The Grumman F-14 Tomcat is still the finest naval fighter after 19 years in service. The only carrier-borne aircraft with variable-geometry ("swing-wings"), it has a maximum speed of Mach 2.34 and has proved itself in operations against Libya and Iraq. In 1991 nearly 500 F-14s were in service, of which some 253 were with 26 active navy squadrons, 58 with four NRF squadrons and 125 were in storage.

The McDonnell-Douglas F/A-18 Hornet multi-purpose fighter was as controversial in its early years as most navy equipment, but today it is accepted as a highly-effective addition to the fleet. There are more than 500 in service in 19 active and three reserve fighter squadrons.

**Below:** An F-14 Tomcat, afterburners roaring, wings fully extended and flaps lowered for maximum lift, climbs away from the flight-deck of the carrier, USS *Kittyhawk*.

**Below:** USAF KC-135 refuels an F-14 Tomcat, while a second awaits its turn. The USAF uses a flying-boom which requires a special hose adapter for naval and USMC aircraft.

The Grumman A-6E Intruder is in service in large numbers (over 300) and its navy use will increase with the transfer of some 40 aircraft from the Marine Corps to balance the new wing organization. A very effective attack aircraft, the A-6E can carry 18,001lb (8,165kg) of stores, including HE and nuclear bombs, rockets, Harpoon, HARM, Maverick, Sidewinder and Walleye.

A derivative of the basic Intruder design, the Grumman EA-6B Prowler, specializes in ECM and there are over 100 in service. As with other ECM aircraft it more than proved its worth in the Gulf War, enabling large-scale Coalition raids to fly over Iraqi and Kuwaiti territory with virtual impunity. A tanker version, KA-6D, is in service too, with over 60 examples flying.

A further Grumman aircraft, the E-2C Hawkeye, is unique because it is the only carrier-borne airborne early warning (AEW) aircraft in service. With a five-man crew and a very sophisticated radar it is able to track over 600 air and surface targets in a 250nm radius and to control 25 simultaneous intercepts. Over 100 are in service. A variant of the E-2, the C-2A Greyhound, has a larger fuselage and is used for carrier on-board delivery (COD) of personnel and various stores.

Long-range ASW for carrier air wings is the responsibility of the S-3A/B Viking, a twin-jet, four man aircraft with a nine hour endurance. Despite its small size the Viking carries a full range of ASW sensors and weapons. Closer range ASW is provided by 36 squadrons of helicopters: 10 with Sikorsky SH-60B Seahawks, 11 with Kaman SH-2F/G Seasprites and 15 with Sikorsky SH-3G/H Sea Kings (to be replaced by Sikorsky SH-60B/F Seahawks).

The shore-based air fleet is equally varied. The Boeing E-6A Hermes took over from the Lockheed EC-130G Hercules in the early 1990s in the TACAMO role. TACAMO (Take Charge And Move Out) is one of several means of communicating with submerged SSBNs in war and involves an aircraft with long antenna broadcasting at Very Low Frequencies (VLF).

The most important of all the shore-based aircraft is the Lockheed P-3C Orion, with several hundred ASW versions currently in service. The P-3C has an excellent ASW capability and can also carry four Harpoon anti-ship missiles.

The NRF makes a significant contribution to the naval air component. There are two carrier air wings and numerous land-based units comprising 36 squadrons, 217 combat aircraft and 58 armed helicopters in all.

In 1943 the first of the Iowa class battleships was commissioned, followed by three more over the next 16 months. They were armed with nine 16in (406mm)/50 guns in three triple turrets and 20 5in (127mm)/38 DP guns in twin turrets; with a maximum speed of 33kts they were the fastest battleships ever built. They were also exceptionally well armoured, with a 12in (305mm) main belt. All four of these ships fought in the Pacific campaign and were then placed in reserve. They were reactivated during the Korean War (1950-53) and later decommissioned again.

The appearance of the Soviet navy's Kirov class battlecruisers in the 1980s led to a decision to reactivate once more. The aim, in the words of Caspar Weinberger, was to provide "a valuable supplement to the carrier force in performing presence and strike missions, while substantially increasing our ability to provide naval gunfire support for power projection and amphibious assault missions". As a result, USS *New Jersey* rejoined the fleet in late 1982 and was soon in action conducting fire missions in support of US Marines in Lebanon. USS *Iowa* followed in 1984, USS *Missouri* in 1986 and USS *Wisconsin* in 1988. Reactivation involved the modernization of all electronics; the renovation of accommodation and domestic utilities; a conversion to take US Navy distillate fuel; the reconfiguration of the after deck to accommodate four helicopters; and the removal of all excess equipment.

The main armament still comprises nine 16in (406mm) guns, but four of the original 5in (127mm) turrets have been removed to make way for two quadruple Tomahawk SLCM launchers; two quadruple Harpoon SSM launchers have been fitted, one either side of the after stack; and four 0.8in (20mm) Mk15 Vulcan Phalanx CIWS have also been installed.

The reactivation of these units has been a triumph and they operate in autonomous "surface action groups" (SAG) in company with a number of escorts and replenishment vessels. In April 1989 an accidental explosion in a turret aboard USS *Iowa* resulted in major loss of life and contributed to the decision to take her and USS *New Jersey* out of service. The remaining two, USS *Missouri* and USS *Wisconsin*, served successfully in the Gulf War, launching Tomahawks against targets deep in Iraq. With the war won and the Cold War thawing the future of these two remaining battleships must be in doubt.

There are 46 guided-missile cruisers in service, with eight more currently building/renovating and two in reserve. These ships are usually deployed as escorts in aircraft carrier battle groups or surface action groups, but could also be employed on independent missions.

The oldest are nine ships of the Leahy class (8,200tons) which were commissioned between 1962 and 1964. They were designed as air-defence escorts for carrier battle groups and have been refitted and modernized during their service. Their armament now includes eight Harpoon SSM launchers and two Mk 10 launchers for Standard

**Above:** Sikorsky MH-53E Sea Dragon towing an ALQ-166 mine counter-measures sled. The sled rides on hydrofoils and can be towed at speeds of up to 30kts. Note the enlarged sponsons which hold extra fuel of 4,478lbs (2,031kg).

**Left:** A maintenance engineer works on a complex rotor-head during the Gulf War.

SM-2ER SAMs. There is a helicopter landing facility on the quarterdeck but no hangar. Five serve in the Atlantic Fleet and four in the Pacific Fleet.

The nine Belknap class (8,065-8,600tons) were laid down two years after the Leahy class and were designed as general-purpose escorts for carrier battle groups. Their armament has been changed several times during refits and is now the same as the Leahy class except for one less Mk 10 launcher and the addition of a single 5in (127mm) gun. A flight-deck and hangar are installed for a single Kaman SH-2F Seasprite helicopter. The USS *Belknap* (CG-26) is the permanent flagship for the Sixth Fleet. Four of these ships serve with the Atlantic Fleet, the balance with the Pacific Fleet.

The current class of oil-fuelled cruiser is the 19-strong Ticonderoga class (9,500tons) which has been the subject of more ill-informed criticism than any other recent warship type. The ships and their electronics systems have, however, survived a number of rigorous tests and several of the class have served in the Persian Gulf over a period of three years with great success.

The heart of these ships is the Aegis Combat System which was developed in response to the threat of saturation attacks by Soviet missiles and is one of the most important naval technological breakthroughs of recent years. It requires sensors with virtually instantaneous reactions and an almost unlimited tracking capability and has led to a radar system with four fixed planar arrays mounted on the ship's superstructure. This remarkable system can handle, simultaneously, four surface-to-air missiles in their terminal phase as well as 18 others in flight.

The principal air-defence system is the Standard SM-2MR missile. In the first five ships this is launched from two twin-arm Mk 26 launchers, while in the remaining ships a modified version of the same missile is fired from vertical launchers; both systems can also launch ASROC ASW missiles. The first five ships have eight Harpoon launchers in a very exposed position on the stern, while the remaining ships can fire Tomahawk missiles from their VLS. (More recently, the SLAM missile has been test fired from the Harpoon launchers.) All ships have two 5in (127mm) guns in single turrets (although these cannot be used in an air-defence role as no suitable radar is fitted), together with six 12.7in (324mm) ASW torpedo tubes and two 0.8in (20mm) Vulcan Phalanx CIWS. All are fitted for helicopter operations, with the first two ships operating two SH-2F Seasprites and the remainding two SH-60B Seahawks. All ships are outfitted as flagships.

The first surface warship in the world to have nuclear-propulsion was the cruiser USS *Long Beach* (CGN-9) which was completed in 1961 and looks set to serve with the Pacific Fleet well into the next century. She is very large for a cruiser, displacing 17,525tons, and her several rebuilds mean that her armament and sensors now differ very considerably from those she had when she was commissioned. There are eight Tomahawk strategic cruise missile

**Above:** USS *Wisconsin* (BB-64) is one of two Iowa class battleships which remain in service. Here, looking spruce and powerful, she undergoes her first sea trial on 30 August 1988, prior to re-commissioning on 22 October of that year.

**Right:** USS *Wisconsin*, showing her huge helicopter flight-deck, but there is no hangar.

**Above:** USS *Horne* (CG-30), a Belknap class cruiser. Constructed in the 1960s the whole class is being modernized and has many years of service ahead.

**Above:** USS *Ticonderoga* (CG-47), name ship of her class. They are the most capable anti-aircraft ships in any navy, using the Aegis Mk 7 system for target handling.

**Right:** A Sikorsky SH-60B Seahawk LAMPS-III ASW helicopter flies past USS *Crommelin* (FFG-37), one of the 51 ubiquitous Oliver Hazard Perry class.

launchers and a further eight launchers for the shorter range Harpoon SSMs. There are two launchers, of slightly different types, for Standard SM-2ER SAMs and two 0.8in (20mm) Mk 15 CIWS. As built, USS *Long Beach* had an all-missile armament, but two 5in (127mm) guns of a rather antiquated pattern were added in 1962 and these are still retained today.

A visual characteristic of the ship is her huge box-like bridge which was designed to accommodate four "billboard" planar radar arrays. Those arrays have long since been removed, but the unique and identifiable bridge remains.

The USS *Long Beach* was followed by the USS *Bainbridge* (CGN-25) and USS *Truxtun* (CGN-35), two rather similar ships with virtually identical dimensions and displacement but actually belonging to separate classes.USS *Bainbridge* (9,100tons) is, to all intents and purposes, a nuclear-powered version of the Leahy class.

The USS *Truxtun* (9,127tons) was constructed as a nuclear-powered version of the Belknap class at the insistence of the US Congress. She also has eight Harpoons, but only one missile launcher which handles both Standard SAMs and ASROC. She has a 5in (127mm) gun on the foredeck, full facilities for an SH-2F Seasprite helicopter and is instantly recognizable by her unusual twin girder masts.

The two California class (10,530tons) cruisers were designed as escorts for the Nimitz class carriers. They are larger and have more sophisticated weapons and electronics systems than the previous two CGNs. USS *California* (CGN-36) and USS *South Carolina* (CGN-37) joined the fleet in 1974 and 1975 respectively and were to have been joined by a third but she was cancelled. Their weapons fit is very similar to that of USS *Bainbridge*, but with Mk 13 rather than Mk 10 launchers and two less ASW torpedo tubes. There are no helicopter facilities but the "gun lobby" was able to ensure that they were given guns in addition to their missiles; this meant they were, in fact, the first ships in the fleet to receive the (then) brand-new lightweight 5in (127mm) Dual Purpose gun.

The third California class cruiser was cancelled because a much improved design was in prospect — the Virginia class. These four ships, launched between 1976 and 1980, have an armament generally similar to that of the previous cruisers with eight Tomahawks, eight Harpoons, two Mk 26 launchers for Standard/ASROC missiles, two 5in (127mm) guns, two 0.8in (20mm) Mk 15 CIWS and six ASW torpedo tubes. Their internal hangar has been taken over by the Tomahawk launchers.

The oldest destroyers in service date from the late-1950s to early-1960s. There are five of the Coontz class which were built for the air-defence mission. They are the only destroyers in the US Navy to be armed with Standard SM-2ER SAMs. By the end of 1992 it is likely that all will have been withdrawn from the active fleet. During the same period, 23 Charles F. Adams class were constructed for the US Navy. For many years this class was the backbone of the US Navy's

**Below:** USS *Long Beach* (CGN-9) was the first nuclear-powered US surface warship and dates from the late 1950s. The fixed, "billboard" antennas have been removed since this particular picture was taken.

**Above:** USS *Mississippi* (CGN-40) is a Virginia class nuclear-powered cruiser. Her primary mission is to help provide the air-defence escort for a nuclear-powered carrier.

**Above:** No less than 31 Spruance class destroyers were built between 1972 and 1983. This ship is USS *John Young* (DD-973), eleventh of the class to be completed.

Anti-Air-Warfare (AAW) destroyer force, providing, with the cruisers, air-defence for carrier battle groups. The first 13 ships have the twin-arm Mk 11 launcher, the remainder the Mk 13 single-arm launcher; in both cases these are used to launch either Standard SM-1MR SAMs or Harpoon SSMs. An ASROC launcher is placed in an unusual position for the US Navy: between the two stacks. Two 5in (127mm) guns and six 12.7in (324mm) ASW torpedo tubes complete their armament. These ships have been very popular in the US Navy but just eight vessels remain in service. Of these eight, three possess the Mk 11 launcher.

In one of the largest post-war surface ship programmes ever, 31 Spruance class destroyers were built between 1972 and 1983. These are large, gas-turbine ships displacing 8,040tons and would be designated cruisers by most navies. They have large magazines below the decks and their electronics are very sophisticated.

Although the last was only commissioned in 1983 an extensive programme of modernization throughout the class was begun in 1986. This will enhance their ASW capabilities and ensure they serve well into the next century. Among other improvements is the fitting of the Mk 41 VLS system (for launching both Tomahawk and Standard SM-2MR) to all but seven ships; this will eventually incorporate ASROC too. All ships have a Mk 29 launcher for Sea Sparrow SAMs, two 5in (127mm) guns, two Mk 15 0.8in (20mm) CIWS, six 12.7in (324mm) tubes for Mk 46 ASW torpedoes, and a large hangar and flight-deck for Sikorsky SH-60B Seahawk helicopter. The seven unmodifed vessels have eight Tomahawk SSMs in two quadruple box launchers and an ASROC launcher. Finally, the ships are very stable, the hull having been designed to render stabilisers unnecessary.

The US Navy was fortunate to receive the four ships of the Kidd class (9,574tons). They were originally ordered by the Shah of Iran as cruisers to form the central core of his fleet, which would have been the most powerful maritime force in the Middle East. Optimized for the air-defence role, they were ordered in 1974 and cancelled by the revolutionary government in 1979. The US Congress then authorized their completion at the "bargain" price of 510 million US Dollars per ship and they were commissioned in 1981-82. They are armed with two Mk 26 launchers which handle both Standard SM-2MR and ASROC missiles, and also have eight Harpoon SSM launchers between the forward stack and the mainmast. There are two 5in (127mm) DP guns, plus a hangar and flight-deck for two Kaman SH-2F Seasprite ASW helicopters. The ships were given very powerful air-filtration and air-conditioning systems for their anticipated service with the Iranian Navy and this has made them very suitable for Indian Ocean and Persian Gulf deployment with the US Navy's task groups.

The last of the Spruance class destroyers left the maker's yard in 1983 at a time when design work had already started on the next destroyers: the Arleigh Burke class (8,315tons) is intended to replace the Coontz and Charles F. Adams classes. USS *Arleigh Burke* was commissioned in 1991 and the class will be the US Navy's standard general-purpose destroyer for the next two decades, with the navy wanting at least 32 ships and hopefully 50. Made of steel with Kevlar armour protection, the ship has a thorough NBC Warfare system installed, stealth technology features, and sprinkler systems throughout.

She is armed with two Mk 41 VLS systems launching Standard SM-2MR SAMs, ASROC and Tomahawk missiles. There are eight Harpoon launchers, a single 5in (127mm) gun, two 0.8in (20mm) CIWS and six ASW torpedo tubes, to give these ships an excellent all-round capability. Learning lessons from the USS *Stark* incident and the Falklands War, the ships have a steel (rather than aluminium) superstructure, considerable armoured protection and a very sophisticated EW capability. A controversial issue is that the earlier ships do not have a helicopter hangar, merely a flight-deck. This omission will only be made good from the 33rd ship onwards, extending the design by 40ft (12.2m) to accommodate the changes. The Aegis radar system is installed, giving these excellent ships an outstanding air-defence capability. The Arleigh Burke class have a rather greater beam than has been the case with recent US warships, giving a length:beam ratio of 7.89 compared to 9.62 for the Kidd class, suggesting that the controversy about modern ships being too long and too narrow may have some validity.

The US Navy now operates 97 frigates, 46 of the Knox class (4,260tons) and 51 of the newer Oliver Hazard Perry class (3,210-4,100tons). The Knox class were constructed between 1965 and 1972 and have proved to be very useful escort ships. They are armed with a Mk 16 ASROC launcher with an automatic loading magazine immediately behind it under the bridge. This magazine also stows eight Harpoon missiles, which are fired from the port pair of the eight-cell launcher. A 5in (127mm) DP gun is mounted forward of the ASROC/Harpoon launcher, while the Mk 15 0.8in (20mm) CIWS is well aft on the quarterdeck. The four 12.7in (324mm) ASW torpedo tubes are in fixed mountings at the forward end of the hangar which houses a Kaman SH-2F Seasprite helicopter.

**Above:** USS *Gray* (FF-1054), one of 46 Knox class frigates. Visible on the foredeck are a single 5in (127mm) Mk42 DP gun and an eight-cell Mk 116 ASROC launcher.

**Below:** The powerful looking USS *Kidd* (DDG-993), one of four built for the Imperial Iranian Navy's hot climates, finds herself in Arctic waters under the US flag!

The Oliver Hazard Perry class originated in the 1960's Patrol Frigate Programme, and were to be the cheaper component in a fleet-wide high/low technology mix, providing large numbers of escorts with reduced capabilities and thus (it was hoped) reduced price. Maximum use was made of prefabrication and major efforts were made to keep costs down. During their service these ships have become more integrated into the fleet and many improvements have been made to keep them up-to-date.

The overall result has been very successful; the class has proved flexible and capable of absorbing much new equipment. The original design allowed for a 3,600tons full load displacement with a 39tons growth margin, but the later ships have a full load displacement of 4,100tons. The armament is air-defence oriented, with a Mk 13 launcher for Standard SM-1MR SAMs forward and an OTO Melara 3in (76mm) DP gun mounted just forward of the stack. A Mk 15 CIWS is mounted on top of the hangar. The major anti-ship system is the Harpoon SSM, which is also launched from the Mk 13 launcher. ASROC is not fitted, but there are two adjacent hangars and a flight-deck aft for two Sikorsky SH-60B Seahawk helicopters. In order to take full advantage of the SH-60B extra length was required and this was achieved by increasing the rake of the stern, thus gaining an extra 8ft (2.4m) in overall length.

Of the ships built, 31 are now with the NRF. The active navy ships are split between the Atlantic and Pacific Fleets, and a number have seen active service in the Persian Gulf, both during the Iran-Iraq War and in the more recent conflict. During the earlier deployment USS *Stark* (FFG-31) was hit by two Iraqi Exocets in May 1987. Over 30 crewmen died but the ship survived and after refitting she returned to the fleet in September 1988. USS *Samuel B. Roberts* (FFG-58) was then hit by a mine in April 1988; she too has since been repaired.

With its enormous surface capabilities, the US Navy has only a limited requirement for patrol boats. Six Pegasus class missile-armed, patrol hydrofoils (PHM) were acquired in the early 1980s. These 241ton boats are armed with eight Harpoon SSMs and an OTO Melara 3in (76mm) gun; they are capable of a top speed of some 50kts. The design is sound, but they have proved of limited value in naval terms.

A number of more conventional patrol boats are in service, used mainly by SEALS, for NRF seamanship training and for inshore work in the Panama Canal Zone. The SEALs are also considering the Israeli Shaldag design of fast patrol craft. Of those currently used, approximately 60 date from the 1960s and 1970s and the remainder are more modern acquistions; these include 24 Seafox class boats armed with light machine-guns and used for swimmer delivery, six more heavily armed Stinger class and 18 Mk III and MK IV patrol boats which carry one 1.6in (40mm) Bofors and one 0.8in (20mm) Oerlikon. These have been active in the Persian Gulf. In addition to these, eight Modified Ramadan class boats are currently on order.

**Above:** USS *John L. Hall* (FFG-32) in the Suez Canal on 8 August 1990. Designed as cheap escorts the Oliver Hazard Perry class is now used as general-purpose destroyers.

**Below:** The Pegasus class patrol hydrofoils are very effective and fast, but are so much more expensive than conventional patrol boats that the US Navy cannot afford them.

**Above:** USS *Wasp* (LHD-1), the first of a new class of assault ship. She is designed to operate AV-8Bs, but no ski-jump is fitted because of the need for deck parking space.

**Left:** The flight-deck of USS *Nassau* (LHA-4) is crowded with USMC aircraft, including two UH-1N Hueys, AH-1 Sea Cobra gunships and four AV-8B Harrier IIs.

The US Navy's experience of amphibious warfare is second to none and she has maintained a large and highly-efficient capability since WWII. The aim is to deliver the US Marine Corps across the beaches in any part of the world. A great variety of ships are operated to achieve this task and the largest are the assault helicopter carriers. Experiments with the use of helicopters for "vertical assault" started in the late 1940s, and in 1955 the US Navy converted an escort carrier into a helicopter assault ship. The success of the concept led to the design of a class of purpose-built Amphibious Assault Ship (LPH), the first of which, USS *Iwo Jima* (LPH-2), entered service in 1961. The seven ships were not required to fulfil full fleet performance and so a merchant-ship hull design was selected with a single propeller. They have a large, un-angled flight-deck with two folding deck-edge lifts which give access to a hangar which can accommodate up to 19 Boeing CH-46 Sea Knight or 11 Sikorsky CH-53 Sea Stallion helicopters. Some 2,000 marines can be carried in living-spaces fore and aft of the hangar, and there is a 300-bed hospital.

In addition to their amphibious warfare role these ships can also act as carriers for Sikorsky's RH-53 Stallion and MH-53E Sea Dragon minesweeping helicopters, as well as McDonnell-Douglas AV-8B Harriers. They have proved their worth repeatedly over the past 30 years and have taken part in numerous operations in the Far East, Middle East and Central America. Their major limitations have been the lack of a docking-well (which confines them to helicopters for ship-to-shore movements) and the use of only a single propeller (which limits speed and manoeuvrability). They are due to be replaced by the Wasp class in the 1990s.

By the 1960s the US Navy and Marine Corps found themselves with two types of amphibious warfare ship. One was the specialized LPH of the Iwo Jima class and the other was the Amphibious Transport Dock ships (LPDs) of the Austin and Raleigh classes (see below). It was, therefore, decided to combine these two into one general purpose type of amphibious assault ship (LHA), the Tarawa class. Inevitably, these were much larger with a full-load displacement of 39,300tons.

These five highly-capable ships incorporate both a hangar and a docking-well and can accommodate up to 12 Boeing CH-46 Sea Knights, six Sikorsky CH-53D Sea Stallions, four AH-1J Sea Cobra gunships and four UH-1N Iroquois Twin Huey utility helicopters. There are nine landing spots for the helicopters on the flight-deck and McDonnell-Douglas AV-8A/Bs are also regularly embarked. The docking-well accommodates four LCUs and four more smaller landing-craft are carried on the flight-deck. The armament is two 5in (127mm) Mk 45 DP guns, two 0.8in (20mm) Mk 15 CIWS and six 0.8in (20mm) Mk67 AA guns. The five are normally split between the Pacific Fleet and the Atlantic Fleet. They are almost invariably roled as flagships and there are extensive facilities for the Commander Amphibious Task Group (CATG) and the Landing Force Commander (LFC) and their respective staffs.

The Wasp class (40,532tons) multi-purpose assault ships (LHD) are by a wide margin the largest and most powerful amphibious warfare ships in the world. They serve as either an amphibious warfare ship, carrying some 1,800 troops and 30 helicopters, or as an ASW carrier, with a combat load of 20 McDonnell-Douglas AV-8Bs and six Sikorsky SH-60B Seahawks. One design criterion was maximum deck-space, which led to the decision not to install a ski-jump on the strengthened flight-deck which is constructed of HY100 steel. As with many other recent US warships, Kevlar armour is used to protect vital spaces. The stern gate in the Tarawa class lifts to open, but in the Wasp class it lowers as in earlier LPDs and LSDs. Among the facilities provided by these ships are three hospitals with a total capacity of 600 beds. The armament comprises two Mk 29 launchers for Sea Sparrow and RAM missiles, and three 0.8in (20mm) Mk15 CIWS.

The remainder of the large amphibious warfare shipping is made up of four types: Amphibious Cargo Ships (LKA), Tank Landing Ships (LST), Dock Landing Ships (LSD) and Amphibious Transport Docks (LPD). There are two ships of a fifth type, a class known as the Amphibious Command Ship (LCC). The USS *Blue Ridge* and USS *Mount Whitney* displace over 18,000tons and provide integrated command and control facilities for the complex organization amphibious operations entail. The vessels were commissioned in the early 1970s and carry protective armament of Sea Sparrow SAMs, four 3in (76mm) guns and two 0.8in (20mm) Mk 15 CIWS.

Of the LKAs, there are five Charleston class (18,600tons) which can carry 363 troops, plus vehicles, ammunition and general cargo. They do not have a dock nor do they carry landing craft of their own, but they do have a large helicopter flight-deck and cranes for offloading to a jetty or landing ships lying alongside.

**Above:** The ramp of the Newport class enables them to do without the clam-shell doors previously fitted to LSTs, so that they can now match the speed of other amphibians.

All 20 LSTs now in service are of the Newport class (8,450tons). It was an essential part of the operational requirement for these ships that they should be capable of keeping up with the 20kts speed of other amphibious shipping. This meant that the traditional LST bow doors could not be used and they have been replaced by the unique fixed derricks which are used to lower and raise a 112ft (34m) ramp. There is a stern door for loading and unloading, and a large helicopter flight-deck. Troop capacity is 400; a tank deck can accommodate 29 M60 tanks or 23 of the USMC's LVTP-7 armoured, amphibious personnel carriers; and the vehicle deck can take up to 29 2.5ton trucks. Of the 20, three are with the NRF.

LSDs are built around a large docking-well which accommodates small landing craft for the transit to the assault area; the stern door is then opened, the dock flooded and the loaded craft emerge and head for the beach. The oldest LSDs in service are five ships of the Anchorage class (14,000tons). The docking-well is 430ft (131m) long, 50ft (15.2m) wide and can accommodate three Landing-Craft Utility (LCU) or nine of the smaller Landing Craft Mechanized-8 (LCM-8). There is a large flight-deck but no hangar for helicopters. Over 350 troops can be accommodated and there is a large vehicle deck.

The Whidbey Island class (15,745tons) is a development of the Anchorage class with an enlarged docking-well to enable it to operate four gas-turbine-powered, air-cushioned, landing-craft designated LCAC by the US Navy. The very large landing-deck can take two Sikorsky CH-53 Sea Stallion helicopters simultaneously, but does not have any hangar or maintenance facilities. Seven Whidbey Island class are in service, one more will follow in 1992, and a variant is under construction designated the Harpers Ferry class.

LPDs seek to combine the attributes of LKAs and LSDs, and the two ships of the Raleigh class (14,865tons) were built in the early 1960s. These ships were designed to combine in one hull the tasks which previously required three different type of ship: attack transport for troops, attack cargo ships for freight, and LSDs for tanks and vehicles. As is inevitable in such a combination, the resulting ship does nothing quite as well as the three individual types; although the personnel capacity is good with a full load of 1,139 troops.

Inevitably the design grew and the 11 Austin class (17,595tons) are essentially lengthened Raleigh class ships. No more LPDs have been built since these and attention has turned to the much more capable and flexible Tarawa and Wasp class.

The amphibious warfare fleet is rounded out by a large number — over 400 — of smaller landing craft. There is also an increasing number of Landing Craft, Air Cushioned (LCAC), with 90 on order.

**Above:** Austin class USS *Shreveport* (LPD-12). The flight-deck can accommodate six large helicopters but the small, telescopic hangar can take only one utility type.

One of the major lessons for the US Navy from its involvement in the Persian Gulf has been that its mine counter-measures capability has been seriously eroded over the past 20 years. There are 23 elderly boats in service, and seven out of 14 of a new class of sweeper have so far been completed. Meanwhile, construction of a new class of coastal minehunter has just started. These are very small numbers, indeed, for such a large navy, not to mention a large country with miles of coastline.

The 14 minesweepers of the Aggressive class (780tons) have been in service since the early 1950s. They are the balance of 93 built, the remainder having been transferred abroad. These, plus two very similar Acme class (924tons), are all in the NRF. The new Avenger class (1,312tons) minehunters are being completed at a slow rate in a programme beset with delays and cost overruns. They have wooden hulls and glass reinforced plastic (GRP) superstructure and can sweep deep-moored mines at depths of up to 590ft (180m) as well as sweep acoustic and magnetic mines.

Construction has started of the Osprey class (895tons), a US-produced version of the Italian Lerici class coastal minehunter. These have a GRP hull and are capable of both minehunting and sweeping. The first boat is due to join the fleet in 1992.

**Left:** A Sikorsky MH-53E Sea Dragon flies over an Avenger class minesweeper/hunter. The Gulf War revealed a gap in the US Navy's mine warfare capabilities.

**Right:** An Oropesa sweep is deployed on an Avenger class. The flagged buoy shows the end of the cable and several "kites" will be attached to the wire to maintain the depth.

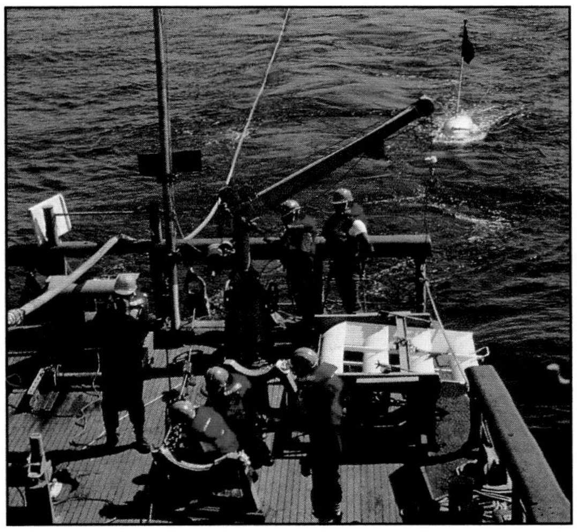

**Above:** Under the "hump" of this Ohio class SSBN are 24 Trident missiles, each with eight 100KT MIRV warheads. This is the most powerful warload ever carried by a ship.

**Below:** A CH-46 helicopter hovers over the deck of USS *George Washington Carver* (SSBN-656), a Benjamin Franklin class SSBN on patrol in the Mediterranean in 1977.

The submarine fleet of the US Navy is so important that it needs to be considered on its own. Following a good performance in WWII the US Navy rapidly established itself as the leading submarine navy, with the largest, most modern and innovative fleet. They pioneered nuclear power for submarines, the submarine-launched ballistic missile (SLBM) and the strategic use of submarines with SLBMs and SLCMs. Today's fleet is large and highly-efficient; it is composed of some 34 nuclear-powered ballistic missile submarines, (SSBNs) 86 nuclear-powered attack submarines (SSNs) and one special forces transport. (The US Navy ceased production of disel-electric submarines in 1959.)

There are four classes of SSBN. The oldest are the Lafayette class (8,250tons), which spawned the Benjamin Franklin and James Madison classes. The difference between these three types lies not only in the weapons they are fitted to carry but also in their machinery. Only two Lafayette class operate and these are armed with Poseidon C-3 missiles; there are eight James Madison class, only two of which are not fitted to take the Trident 1 C-4; and there are 12 Benjamin Franklin class, half of them with the Poseidon C-3 and half with the Trident 1 C-4. The Poseidon-armed ships are being decommissioned in increasing numbers as the Ohio class join the fleet, in order to comply with the SALT-II limits. All these ships belong to the Atlantic Fleet and all those equipped with Trident 1 missiles are home ported in King's Bay, Georgia.

The 12 Ohio class ships are much larger, displacing 18,750tons, and are equipped with 24 Trident missiles. The first operational Trident 1 C-4 missile was fired on 17 January 1982 and USS *Ohio* (SSBN-726) commenced her first operational cruise later that year on 1 October.

The first eight Ohios are based at Bangor in Washington State to carry out their deterrent patrols in the Pacific Ocean, while the remainder will be based at King's Bay, Georgia, from where they deploy into the Atlantic Ocean. The first eight ships were fitted with Trident 1 C-4, but are being refitted to take Trident 2 D-5 at a rate of one every two years. The ninth and subsequent boats are fitted to take the longer-ranged Trident 2 D-5 missile during construction. Their operational cycle is a 70-day patrol, followed by a 25-day refit.

The four Permit class (4,465tons) submarines are the oldest US Navy SSNs in service. They are the survivors of a class of 14 built between 1959 and 1967. Nine have been stricken since 1988, with the remainder to follow shortly.

There are 35 Sturgeon class (4,960tons) boats built between 1963 and 1975 as the successors to the Permit class. They are armed with four 21in (533mm) torpedo tubes, for which they carry a mix of Mk 48 torpedoes, Harpoon and Tomahawk. These tubes are mounted amidships firing outwards at an angle, since the entire bow is taken up by a large sonar array. Each of these remaining boats (there were 37 built) is expected to serve for 30 years, giving a life expectancy through to 2005. A modified Sturgeon class, the USS *Narwhal* (SSN-671), is also in service. It is fitted with the General Electric S5G natural-circulation reactor as opposed to the Westinghouse S5W pressurized water-cooled reactor.

The Los Angeles class (6,927tons) is one of the largest, with 45 in 1991, and also one of the most expensive defence programmes in any country since WWII. It is the finest ASW platform in any navy. The first-of-class, USS *Los Angeles* (SSN-688), was launched in 1976 and the 62nd and final boat will be launched 20 years later in 1996. These are fast and well-equipped submarines designed for long-range ASW missions deep in enemy waters, and one of their principal targets can be assumed to be enemy SSBNs.

Not surprisingly, the design has altered in many respects over the time it has been in production. The armament consists of four 21in (533mm) tubes mounted amidships, for which 22 reloads are carried. Originally, only Mk 48 torpedoes were carried, but Harpoon began to be carried in 1978 and then SUBROC was introduced in 1983 in some boats, only to be totally removed again by 1989. A major modification enabled eight tube-launched Tomahawk missiles to be carried in the first 31 boats, but it was later realized that this was at the expense of other missiles within the 26 total and the later boats have vertical launch tubes for the Tomahawks to be mounted under the casing instead. USS *Scranton* (SSN-756) and later boats can launch mines from their tubes, and ADCAP torpedoes have been test fired successfully.

For many years the US Navy has mounted submarines' forward hydroplanes on the sail. However, the disadvantages of this arrangement have at last been appreciated: in particular there is the fact that it makes both surfacing through ice and control when running at periscope depth much more difficult. As a result Los Angeles class boats from USS *Topeka* (SSN-754) onwards have had their forward 'planes moved forward to the bow position where they are also fully retractable. Another boat, USS *Memphis* (SSN-691), is being converted to a trials configuration and will have two 21in (533mm) torpedo tubes replaced by one new 30in (762mm) tube. This considerable increase in size is to enable bigger torpedoes with larger diameter warheads to be launched against tough targets such as the Soviet Oscars and Typhoons.

One former Ethan Allen class SSBN, USS *John Marshall*, has been converted for use as a transport submarine for special forces. She carries up to 67 SEAL swimmers, and two Dry Deck Shelters (DDS) can be mounted on their upper casing, each of which holds one Swimmer Delivery Vehicle (SDV). On arrival in the operational area swimmers enter the DDS from the submarine below, activate the SDV and then open the DDS outer door to depart from the still submerged submarine.

Two specially-built research submarines are in service. USS *Dolphin* (AGSS-555) is operated as a naval auxiliary and is, in fact, positively the last diesel-electric submarine in the US Navy inventory. The other submarine is simply designated *NR-1* and is a small (700tons) nuclear-powered boat with a maximum operating depth of 2,625ft (800m). Two air-transportable Deep Sea Rescue Vehicles (DSRV) can rescue up to 24 men at a time from suitably fitted submarines at depths of up to 4,920ft (4,500m).

The first of the successor class to the Los Angeles is already under construction: the USS *Seawolf* (SSN-21). Somewhat larger than its predecessor (displacing 9,150tons) three of these boats are currently planned, the small number being due to their very high costs — estimated to be 2 billion US Dollars each. They will be armed with eight of the new, larger 30in (762mm) torpedo tubes and will fire Sea Lance, Tomahawk and Harpoon missiles, as well as Mk 48 ADCAP torpedoes. They are designed with better sensors and to be quieter, faster, and more efficient than the Los Angeles class. As with the later Los Angeles boats the forward hydroplanes will be low on the bows, while a British-style pump-jet will replace the more traditional seven-bladed propeller.

It is also intended to develop a smaller (6,000ton) and cheaper attack submarine, currently designated "Project Centurion". This will be needed to maintain the current goal of 80 attack submarines from 1997 onwards, since the final boats of the Los Angeles class and the subsequent Seawolf class will not keep pace with the retirement of older boats. Whether or not the US Congress will agree remains to be seen.

**Above:** The 35,000hp nuclear propulsion system drives the USS *City of Corpus Christi* (SSN-705), one of 62 impressive Los Angeles class being built.

**Below:** Three USN Sturgeon class SSNs at the geographic North Pole in May 1987: (left to right) USS *Ray* (SSN-653), USS *Hawkbill* (SSN-666) and USS *Archerfish* (SSN-678).

**Left:** The US Marine Corps is the largest marine force in the world. Its flexibility, strength and high standard of training make it a key element in US foreign policy.

The USMC is over 200-years old and has just under 200,000 men and women in its ranks. Its range of equipment gives it greater power than most other countries' armies. Its principal missions are: to maintain an amphibious capability to be used in conjunction with fleet operations; to seize and defend advanced naval bases; and to conduct land operations essential to a naval campaign. Among other things it is also tasked with carrying out any other operations defined by the president — a "catch-all" authority which covers such commitments as the peace-keeping force in the Lebanon.

The USMC traditionally pairs a Marine division and a Marine air wing, plus the necessary logistic units, into an expeditionary force with a total strength of some 58,000 men and women. There are three regular expeditionary forces, two operating in the Pacific area under Fleet Marine Force Pacific (FMF PAC) and one in the Atlantic under Fleet Marine Force Atlantic (FMF LANT). There is a fourth which serves as a reserve cadre.

The basic 'building block' in the USMC organization is the infantry battalion. This is combined with air elements, tanks, artillery, helicopters and a support unit to form a Marine Expeditionary Unit (MEU) with a strength of some 2,500 personnel. Next in size is a Marine Expeditionary Brigade (MEB): this consists of one Regimental Landing Team (RLT) (usually two, sometimes three, battalions strong and each of 822 men), a mixed air group of 110 fixed-wing attack aircraft and 120 helicopters, plus tanks, artillery and elements from the Fleet Marine Force, for a grand total of some 15,500 personnel.

In a typical divisional organization the infantry would be formed into three regiments, each of three infantry battalions, each of three rifle companies, a weapons company and an HQ company. Each division also has a light armoured assault battalion (LAAB) equipped with the LAV-25 wheeled, amphibious APCs. Fire-support is provided by an artillery regiment of three artillery battalions, which are armed with a mixture of wheeled and tracked howitzers. Other divisional units include a tank battalion (currently equipped with the M60A1, but about to receive the M1A1), an armoured amphibian battalion (equipped with LVTP-7), a combat engineer battalion, a reconnaissance battalion and an HQ unit.

The USMC aviation element is an integral part of their "air-ground task force" concept, in which each combined-arms taskforce is tailored to meet the needs of its specific mission. Thus, while there are three active wings (plus one reserve air wing), their organization can be altered to meet the requirements of a particular mission. A USMC wing consists, typically, of between 286 and 315 aircraft in 18-21 squadrons, comprising three fighter/attack groups, a helicopter group, an air control group and a support group, plus an EW squadron, a reconnaissance squadron, an airborne refuelling squadron and an HQ squadron.

The standard attack fighter of the USMC is the McDonnell-Douglas F/A-18 Hornet, of which there are 13 active squadrons with 12 aircraft each, one 12-aircraft squadron in the Marine Corps Reserve (MCR) and 36 in training units. The USMC was one of the earliest supporters of the British V/STOL Harrier and has now fully re-equipped with the McDonnell-Douglas AV-8B Harrier II version, of which there are some 150 fighter/ground attack versions in service with eight active squadrons, together with 32 two-seater TAV-8A/Bs for training.

Four squadrons (40 aircraft) of the Grumman A-6E Intruder attack aircraft serve in the attack and interdiction role and there are two squadrons of the Grumman EA-6 Prowler specialized ECM version in service (one squadron of four EA-6As with the reserves and one squadron of 18 EA-6B with the active element).

There is a large force of some 600 helicopters. The active units comprise six squadrons of attack helicopters, 15 medium transport squadrons and nine heavy squadrons. The reserve has two attack squadrons, one utility squadron, two medium transport squadrons and one heavy squadron. There are also numerous aircraft in the forward air controller (FAC), transport, airborne refuelling and training roles.

It is essential that any appreciation of the USMC must include an understanding of the size of its units, which are far larger than those in other services with similar titles.

**Below:** After an intensely fought competition the Swiss-designed, wheeled LAV-25 was selected as the USMC's standard infantry armoured personnel carrier.

**Below:** An LTPV-7 amphibious vehicle enters the water over the ramp of *2nd Lieutenant John P. Bobo*, a 40,000ton Ro-Ro ship of Military Sealift Command's Fleet.

**Above:** An AV-8B Harrier II of USMC squadron VMR 513 over the Gulf where this V/STOL aircraft performed with some distinction in combat for the first time.

**Below:** Boeing Vertol CH-46 Sea Knights operating from the deck of the assault ship USS *Tripoli* (LPH-10). The USMC operates 15 squadrons, each with 12 of these aircraft.

Thus, for example, a Marine air wing is much larger than those of the USAF and USN with maximums of 72, 86 and 315 aircraft respectively. Similarly, the Marine division is a very large organization which is considerably stronger in manpower terms than a conventional army division.

The United States Marine Corps is a very large, powerful and flexible fighting force whose effectiveness has been demonstrated repeatedly during the twentieth century. Its combination of amphibious capability, an integral air force, sophisticated infrastructure and a homogenous organization give it a military potential without parallel in the world.

### EQUIPMENT

**Aircraft Carriers:**
Forrestal class
Kitty Hawk class
Enterprise class
Nimitz class
**Battleships:**
Iowa class
**Cruisers:**
Long Beach class
Bainbridge class
Truxtun class
California class
Virginia class
Leahy class
Belknap class
Ticonderoga class
**Submarines:**
**SSBN:**
Lafayette class
Benjamin Franklin class
James Madison class
Ohio class
**SSN:**
Permit class
Sturgeon class
Narwhal class
Los Angeles class
Ethan Allen class
**Destroyers:**
Coontz class
Charles F Adams class
Spruance class
Kidd class
Arleigh Burke class
**Frigates:**
Knox class
Oliver Hazard Perry class
**Patrol Boats:**
Pegasus class
Stinger class
Seafox class
**Amphibious Warfare:**
Blue Ridge class
Iwo Jima class
Tarawa class
Wasp class
Raleigh class
Austin class
Anchorage class
Whisbey Island class
Newport class
Charleston class
**Mine Warfare:**
Aggressive class
Avenger class
**Naval Aircraft:**
Bell AH-1J, T & W Sea Cobra
Bell UH-1E & UH-1N Iroquois
Boeing E-6A Hermes
Boeing-Vertol CH-46A, D & E Sea Knight
Kaman SH-2F & G Seasprite
Grumman F-14A, A-Plus & D Tomcat
Grumman A-6E & KA-6D Intruder
Grumman EA-6A/B Prowler
Grumman E-2C Hawkeye
Grumman C-2A Greyhound
Lockheed S-3A & B Viking
Lockheed P-3C Orion
Lockheed C-130, LC-130, DC-130, EC-130G & KC-130T Hercules
McDonnell Douglas F/A-18A, B, C & D Hornet
McDonnell Douglas AV-8B, TAV-8A & Harrier II
Rockwell OV-10D Bronco
Sikorsky SH-3D/G/H Sea King
Sikorsky SH-60B Seahawk
Sikorsky SH-60F Oceanhawk
Sikorsky CH-53 D Sea Stallion
Sikorsky CH-53E Super Stallion
Sikorsky RH-53D Stallion
Sikorsky MH-53E Sea Dragon
Vought A-7E Corsair II
**Marines:**
Three active divisions
One reserve division
Three Forces Service Support Units (three active, one reserve)
Two Security Force battalions

# CENTRAL AND SOUTH AMERICA

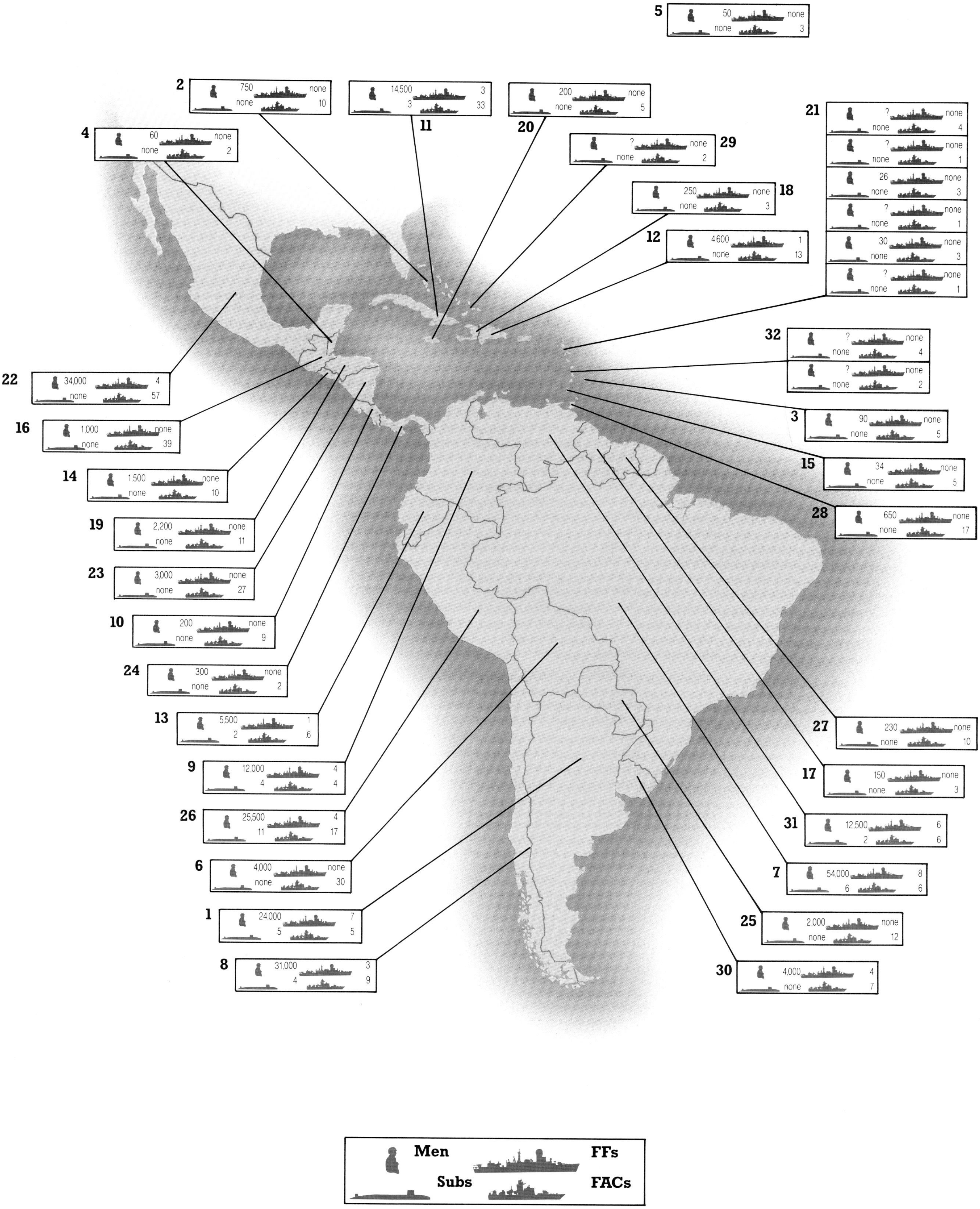

5 50 none none 3
2 750 none none 10
11 14,500 3 3 33
20 200 none none 5
21 ? none none 4
? none none 1
26 none none 3
? none none 1
30 none none 3
? none none 1
4 60 none none 2
29 ? none none 2
18 250 none none 3
12 4600 1 none 13
32 ? none none 4
? none none 2
22 34,000 4 none 57
16 1,000 none none 39
3 90 none none 5
14 1,500 none none 10
15 34 none none 5
19 2,200 none none 11
28 650 none none 17
23 3,000 none none 27
10 200 none none 9
24 300 none none 2
13 5,500 1 2 6
27 230 none none 10
9 12,000 4 4 4
17 150 none none 3
26 25,500 4 11 17
31 12,500 6 2 6
6 4,000 none none 30
7 54,000 8 6 6
1 24,000 7 5 5
25 2,000 none none 12
8 31,000 3 4 9
30 4,000 4 none 7
Men
FFs
Subs
FACs

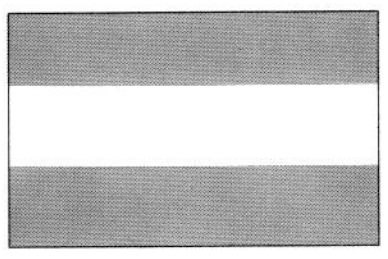

## ARGENTINA

THERE are three major areas which dominate the Argentinian view of national defence. First is a traditional Argentina-Brazil rivalry for the honour of being the dominant country in South America. Secondly, Argentina and Chile have several major border disputes and repeated efforts at arbitration have failed to reach a final settlement. Thirdly, there is the Argentinian claim to the Falkland Islands (Malvinas). Nowhere has this competition been more evident than in naval matters.

The navy was not involved in either of the two world wars. It did, however, participate in the 1962 naval blockade of Cuba in support of the US Navy. When the Falklands War broke out in 1982 the Argentine fleet comprised one ex-British aircraft carrier, one ex-US heavy cruiser, and a number of destroyers, frigates and submarines. There was considerable naval action during the war, including the loss of the cruiser *General Belgrano*, sunk by the British nuclear submarine (SSN) HMS *Conqueror*, and the submarine *Sante Fe*, which was seriously damaged by helicopters in South Georgian waters. The Argentine Navy tried desperately hard to sink British ships and naval aircraft did succeed in sinking the warships HMS *Sheffield*, HMS *Ardent* and HMS *Antelope*, and the merchantman *Atlantic Conveyor*. The submarine *San Louis* operated in the area of the British task force and launched six torpedoes, but without success.

After the war Argentina returned to democratic rule and a protracted period of political and economic instability. The funding available for defence has reduced very considerably and this has affected the navy in many ways: for example, purchases have been delayed, refits postponed, manpower cut and steaming days reduced to 20 per ship. Also, a plan to develop a nuclear-propelled submarine was cancelled by President Alfonsín.

The current missions of the navy are to defend Argentine territorial waters and national interests in the Antarctic. The long-standing maritime disputes with Chile continue, particularly in the Cape Horn area, and the navy has also kept a wary eye on the Brazilian Navy. Finally, there is an unspoken mission eventually to attempt to recapture the Falkland Islands.

There are three naval regions: Central Naval Region extends from the River Plate to 42 deg S, with its HQ at Puerto Belgrano; Southern Naval Region covers the remainder of the national coastline with its HQ at Ushuaia; and the third is Antarctica Region. There are other naval bases at Buenos Aires and Puerto Deseado, and a submarine base at Mar del Plata. There are some 18,000 men in the navy, 2,000 in the naval air force, and 4,000 marines. There is

**Above:** An Argentine destroyer of the Almirante Brown (MEKO 360) class. Designed on the modular principle, these are four excellent modern ships.

**Below:** Argentina bought two British Type 42 destroyers in the 1970s. Since the war in 1982 both have been offered for sale, but no takers have been found for these ships.

also a fairly large coastguard service (Prefectura Naval), with some 1,200 officers and 12,000 men, which operates a number of patrol ships and craft.

Flagship of the fleet is the aircraft carrier *Vienticinco de Mayo*, an ex-British light fleet carrier of 19,896tons which the Argentine Navy bought from the Dutch with whom it had served as *Karel Doorman*. Launched in 1942 her machinery is worn out and she has been in refit since 1986 while various plans have been made to bring her up to an operational standard. Even so, she can only operate using rather dated A-4Q Skyhawks, having proved unsuitable for Super Etendards.

Principal units of the surface fleet are four destroyers of the German MEKO 360 type, built by Blohm und Voss between 1980 and 1984. These large (3,360tons) and capable ships are armed with Exocet ship-to-ship missiles (SSMs), Albatross surface-to-air missiles (SAMs), a 5in (127mm) dual-purpose (DP) gun, six 1.6in (40mm) anti-aircraft (AA) guns and six torpedo tubes. They were to have had Lynx helicopters but this order was cancelled by the British and for several years they have operated French Aerospatiale SA.316/319 Alouette IIIs. Recently, however, a batch of Kaman SH-2F Seasprites has been delivered from the US. There are also two British-designed destroyers, one of which was built in Britain (completed in 1976) and the other built in Argentina (completed in 1981). Despite numerous reports that these have been offered for sale they are both still operational with the Argentine Navy.

There are seven frigates: four of the MEKO 140 type (1,790tons) and three of the French Type A-69 (1,250tons). One of the latter, *Guerrico*, was serious damaged by fire from the shore during the invasion of South Georgia in 1982 but has since been repaired. There are also numbers of patrol boats, minesweepers, amphibious warfare ships and craft, and auxiliaries.

Planned submarine strength is seven, of which five are currently operational: two Salta class (Type 209), commissioned in 1974, and three Santa Cruz class (TR-1700). The TR-1700s are being built at a very slow rate: only three were commissioned between 1984 and 1991, with two more still building. Both of the German designs, the Type 209s, are currently undergoing a major refit and rumours that some or all of these boats have been offered for sale have not been substantiated.

The marine force is quite substantial. There are two groups, each of two marine infantry battalions, an artillery battalion, and reconnaissance (recce), anti-tank and engineer companies. There are also independent infantry battalions; however, there is only one major landing ship, *Cabo San Antonio*, which was built in Argentina in 1978 to a US design and subsequently used in the invasion of the Falkland Islands.

The Argentine Navy is unique among South American navies in having recent combat experience, and there can be no doubt that, despite its losses, it did very well against the much larger and more experienced Royal Navy in 1982. Since then it has been subjected to swingeing cuts, severe limitations have been put on its operations and several of its ships have been offered for sale. Despite this, in 1990 President Menem decided to send two of the destroyers to the Persian Gulf as part of the UN force, the only South American country to make such a contribution.

**Above:** A flight of five Dassault Super Etendard strike fighters of the Argentine Navy. These aircraft operated from land bases during the Falklands War, their pilots impressing the world with their daring and courage.

**EQUIPMENT**

**Aircraft Carriers:**
Vienticinco de Mayo (British Colossus) class
**Submarines:**
Santa Cruz (German TR-1700) class
Salta (German Type 209) class
**Destroyers:**
Hercules (British Sheffield) class
Almirante Brown (German MEKO 360 H2) class
**Frigates:**
Espora (German Meko 140 A16) class
Drummond (French Type A-69) class
**Patrol Boats:**
German TNC45 class
Israeli Dabur class
**Amphibious Warfare:**
Cabo San Antonio (US De Soto) class
**Naval Aircraft:**
Aerospatiale SA.316/319 Alouette III
Dassault Super Etendard
Douglas A-4Q Skyhawk
Grumman S-2E Tracker
Kaman SH-2F Seasprite
Sikorsky SH-3D/H Sea King
**Marines:**
Ten battalions

## THE BAHAMAS

THE defence of the Commonwealth of the Bahamas is vested in the Royal Bahamian Defence Force, of which the naval arm is some 750 strong. Its main base is at Coral Harbour on New Providence Island and it is employed on anti-smuggling and, particularly, on anti-drug work. It operates ten patrol boats of some 100tons displacement and a number of smaller craft.

**Below:** The Bahamian patrol boat *Yellow Elder*, together with two sisters, belong to the Protector class, was built in Britain by Vospers and delivered in 1986.

## BARBADOS

THIS Caribbean island became independent from the UK in 1966 and remains part of the British Commonwealth today. The defence force has a navy based at Bridgetown which is equipped with one large Brooke Marine patrol boat, *Trident*, of the Kebir class which displaces nearly 200tons and carries an armament of one light machine-gun and one 0.8in (20mm) cannon; one Enterprise class patrol boat, *Excellence*, of 40ton displacement armed with a 0.30in (12.7mm) machine-gun; and three UK-built Guardian-II class boats of 11 tons displacement. All are used for patrols and search and rescue.

## BELIZE

FORMERLY known as British Honduras, the Central American state of Belize on the Caribbean Sea became independent in 1981. It retains a British garrison to deter neighbouring Guatemala but also has its own small force with a tiny maritime element of 60 men. It has two small patrol boats, *Dangriga* and *Toledo*, of the 65.5ft (20mm) Wasp type.

## BERMUDA

THIS British colony has no distinct navy but its police and customs service do operate three Heron class craft.

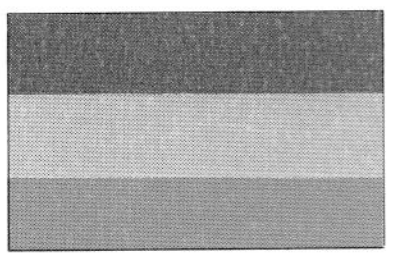

## BOLIVIA

BOLIVIA was the last South American colony to achieve its independence, in 1825, and since then it has been involved in a number of wars. In alliance with Peru it fought Argentina and Brazil from 1835 to 1839, and then Chile from 1879 to 1883, the latter conflict ending with the loss of access to the Pacific. It fought Brazil again in 1904 and Paraguay in 1932-35 (the Chaco War).

The lack of access to the Pacific is a deeply felt problem and there is constant hope of being ceded a corridor running between Peru and Chile. This long-term aim gives rise to an 1,800 strong navy which is, at least for the time being, a riverine force only. The command structure includes six naval districts, each of which has a flotilla; one district is on Lake Titicaca, the others on the major rivers.

The largest ship is an ocean-going freighter, *Libertador Bolivar*, which is naval manned to provide proper sea training for the day when the corridor is gained and the navy can operate out of a Bolivian port on the Pacific coast. In the meantime the ship is used as a normal commercial freighter and generates revenue for the Navy Ministry. It is home-ported in Argentina and was donated by Venezuela.

The remainder of the navy consists of some 30 patrol boats and launches, and there is one naval-owned Cessna U206 patrol aircraft. There are about 2,000 men in the marines. The main unit is the Almirante Grau Marine Battalion, which detaches a company to each of the naval districts.

### EQUIPMENT

**Marines:**
Two battalions

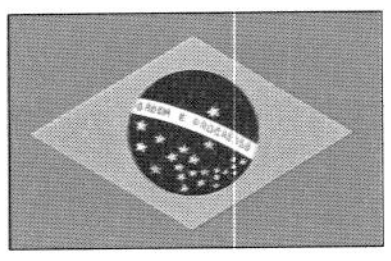

## BRAZIL

WITH an area of 3,290,000 sq miles (8,521,100sq km) and a population of over 150 million Brazil is by far the largest and most populous country in Latin America. Its armed forces, with a strength of 324,200, are the second largest in the Americas.

Brazil joined the Allies early in WWII and took part in the Atlantic, Pacific and Mediterranean campaigns. After the war the fleet was made up mainly from ex-US vessels, but in the 1970s the navy started another expansion programme.

Largest unit in the fleet is the ex-British aircraft carrier *Minas Gerais*, a 19,890tons light fleet carrier purchased in 1956. She was taken out of commission in 1987 but the promised refit has not yet been started and it looks possible that she might not return to service.

There are 11 destroyers, all ex-US Navy. Seven of these are of WWII vintage, two Gearing class and five Sumner class, and despite several modernizations they are now nearing the end of their useful lives. More up-to-date are four Garcia class (Para class in Brazilian service) which, although classified as frigates by the US Navy, have been given "D" pennant numbers in Brazil. Constructed in the 1960s and displacing 3,560tons these were acquired in 1989 and are the only Brazilian vessels to be equipped with ASROC.

Mainstay of the frigate force are six British-designed Mark 10s: four are optimized for anti-submarine warfare (ASW) missions and two are rated as "General Purpose" (GP); four were built in the UK and two in Brazil. All six are armed with Exocet missiles, a 4.5in (114mm) gun (the GP version has two), US Navy Mk 15 Vulcan Phalanx close-in weapons system (CIWS), ASW rocket launchers and torpedo tubes, and they carry a Lynx helicopter. The ASW version has a special version of the Australian Ikara ASW missile, known as the Branik (Brazilian Ikara).

Latest to join the fleet is the Inhauma class which originated as a proposal for 12 corvettes to undertake economic zone patrols for the coastguard. It grew while on the drawing-board into a 1,930tons displacement frigate for the navy. Designed and built in Brazil, four will have been commissioned by 1992 but there are no further orders at the present. They are armed with four Exocet launchers, a single 4.5in (114mm) gun, a CIWS, two 1.6in (40mm) AA

**Left:** Brazilian frigate *Niteroi*, one of four ASW versions of this class. There are also two general-purpose versions optimized for surface warfare.

**Left, above:** The carrier, *Minas Gerais*. On her flight-deck are a single Gaviao and three Sea King helicopters, together with six Tracker ASW aircraft.

**Above:** The Brazilian Navy has a vast commitment to riverine operations. This is *Roraima*, a 365ton vessel armed with one 1.6in (40mm) gun, six 0.5in (12.7mm) MGs and two 3.2in (81mm) mortars.

guns, six torpedo tubes, and carry a Lynx helicopter.

An unusual type of warship is the "vedette," a corvette or small patrol vessel of which there are a number in service. The Imperial Marinheiro class is based on an ocean-going tug design, modified for naval service and armed with one 3in (76mm) gun and four 0.8in (20mm) cannon. They are used to patrol the 200-mile economic zone together with 20 patrol craft of various sizes. A new class of large (410tons) Vosper-designed boats is under construction for the same purpose.

Like many South American countries Brazil has thousands of miles of river, for which the navy needs river patrol ships. There are six of these in service, with one new ship being built for duty on the Paraguay River.

There is a substantial amphibious fleet, of which the largest is the 12,150tons dock landing ship (LSD), *Ceara*, which was purchased from the US Navy in 1989. With a capacity of some 350 troops, 38 tanks and a number of wheeled vehicles, she is the most capable amphibious warfare vessel in any Latin American navy. The Brazilians are reported to be seeking to purchase another such ship. *Ceara* is backed-up by the tank landing ship (LST) *Duque de Caxias*, another ex-US ship, originally of the De Soto class, which can carry up to 700 men. These two large ships are supported by a variety of smaller landing craft.

The submarine fleet's most recent acquisition is the German-designed Type 1400. The first, *Tupi*, was built in Kiel while the remainder are being constructed in Brazil. These are among the largest and most powerful diesel-electric submarines in service in any navy. They have a displacement of 1,900tons and an armament of eight tubes for which 16 British Tigerfish torpedoes are carried. Also in service are three Humaita class submarines which were built in Britian in the 1970s and are identical to the Oberon class. Finally, there are two very elderly ex-US Navy Guppy submarines, the last of a number purchased from the US which will waste out as the Tupi class enters service. There are already plans for a new class to replace the Humaita class which will be designed and built entirely in Brazil, of which at least one is planned to have nuclear propulsion.

Fixed-wing aircraft support is provided by the air force and includes the squadron of Grumman S-2E Trackers which operate from the carrier (when she is in service). This leaves the navy to operate only helicopters. The primary type for ASW duties afloat is the Westland Lynx, of which nine are currently in service with a further eight planned. There are also six Exocet-armed Super Pumas, eight Sea Kings, 17 Agusta-Bell JetRangers and nine old Westland Wasps. Eight Brazilian-built versions of the Aerospatiale Lama are on order.

The marine force, the Fuzililieros Navais, is rather large with a current strength of some 14,613 officers and men. The principal formation is an amphibious division (which is, in effect, a brigade) composed of one special operations, one artillery and three infantry battalions. There is a Reinforcement Command comprising four infantry and one engineer battalions, and an Internal Security Force of six regional and one special operations groups.

### EQUIPMENT

**Aircraft Carriers:**
Minas Gerais (British Colussus) class
**Submarines:**
Tupi (German Type 1400) class
Humaita (British Oberon) class
Goais (US Guppy) class
**Destroyers:**
Marcilio Diaz (US Gearing) class
Mato Grosso (US Sumner) class
Para (US Garcia) class
**Frigates:**
Niteroi (Vosper Thornycroft Mark 10) class
Inhauma class
**Corvettes:**
Imperial Marinheiro class
**Amphibious Warfare:**
Ceara (US Thomaston) class
Duque de Caxias (US De Soto) class
**Naval Aircraft:**
Aerospatiale AS.332M Super Puma
Aerospatiale AS.350 Esquilo
Agusta-Bell AB.206B JetRanger
Helibras SA.315B Gaviao (Aerospatiale Lama)
Westland Wasp HAS.1
Westland Mk21 Lynx
Sikorsky SH-3H Sea King
**Marines:**
Eighteen battalions

**Right:** A wooden-hulled, Brazilian Navy EDVP class landing craft disembarks its load of 36 marines during a training exercise. The 14,613 strong Fuzileiros Navais is one of the world's largest marine corps.

## CHILE

THE Chilean Navy today maintains a small but notably efficient fleet whose main purpose has been to keep an eye on its neighbours, Peru to the north and Argentina to the south. Like other South American navies, Chile for many years operated one battleship with a force of cruisers and destroyers supported by a small number of submarines. A minor curiosity of the Chilean Navy is that some of its major surface vessels appear from time to time in camouflage paint schemes.

The Chilean Navy has some 2,000 officers and 24,000 men (500 of whom are in the naval air component) and just over 5,000 marines. There are three major ship commands: the fleet, the submarine flotilla and naval transport. There are also the usual naval commands ashore, of which the most northern is 4th Naval Zone which covers from the Peruvian border southwards to 32deg S and has its HQ at Iquique. The 1st Naval Zone covers Valparaiso, where it has its HQ, and has boundaries stretching from 32deg S to 36deg S; 2nd Naval Zone (HQ Talcahuano) stretches from the junction with 1st Zone down to 43deg S; while 3rd Naval Zone (HQ Punta Arenas) covers down to Cape Horn from 43deg S. Chile also retains responsibility for Easter Island in the eastern Pacific Ocean.

Largest ship in the fleet is the *O'Higgins* which has the distinction of being the last all-gun cruiser in any of the western world's navies. Originally USS *Brooklyn* (CL-40) she was sold to Chile in 1951. She is armed with 15 guns of 6in (152mm) calibre in five three-gun turrets with another eight 5in (127mm) guns in single mounts.

There is a very strong destroyer force of which the most recent units are the four ex-British County class ships, the Captain Prat class (6,200tons). Transferred between 1982 and 1986 these have been modernized and altered to suit Chilean conditions. Two retain their Sea Slug missile launchers — Chile having purchased all remaining stocks of these missiles from Britain in 1986 — while the other two have had their missile facilities replaced by a new, larger hangar and an enlarged flight-deck to enable them to handle two helicopters.

The two other British-built destroyers, *Almirante Williams* and *Almirante Riveros*, were designed and built in Britain in the 1950s specifically for the Chilean Navy and have been progressively updated since (including fitting Exocet missiles). They are armed with two 4in (102mm) guns in single turrets, the two superfiring turrets having been removed during refits in the late 1980s to reduce topweight and enable a helicopter deck to be mounted on the site of the after turret. There are also two former US Navy Sumner class destroyers, *Ministro Zenteno* and *Ministro Portales*.

Three Leander class frigates were purchased from Britain in the 1980s and it is reported that Chile wishes to take another four if they become available. The major modification carried out by the Chilean Navy is to remove the Limbo ASW mortar and replace it with four Exocet launchers.

There are nine fast patrol boats. Four are the German Lürssen 36m design built by Bazan in Spain in the mid-1960s. These have been supplemented by four Israeli-designed boats: two Sa'ar-IIs built in France in 1969 and two Sa'ar-IVs (Reshev) built in Israel in the late 1970s. Chile has made several attempts to buy four more of the latter, but has not so far succeeded. All the Sa'ar boats are armed with Israeli Gabriel missiles, having had their US-supplied Harpoon missiles removed prior to delivery.

The submarine fleet consists of two German-designed and built Type 1300s, which were purchased in 1984, and two British Oberon class, which were delivered new in 1976. Like the similar Brazilian boats they are now due for replacement and it is understood that there are plans to acquire a further two Type 1300s for this purpose.

The Chilean Navy operates its own small naval air arm. Fixed-wing types include 10 Embraer Bandeirantes, of which three are equipped for maritime reconnaissance,

**Above:** Two of Chile's tough 5,200 strong marine force of shock troops. The navy operates three landing-ships to transport them along Chile's long and rugged coastline.

**Below:** The very handsome *Almirante Williams*, seen here, and her sister *Almirante Riveros* were designed and built by Vickers-Armstrong in England in the 1950s.

**Below:** The Chilean Navy has six of these torpedo-armed Agusta-Bell AB.206A JetRangers. They operate from the Leander class frigates.

and 10 A-36 Halcon strike/trainers, which have been adapted to launch British Sea Skua anti-ship missiles. Helicopters include 10 Alouette IIIs, six Agusta-Bell JetRangers and three Aerospatiale AS.322M Super Pumas, with four more of the latter on order.

The Chilean marines are 5,200 strong. There are four battalion groups, each consisting of an infantry battalion, a commando company, an artillery company and an air-defence company. There is a further amphibious battalion. Amphibious transport is provided by three Maipo class landing ships, which were constructed in Chile to a French design.

### EQUIPMENT

**Cruisers:**
O'Higgins (US Brooklyn) class
**Submarines:**
Thomson (German IKL Type 1300) class
O'Brien (British Oberon) class
**Destroyers:**
Capitan Prat (British County) class
Almirante Williams class
Ministro Zenteno (US Sumner) class
**Frigates:**
Condell (British Leander) class
**Patrol Boats:**
Iquique (Israeli Sa'ar-II) class
Casma (Israeli Sa'ar-IV) class
Guacolda (German Lürssen 36m) class
**Amphibious Warfare:**
Maipo (French Batral) class
**Submarines:**
Thomson (German IKL Type 1300) class
O'Brien (British Oberon) class
**Naval Aircraft:**
Embraer EMB-110 Bandeirante
FAC/Ind-Aer A-36 Halcon (Spanish Casa C-101 Aviojet)
Aerospatiale SA.316/319 Alouette III
Aerospatiale AS.365F Dauphin
Aerospatiale AS.322M Super Puma
Agusta-Bell AB.206 JetRanger

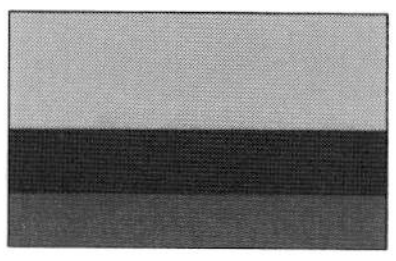

## COLOMBIA

COLOMBIA lies in a strategically important position in the north-west of South America. It has borders with Panama, Venezuela, Brazil, Peru and Ecuador, and its population of some 32 million is among the largest in South America.

It has traditionally possessed a very small navy whose attention has tended to concentrate on riverine tasks, although not to the exclusion of sea-going forces.

Today the Colombian Navy has a strength of 700 officers and 6,500 ratings. The primary military mission is protection of the country's economic zone, but in practice its most important task is drugs interdiction. Main bases are at Cartagena on the Caribbean and Buenaventura on the Pacific coasts, giving good coverage.

The main units in the surface fleet are four Almirante Padilla class frigates which were designed and built by Howaldtswerke in Germany and delivered in 1983-84. Displacing 1,850tons, they are armed with eight Exocet SSM launchers, one 3in (76mm) OTO Melara DP gun, two 1.6in (40mm) cannon, and can carry one MBB Bo-105 helicopter. It is an exceptionally neat and workmanlike warship design.

There are two patrol boats of the Quito Sueno class (former US Navy Asheville class) which have proved difficult to maintain. They are supplemented by a number of boats which have been captured from drugs runners and been pressed into use to hunt their former comrades. There are also two river patrol boats.

Considering the small size of the navy overall, the submarine arm is surprisingly strong with four boats. Largest are two German Type 209 submarines commissioned in 1975, Colombia having been one of the earliest of the South American navies to order this type. There are also two Italian S.X 506 midget submarines, survivors of a class of four commissioned in the early 1970s. With a displacement of 70tons they have a crew of five and can carry up to eight fully-equipped frogmen.

The naval aviation branch consists of four Cessna A-37 Dragonfly light attack aircraft and the four MBB Bo-105 helicopters used on the frigates. The marine corps consists of 6,000 men in five battalions.

**Below:** A fine shot of the frigate *Almirante Padilla*; four ships of this FS-1500 class were built for Colombia by HDW in Germany in 1981-83. Main armament is eight Exocet SSM launchers and one 3in (76mm) OTO Melara DP gun. A flight-deck and hangar are fitted.

### EQUIPMENT

**Submarines:**
Pijao (German Type 209 Mod 1) class
Intrepido (Italian S.X. 506) class
**Frigates:**
Almirante Padilla (German FS-1500) class
**Patrol Boats:**
Quito Sueno (US Asheville) class
Rio Hacha class
**Naval Aircraft:**
Cessna A-37B Dragonfly
MBB Bo-105
**Marines:**
Five battalions

## COSTA RICA

COSTA Rica is protected by a paramilitary Civil Guard. The marine element is some 200 strong and is equipped with nine small patrol boats, of which the largest, *Isla del Coco*, displaces 118tons, has a crew of 14 and is armed with three 0.5in (12.7mm) machine-guns (MG) and a 2.4in (61mm) mortar. The air wing of the Civil Guard includes in its inventory two Cessna 337 Skymaster aircraft, equipped for maritime patrol.

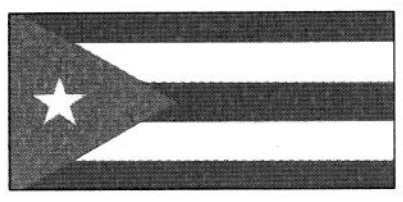

## CUBA

THE Cuban Navy today is some 13,500 men strong, of whom about 60 per cent are conscripts. There are four operational functional flotillas for missile patrol boats, torpedo patrol boats, anti-submarine ships and submarines. Ashore there are three naval districts, with bases at Havana, Cienfuegos, Cabanas, Mariel, Punta Movida and Nicaro. The tasks of the navy are to protect Cuba's territorial waters and to watch the US base at Guantanamo Bay, which is a strange historical quirk.

The navy is inevitably organized on Soviet lines and uses Soviet equipment. The largest ships are three modern Soviet-supplied Koni class frigates (1,600tons) armed with one SA-N-4 Gecko launcher, two twin 3in (76mm) turrets, four CIWS and two RBU-6000 ASW rocket launchers. The first entered service in 1981, the second in 1984 and the third in 1988.

The bulk of the fleet is made up of 33 patrol boats: 13 Osa-IIs, five Osa-Is, four Stenkas, two SO-1s and nine Turyas. Of these the most significant are the Osas which are armed with SS-N-2 missiles, although their age is such that the US Navy (their only possible target) would have little difficulty in countering them. All are Soviet Navy types and it is of interest that none has been supplied since 1983. The surface fleet is completed by 13 coastal and inshore minesweepers (Yevgenya and Sonya classes) and two Polnocny class landing ships. Finally, there are three elderly Foxtrot class diesel-electric submarines which were transferred from the Soviet Navy between 1979 and 1984.

There is no naval air arm, all air support being provided by the air force. This is equipped with fighters and attack aircraft, and also with 14 Mil Mi-14 Haze ASW helicopters. Marine forces comprise one amphibious assault battalion, which is approximately 800 strong.

**Above:** A Cuban Navy Foxtrot class submarine photographed in 1986. Virtually all Cuban naval vessels are of Soviet origin, with most now very elderly and in poor condition.

### EQUIPMENT

**Submarines:**
Soviet Foxtrot class
**Frigates:**
Mariel (Soviet Koni) class
**Patrol Boats:**
Soviet Osa-I & II class
Soviet Stenka class
Soviet Turya class
**Marines:**
One battalion

## DOMINICAN REPUBLIC

THE Dominican Republic lies due east of Cuba and shares the island of Hispaniola with Haiti. A navy was established in 1873, but remained very small; it was officially disbanded in 1916 then re-constituted in 1941. Today, the navy is 4,600 strong and operates a large number of small, mainly elderly vessels. Naval headquarters are at Santo Domingo, with a subsidiary base at Las Calderas.

Principal ship is *Mella*, a Canadian-built version of the British wartime River class frigate, built in 1944 and transferred to the Dominican Republic in 1947. With a displacement of 2,300tons she is armed with one 3in (76mm) DP gun with two 1.6in (40mm) and two 0.8in (20mm) AA guns. Three former US Navy Cohoes class vessels were sold to the Dominican Navy in 1976 and are employed primarily as corvettes, although they also undertake a miscellancy of other duties. Despite their armament of two 3in (76mm) guns and three 0.8in (20mm) cannon, their maximum speed of just over 12kts suggests that their value must be limited. Two former US Navy minesweepers, which have had their minesweeping equipment removed, are also used as corvettes.

The remainder of the navy consists of 13 launches, mainly from the United States, and a number of auxiliaries. Air support is provided by the air force and the navy includes a small force of marines.

### EQUIPMENT

**Frigates:**
Mella (Canadian River) class
**Corvettes:**
Cambiaso (US Cohoes) class
Prestol Botello (US Admirable) class

**Above:** *Capella*, one of four "Commercial Cruiser" patrol boats operated by the Dominican Republic. Many of these US-built boats are supplied to smaller navies.

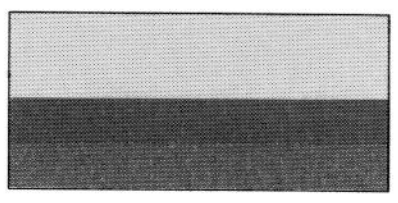

## ECUADOR

ECUADOR'S Navy was first raised in 1828 and it remained very small for a long time despite the strong Peruvian fleet to the south; no expansion occurred until the early 1940s and it was only in the 1970s that a determined effort was made to expand the fleet, so that today Ecuador has a relatively strong navy for its size. The navy has a strength of 300 officers and 3,500 ratings, with bases in Guayaquil, Jaramijo and the Galapagos Islands, and is noticeably better equipped than some numerically larger forces.

Flagship of the fleet is the *Presidente Eloy Alfaro*, a former US Navy Gearing class destroyer. Built in 1945 she was transferred from the USN Reserve and sold to Ecuador in 1978 and completed a major refit in 1980. Displacing 3,500tons she is armed with four 5in (127mm) DP guns, two 0.8in (20mm) AA cannon, six torpedo tubes and two depth-charge racks. She has modern electrical systems and her two geared steam turbine engines give a speed of 32kts.

The navy operates a number of excellent corvettes and fast patrol boats. There are six Esmeraldas class corvettes which manage to accomodate six Exocet and one Albatros missile launchers, one 3in (76mm) gun and one 1.6in (40mm) cannon, together with six ASW torpedo tubes, all on a 700ton hull. These were built in Italy and delivered between 1982 and 1984. There are also two classes of Lürssen patrol boats — the Quito and Manta classes — both of three boats each. The Quito class, the larger of the two, is armed with four Exocet launchers, one 3in (76mm) gun and two 1.4in (35mm) cannon; the Manta class is armed with four Gabriel missile launchers and two 1.12in (30mm) AA. Both are fast, with a top speed of 35kts, and, like the Esmeraldas class corvettes, pack a heavy punch for the size of the hull.

**Above:** A crewman guides a helicopter into a landing on the tiny flight-deck of the Ecuadorian *Esmeraldas*. Six of these well-armed corvettes with good electronics were built in Italy in the early 1980s.

Finally, the Ecuadorean Navy operates two German-built Type 209 diesel-electric submarines: *Shyri* and *Huancavilca*. They were delivered in 1977/78 and refitted in 1983/84. There are the usual numbers of auxiliaries and one LST. Like a number of South American navies, the Ecuadoreans operate a beautiful sail-training ship, the 934ton barque *Guayas*.

The main element of the naval air arm is based at Guayaquil Air Base and contains five Agusta-Bell 206 JetRanger helicopters which operate from the destroyer, frigate and corvettes, all of them having been fitted with a landing deck (although none has a hangar). There are four Cessna T-37 training and light attack aircraft, a Canadair CN-235 amphibian and several other light aircraft, namely one Beech Super King 200T and three Beech T-34Cs.

The 1,900 marines are organized into three battalions, of which one is a commando unit, while the other two are on garrison duties. There are three marine bases: Guayaquil, the Galapagos Island and Oriente.

### EQUIPMENT

**Submarines:**
Shyri (German Type 209) class
**Destroyers:**
Presidente Eloy Alfaro (US Gearing) class
**Frigates:**
Moran Valverde (Canadian River) class
**Patrol Boats:**
Quito (German Lürssen 47m) class
Manta (German Lürssen 36m) class
**Corvettes:**
Esmeraldas (Italian modified Wadi M'ragh) class
**Amphibious Warfare:**
Hualcopo (US LST-542) class
**Naval Aircraft:**
Agusta-Bell AB.206 JetRanger
Canadair CN-235
Cessna A/T-37 Dragonfly
**Marines:**
Three battalions

## EL SALVADOR

EL SALVADOR is a tiny republic on the Pacific coast of Central America which has had a troubled history and today has a protracted civil war.

Despite its 200-mile coastline, the El Salvadorean Navy is unusual in that it is smaller than the marine corps, strengths being 700 and 800 officers and men respectively. Based at La Libertad, the navy operates a number of small patrol boats and craft, the largest of which are the three 100 ton boats of the GC-6 class. Aircraft support is provided by the air force.

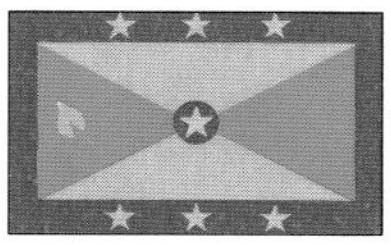

## GRENADA

GRENADA was invaded and occupied by United States armed forces in 1983, since when the Grenadian forces have been very small but are being restructured.

The tiny navy operates five patrol boats, the largest of which is *Tyrell Bay*, a 94ton US-built boat which was delivered new in 1984 and armed with four light machine-guns. Four older craft had been allowed to become derelict prior to 1983, but have since been refurbished extensively and returned to service.

## GUATEMALA

DESPITE having coastlines on both the Pacific and the Caribbean the Central American state of Guatemala has a tiny navy of some 400 men. It operates from a collection of naval bases at Puerto Barrios, Santo Tomas, Puerto Quetzal and Puerto San Jose.

The navy has nine sea-going patrol boats, all relatively new and all constructed in the United States. There are also 30 river patrol craft and two very small (6ton) troop carrying craft. There is no naval aviation, but there is one battalion of marines.

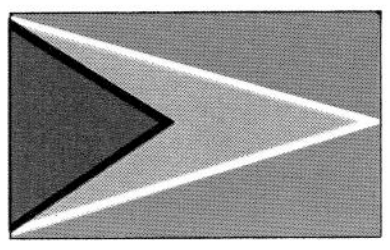

## GUYANA

THE "Cooperative Republic of Guyana" is the former colony of British Guiana which gained independence in 1966. It has one of the smallest armed forces in the Americas, the Combined Guyana Defence Force, which includes naval, ground and air elements numbering about 2,000 men, of whom 150 are in the marine section. This force has bases at Georgetown and New Amsterdam, and operates one 109ton patrol boat, *Peccari*, three converted fishing boats, three ex-German boats and one ex-Dutch LCU.

## HAITI

THE Republic of Haiti shares the island of Hispaniola with the Dominican Republic. It is a turbulent and poverty-stricken country.

The navy was founded in 1860, but priority in Haiti has always been given to the combined army/police force which has some 7,000 men. By way of contrast the navy currently has just 250 men, although the air force is even smaller with a mere 150. The navy operates out of Port au Prince and it consists of one armed tug, three 33ton patrol craft and nine very small motor boats.

## HONDURAS

THE Honduran Navy was formed late in the last century but has never been a significant part of the country's defences. Today, there are some 18,000 men in the Honduran defence forces, but only 1,600 of these are in the navy. Bases are at Puerto Corted and Puerto Castilla on the Caribbean coast and Amapala on the very short stretch of Pacific coast.

There are six large US-built patrol boats, all of which are armed with a 0.8in (20mm) Sea Vulcan gatling gun which would quickly dispose of any hostile boats within range. The two Copan class boats displace 94tons and are capable of 35kts, while the very similar Guaymaras class (three boats) have a top speed of 24kts. The sixth boat, *Chemelecon*, was originally the *Rio Kuringwas* of the Nicaraguan Navy but was used by defectors for their escape and was then pressed into Honduran service where it has remained since.

There are also five smaller patrol boats, the Nacaome class (36tons) and a number of smaller craft. The largest boat in the navy is a landing-craft, *Punta Caxinas*, which displaces 625tons.

Naval air crews operate four Brazilian maritime patrol aircraft. There is also a small marines force of approximately one battalion strength.

### EQUIPMENT

**Patrol Boats:**
Guaymaras class
Copan class
Nacaome class
**Naval Aircraft:**
Embraer EMB-110 Bandeirante
**Marines:**
One battalion

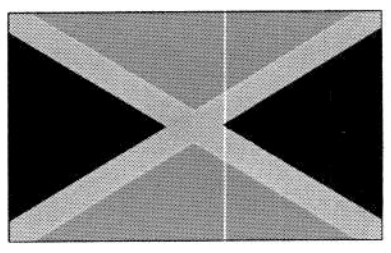

## JAMAICA

THE former colony of Jamaica in the Caribbean is now an independent state within the British Commonwealth. During British rule there was no need for a naval force since such protection was provided by Britain's Royal Navy.

The coastguard element of the unified Jamaican Defence force was formed in 1963 and is surprisingly small. Based at HMJS Cagway, Port Royal, it has some 200 men, with a further 50 in reserve, and is equipped with five lightly-armed patrol boats.

The largest is the 103ton, aluminium construction *Fort Charles* dating from 1974 but extensively modified in 1986. It is powered by two MTU 16V 538 TB90 diesel engines which enable a speed of 32kts. It has one 0.8in (20mm) Oerlikon gun, two 0.5in (12.7mm) MGs and can accommodate 18 soldiers in addition to its 20-man crew.

Even older are the three 60ton boats of the Discovery Bay class which were commissioned in the mid-1960s: *Discovery Bay, Holland Bay* and *Manatee Bay*. These lightly-armed craft (two 0.5in MGs) have been fitted with new, uprated engines several times.

The newest vessel, commissioned in 1985, is the *Paul Bogle* of the Hero class. Again an aluminium build it displaces nearly 100tons and was originally intended as the third of Honduras's Copan class. It has a top speed of more than 30kts and is armed with one 0.8in (20mm) Oerlikon gun and two 0.5in (12.7mm) MGs.

### EQUIPMENT

**Patrol Boats:**
Discovery Bay class
Fort Charles class
Hero class

**Below:** Honduran Navy 106ft patrol boats *Tegucigalpa* and (in rear) *Copan*, dressed overall during a 1986 visit to New York, USA.

**Below:** The Jamaican patrol boat *Discovery Bay*, one of many US "Commercial Cruiser" designs in service with numerous small navies.

**Above:** The Jamaican *Fort Charles*, armed with a 0.8in (20mm) cannon and two 0.5in (12.7mm) MGs. It has an 18-bed dispensary.

**Below:** *Paul Bogle* of the Jamaican Defence Force, provided by US aid, is a sister-ship to the Honduran *Tegucigalpa* (opposite).

## LEEWARD ISLANDS

### ANGUILLA

THIS tiny island has a marine police force with four small patrol craft: one Halmatic M160 class, one each of the Huntsman and Interceptor classes, and two local builds, *Anguilleta* and *Mapleleaf*.

### DOMINICA

THE coastguard has one unarmed 65ft (19.8m) Swift class patrol craft, *Melville*, and two 88.5ft (27m) craft built by Boston Whaler, *Vigilance* and *Observer*, acquired in 1988.

### ST KITTS-NEVIS

THIS small state has a 30-man coastguard operating one large patrol vessel, the 99ton *Stalwart*, plus two small patrol craft of the Fairey Marine Spear class.

### ANTIGUA-BARBUDA

IT has a coastguard which operates one 65ft (19.8m) patrol craft presented by the United States government, a Swift class boat named *Liberta*.

### MONTSERRAT

THE marine police operate one Halmatic M160 class patrol craft of 18tons displacement armed with a 0.30in (7.62mm) machine-gun.

### VIRGIN ISLANDS

STILL a British dependency, the marine police operate one 17ton Halmatic M140 patrol craft, *St Ursula*, financed by the UK and commissioned in 1988.

## MEXICO

**Above:** The naval air arm of the Mexican Navy operates 11 MBB Bo-105. A popular helicopter it has a range of 407nm (754km) and a ceiling of 9,845ft (3,000m).

**Below:** Mexican Navy ships in Acapulco harbour, with the sail training ship *Cauahtemoc* taking pride of place and the old destroyer *Quetzalcoatl* behind.

**Left:** The patrol boat *Miguel Ramos Arizpe* is one of the 31 Azteca class. Twenty-one were built in the UK between 1972 and 1976, with the remainder being built in Mexican shipyards.

THE third largest country in the region and with long coastlines on both the Gulf of Mexico and Pacific, Mexico has never had a large navy — possibly due to the proximity of the mighty US Navy to the north. Certainly she has never become involved in the battleship races, which have cost some of the South American navies so much, and even today when her navy is much larger she maintains no "prestige" ships, such as cruisers or aircraft carriers, and is virtually the only one among the larger navies in the area never to have operated a submarine force.

The present-day Mexican Navy is some 25,000 strong and the command is split two ways: Gulf Area, with its HQ at Vera Cruz, and Pacific Area, with its HQ at Acapulco. The largest units in the fleet are three very elderly ex-US Navy destroyers. *Quetzalcoatl* and *Netzahualcoyotl* are Gearing class destroyers of 3,528tons displacement which were first commissioned in 1945; they are armed with four 5in (127mm) DP guns and an ASROC launcher. The third destroyer, *Cuitlahuac* (2,850tons), is two years older and is almost certainly the last of the once very numerous Fletcher class destroyers still in service.

Next in size come four former US Navy high-speed transports now used as frigates. Armed with a single 5in (127mm) gun and a number of AA cannon these 2,130ton ships are very old, having originally entered service in 1943-45 and will have to be replaced soon. None of the destroyers or frigates has the facility to operate helicopters.

The large force of corvettes includes 29 former US Navy fleet minesweepers (17 of the Auk class and 12 of the Admirable class) all of which have had their minesweeping and ASW equipment removed. The Mexicans have used them as large patrol vessels, primarily to protect the 200mile economic zone; but, again, all were first commissioned in 1942-44 and are now of rapidly decreasing operational value.

Six new corvettes were purchased in 1982-83. Displacing 910tons, the Cadette Virgilio Uribe class consists of six ships all built in Spain to the Halcon class design. (They are very similar to five ships built for the Argentine coastguard.) They have a large helicopter deck aft and operate an MBB Bo-105S helicopter. Armament is a token, single 1.6in (40mm) Bofors. These are being supplemented by four new ships of a design based on that of the Uribe class, but slightly smaller and with better armament and performance, which are being constructed in Mexican shipyards. Known as the Aquila class, they have an additional 2.25in (57mm) Bofors DP gun and a slightly smaller helicopter deck.

The main strength of the patrol boat fleet lies in 31 boats of the Azteca class, of which 11 were built in Mexico and the remainder in Great Britain. Of very light construction they are armed with machine-guns and some also have a 1.6in (40mm) Bofors. Now under construction in Spain are six Cormoran class boats which are somewhat larger (300tons displacement) and are intended to replace some of the aged Auk and Admirable class. They will be armed with an OTO Melara 3in (76mm) compact gun, a 1.6in (40mm) gun, and may also carry SSMs, making them the first warships in the Mexican Navy to carry missiles.

There are also a number of smaller patrol

craft and auxiliaries but there are no amphibious landing craft, although there are two Mexican-designed and built troop transports.

There is a small naval air force of some 500 men. This operates 21 land-based aircraft in the maritime reconnaissance role, with a further 11 helicopters operating from the modern corvettes; all are unarmed. Remaining aircraft are operated in the transport and liaison roles.

The large (9,000 men) force of marines has a main operational force of one brigade of two battalions but no landing-craft or ships for amphibious landings. The marines also provide the Presidential Guard Battalion and some 35 "security companies."

### EQUIPMENT

**Destroyers:**
Quetzalcoatl (US Gearing) class
Cuitlahuac (US Fletcher) class
**Frigates:**
Zacatecas (US Charles Lawrence) class
Usumacinta (US Crosley) class
**Patrol Boats:**
Cormoran class
Azteca class
**Corvettes:**
Cadette Virgilio Uribe (Spanish Halcon) class
Leandro Valle (US Auk) class
DM-01 (US Admirable) class
**Naval Aircraft:**
Casa 212 Aviocar
MBB Bo-105S
Grumman HU-16A Albatross
**Marines:**
Three battalions

## NICARAGUA

THE troubled Central American republic of Nicaragua is recovering from years of civil war, although the navy, like the other two services, will show the remnants of the equipment bought during that period for years to come. The navy is about 3,700 strong and consists of a number of classes of small patrol craft, together with two classes of minesweeper and some auxiliary vessels.

The main part of the navy is equipped with 27 patrol craft, the newest of which are 10 of the North Korean Sin Hung class. These were built as torpedo boats but have been delivered with the tubes removed; they are small boats, displacing just 25tons, armed with two 0.6in (14.5mm) MGs. The largest units are 11 Soviet Zhuk class patrol craft.

### EQUIPMENT

**Patrol Boats:**
North Korean Sin Hung class
Soviet Shuk class

## PANAMA

DESPITE bordering on two oceans and being responsible for one of the world's two great international canals the Republic of Panama has never had a navy of any significance. The territory was a part of Colombia until 1903, when it seceded with the active support of the US. Always an unstable state, Panama was invaded by American forces in 1989 who linked-up with the strong US garrison permanently based in the Canal Zone.

Immediately prior to the US intervention the naval arm of the National Guard was equipped with five patrol boats, of which the largest were two 65ft (19.8m) Comandante Torrijos class vessels displacing 31tons and armed with two MGs. The naval HQ was at Balbao, with a second base at Colon. These boats were subsequently destroyed or seriously damaged. Replacements are being supplied by the US, but at a slow rate.

There are no marines and naval air support is supplied by the air force.

## PARAGUAY

PARAGUAY and the adjacent Bolivia are the only two South American states without direct access to the sea, but, as with virtually all the countries in the continent, there is a vast network of rivers. As a result Paraguay has a very small navy of some 2,000 men, a figure which includes the coastguard and a riverguard. The main bases are at Asuncion, Bahio Negra and Ciudad Deo Este. The equipment is mostly elderly and of little tactical value. One notable vessel is the *Capitan Cabral* which patrols the Upper Parana River and was built as a tug in 1908.

The most modern of the river gunboats is *Itaipo*, a 220ton vessel built in Brazil, commissioned in 1985. Armed with one 1.6in (40mm) gun, six machine-guns and an 3.2in (81mm) mortar, it is also fitted with a small helicopter deck. There are three ships of the Nanawa class, which were built as ocean minesweepers for the Argentine Navy in the late 1930s. Displacing 450tons, they are armed with four 1.6in (40mm) and two MGs. The largest vessels in the navy, displacing 63 tons, are two ships of the Humaita class which were built in Italy in 1930 and four 4.7in (120mm) guns.

An unusual feature of the navy is that it operates a cargo ship, the *Guarani* (1,800tons), which both generates revenue and provides ocean-going experience for naval cadets.

There is a small naval air arm equipped with a variety of elderly aircraft. There are also some modern helicopters, including two Helibras AS.350B, two SA.315B and four Bell H-13 Sioux.

### EQUIPMENT

**Patrol Boats:**
Haipo class
Itaipo class
Humaita class
Nanawa class
**Naval Aircraft:**
Helibras SA.315B Gaviao
Helibras AS.350B
Bell H-13 Sioux

**Below:** A very smart Cessna 150M of the Paraguyan Navy. A growing number of navies are forming their own air arms, mainly to patrol the new economic zones.

## PERU

THE Republic of Peru operates one of the two large navies on the Pacific coast of South America, the other being Chile.

The fleet today centres on a strong force of two cruisers, eight destroyers, four frigates and 11 submarines. The two former Dutch cruisers, *Aguirre* and *Almirante Grau*, were originally identical ships of the Dutch De Zeven Provincien class completed in 1953. They now differ somewhat from each other: *Aguirre* is armed with four 6in (152mm) guns forward, while aft she has a large hangar and flight-deck from which no less than three Sea King helicopters can operate; *Almirante Grau* has eight 6in (152mm) guns and eight Otomat SSM missile launchers, and does not have the helicopter facilities of the *Aguirre*.

Six of the destroyers are also former Dutch ships, having been built in the 1950s as the Royal Netherlands Navy's Friesland class. Originally eight were purchased by Peru, all in the early 1980s, but two have since been stricken. Their main armament is four 4.7in (120mm) guns and two 14.75in (375mm) ASW rocket launchers, but it is a little difficult to gauge their role as they are not particularly capable in any field and the absence of a helicopter deck is especially noticeable. There are also two British ex-Daring class destroyers, purchased in 1969, which have both been fitted with a helicopter deck, although only one has a hangar. Both are armed with 4.5in (114mm) guns (one having four, the other six), and are fitted with four 1.6in (40mm) Breda Dardo air-defence systems.

Much more modern are the four Carvajal class frigates, which are very similar to the Italian Navy's Lupo class; two were built in Italy and two in Peru. Displacing 2,500tons these ships have a single 5in (127mm) DP gun, eight Otomat SSM launchers, an Albatros air-defence system using Aspide missiles, four 1.6in (40mm) Breda Dardo guns and six torpedo tubes. A flight-deck and hangar are also provided for an Agusta-Bell helicopter which is used for both ASW and over-the-horizon targetting for the Otomat SSMs.

The surface fleet is completed by six corvettes/fast patrol boats of the Velarde class. Built in France, they were all delivered in 1980-81. They displace 610tons and are armed with four Exocet SSMs, a single 3in (76mm) and two 1.6in (40mm) guns.

There is a strong amphibious flotilla of four large LSTs which were acquired in 1985. Formerly serving with the US military Sealift Command, they displace 6,225tons at full load and represent a far greater amphibious capability than most other South American navies.

The Peruvian Navy also operates no less than 11 submarines. Six are of the ubiquitous

**Above Left:** The submarine *Islay* is one of six highly-effective German Type 209s serving with the Peruvian Navy.

**Left:** Two of the five Beechcraft T-34C Mentor trainers operated by the small, but efficient Peruvian naval air arm.

**Above:** As in many other South American navies, these Peruvian marines have a major commitment on the country's many large rivers. There are some 2,500 marines in total, formed into a brigade which consists of two battalions, plus two, elite commando and recce companies.

German Type 209, which entered service between 1975 and 1983. These modern boats are supplemented by four Dos de Mayo class submarines, which were built in the 1950s in the United States to a design based on a rather unsuccessful US Navy submarine, the Marlin class. The Peruvian submarines have two unusual distinctions: they were the last submarines built in the USA for export and two of them are the last submarines in the world to mount a deck gun. Finally, there is one remaining ex-US Navy Guppy-IA, the sister of *Pacocha* which sank in 1988 with the loss of five lives.

The naval air force is again quite strong. There are some 24 helicopters: nine Sea Kings armed with Exocets, six AB.212s which operate from the Carvajal class frigates, and a number of smaller types. Fixed-wing assets include two C-130H patrol aircraft, nine Grumman S-2E Tracker ASW aircraft and a number of others.

The marine force is some 2,500 men strong, forming a brigade of two battalions, together with independent recce and commando companies.

### EQUIPMENT

**Cruisers:**
Almirante Grau (Dutch De Zeven Provincien) class
**Submarines:**
Dos de Mayo (US Marlin) class
Casma (German Type 209) class
**Destroyers:**
Palacios (British Daring) class
Bolognesi (Dutch Friesland) class
**Frigates:**
Carvajal (Italian Lupo) class
**Patrol Boats:**
Velarde (French PR-72) class
Pedrera (US Guppy-IA) class
**Naval Aircraft:**
Grumman S-2E Tracker
Beech SuperKing Air
Agusta-Bell AB.212
Sikorsky SH-3D Sea-King
**Marines:**
Two battalions, two companies

## TRINIDAD & TOBAGO

INDEPENDENT from the UK since 1962, the islands have a 650-man coastguard which has a main base at Staubles Bay. It operates two CG-40 class vessels from Sweden which displace 210tons and are armed with one 1.6in (40mm) Bofors gun and one 0.8in (20mm) Oerlikon cannon. There are 15 other craft — including six Wasp class, a large Vosper-build and a Swedish CG-7 of 350tons displacement — and one Twin Beech aircraft.

## SURINAME

ONCE a Dutch colony, Suriname became independent in 1975 and operates a small navy as part of its tri-service force. Its three Dutch-built patrol craft of 140 tons displacement have their main base at Paramaribo and are armed with two Bofors 1.6in (40mm) AA guns and one light machine-gun. There are seven smaller craft in service armed with 0.30in (7.62mm) machine-guns. Four Britten-Norman BN.42 Maritime Defender aircraft undertake coastal patrols as part of the small air force.

## TURKS & CAICOS ISLANDS

THIS British Protectorate has a marine police force which operates two small patrol craft: a Fairey Marine Dagger class displacing 8tons and *Sea Quest*, a Halmatic M160 class displacing nearly 19tons.

**Below:** Souter Wasp patrol craft of the Trinidad coastguard. Many countries are devoting greater resources to policing their extensive 200mile economic zones.

## URUGUAY

**U**RUGUAY'S main claim to naval fame is that it was the unintentional host to the German pocket-battleship *Admiral Graf Spee* during the Battle of the River Plate in 1939 Despite its long coastline Uruguay itself has never attempted to be a major naval power and, with Brazil to the north and Argentina to the south, its navy finds itself sandwiched between the largest and the second largest navies in South America. It does not try to match either, concentrating instead on its task of coastal patrol. The 4,500 men are based at Montevideo and La Paloma.

Largest ships in the navy are three former French Commandant Riviere class frigates. Displacing 2,230tons they are armed with two 3.9in (100mm) guns, an ASW mortar and torpedo tubes; the Exocets, which were fitted when in French service, have been removed. The other major unit is the former USS *Dealey* of the US Navy's class of destroyer-escorts, now named *18 de Julio*. Her armament is similar to the other frigates, with four 3in (76mm) guns, six torpedo tubes and a depth-charge rack.

There are three large patrol boats of the 25 de Agosto class armed with a single 1.6in (40mm) DP, plus a number of other smaller vessels. Like some other South American navies, the Uruguayans operate a merchant-ship, in this case a large tanker, to give their cadets experience. This ship was taken on in 1988; in 1989 it managed to run aground, spilling 1,500,000 gallons of oil.

The naval air force operates a flight of six Grumman S-2E Trackers, a SuperKing Air on maritime patrol and a number of other smaller fixed- and rotary-wing aircraft, including a Sikorsky CH-34A and a Bell.222.

### EQUIPMENT

**Frigates:**
Uruguay (French Commandant Riviere) class
18 de Julio (US Dealey) class
**Patrol Boats:**
25 de Agosto (French Vigilante) class
**Naval Aircraft:**
Grumman S-2A/E Tracker
**Marines**
One battalion

## VENEZUELA

**I**N a continent where most naval ships are bought from abroad the Venezuelan Navy probably holds the record for buying from more countries than any other navy, with vessels from the United States, Germany, Italy, the United Kingdom, Spain and Norway.

The major surface units are six Italian Lupo class frigates, very similar to those in service with the Peruvian Navy. These are supported by six Constitucion class guided-missile patrol boats, built in the UK, which have two different armament fits: three have four Harpoon SSM launchers and a 3in (76mm) gun, while the other three have two Otomats and a 1.6in (40mm) cannon.

There are four very modern LSTs built in South Korea and delivered in 1984. These are supplemented by a single ex-US LST, currently being refitted after running aground. These ships give the Venezuelan Navy a strong amphibious warfare capability.

**Above:** *General Salom*, a Lupo class frigate of the Venezuelan Navy. These ships have a very heavy armament for their size. Seen here are the 5in (127mm) gun on the forecastle, four (of eight) Otomat SSM launchers, the Albatros eight-cell SAM launcher atop the hangar, and one of the two Dardo twin 1.6in (40mm) anti-aircraft gun turrets. The tail of the AB.212 helicopter can just be seen on the flight-deck aft.

**Above:** Venezuelan Navy Agusta-Bell AB.212 helicopter, armed with an Otomat Sea Killer/ Marte anti-ship missile. The AB.212 is based on the Bell 212, which was developed from the famous Bell UH-1 "Huey". Unusually, it has retained its skid undercarriage.

The fleet is rounded-out by two submarines, both German Type 209s. There are reports that three more submarines are to be acquired, one of which may be the USS *Blueback* (SS-581) the last diesel-electric submarine in service with the US Navy which was stricken in 1990. The other two submarines will probably be new-builds, possibly more Type 209s but other designs are known to be under study.

Naval aviation operates both fixed-wing aircraft and helicopters. Casa 212A Aviocars are used for maritime recce and there are a number of other types in the transport and liaison roles. Eight Agusta-Bell AB.212 helicopters operate from the Mariscal Sucre frigates.

There are 6,000 marines, organized into four infantry battalions and supported by artillery and amphibious vehicle battalions plus two paratroop/commando units.

The coastguard is a separate command within the navy with responsibility for patrolling the 200-mile economic zone. It operates a number of vessels which were previously part of the fleet command, including two Almirante Clemente class frigates and two former US Navy fleet tugs, as well as some smaller patrol boats.

**Below:** A German Type 209 submarine of the Venezuelan Navy, which has operated two such boats since 1976/77 and is seeking to buy even more. Both are being refitted and re-engined between 1990 and 1994, enabling them to serve well into the next century.

### EQUIPMENT

**Frigates:**
Mariscal Sucre (Italian Lupo) class
**Patrol Boats:**
Constitucion class
**Amphibious Warfare:**
Capana class
**Naval Aircraft:**
Casa 212 Aviocar
Agusta-Bell AB.212
**Marines:**
Six battalions

## WINDWARD ISLANDS

### ST LUCIA

THE small coastguard operates a 65ft (19.8m) Swift class boat, *Defender*, plus three smaller vessels: *Vigilant II*, built by Phoenix Enterprises in Florida, and two Boston Whalers acquired in 1988.

### ST VINCENT & THE GRENADINES

THIS island group has a marine police force with two small, locally built craft, a 75ft (23m) Vosper Thornycroft boat (*George McIntosh*) and a 120ft (36.6m) Swiftships craft, *Captain Mulzac*.

# ASIA AND FAR EAST

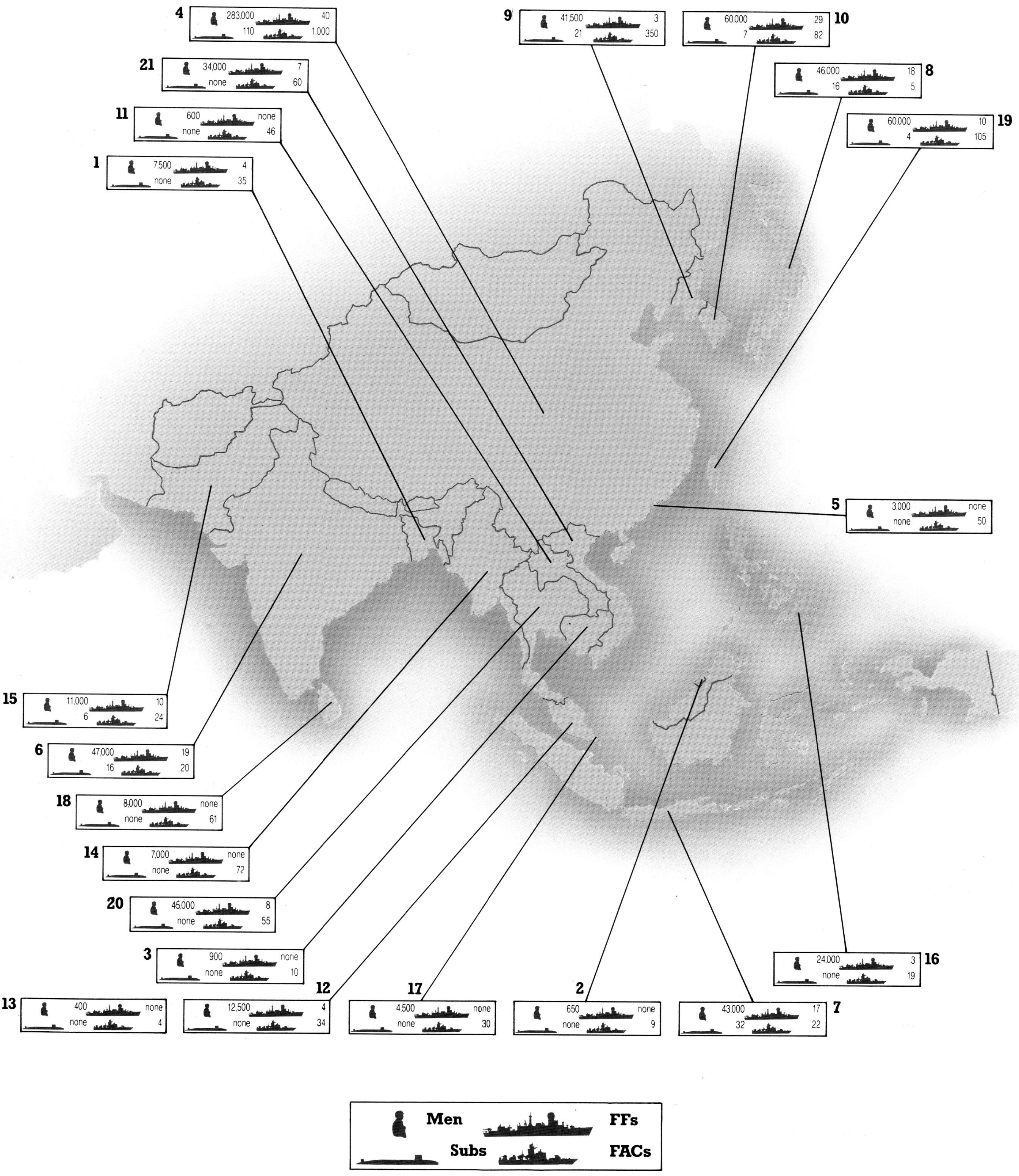
4 283,000 40 110 1,000
21 34,000 7 none 60
11 600 none none 46
1 7,500 4 none 35
9 41,500 3 21 350
10 60,000 29 7 82
8 46,000 18 16 5
19 60,000 10 4 105
5 3,000 none none 50
15 11,000 10 6 24
6 47,000 19 16 20
18 8,000 none none 61
14 7,000 none none 72
20 45,000 8 none 55
3 900 none none 10
16 24,000 3 none 19
13 400 none none 4
12 12,500 4 none 34
17 4,500 none none 30
2 650 none none 9
7 43,000 17 32 22
Men
FFs
Subs
FACs

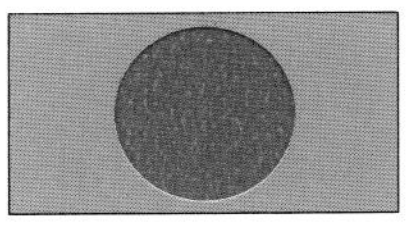

## BANGLADESH

WHEN India gained its independence in 1947 the Muslim state of Pakistan was created. It consisted of two areas separated by the hostile territory of India and as time passed the two found it increasingly difficult to work together. When war broke out in December 1971 between India and Pakistan, the Indians overran the eastern enclave of Pakistan and it became the separate state of Bangladesh, with its own armed forces.

The Bangladesh Navy is a small force which uses a mixture of British and Chinese equipment. Naval HQ is at Chittagong, with other bases at Dhaka, Khulna and Kaptai. The latest warship to join the fleet is the *Osman* (1,900tons), a Chinese Jianghu-II class frigate armed with SSMs, four 3.9in (100mm) guns, 12 AA cannon and depth-charges. *Osman* supplements three former Royal Navy frigates which were built in the mid-1950s and transferred in 1976-1978; all are now of limited operational value.

The remainder of the fleet consists of some 35 patrol boats of various classes, most bought from China with the newest being six years old. Largest of them are two Durjoy class (Chinese Hainan class) vessels, displacing 400tons, which were delivered in the early 1980s. There are no amphibious warfare vessels and neither the navy nor the air force operate maritime aircraft.

### EQUIPMENT

**Frigates:**
Osman (Chinese Jianghu-II) class
Abu Bakr (British Leopard) class
Umar Farooq (British Salisbury) class
**Patrol Boats:**
Durjoy (Chinese Hainan) class
Chinese Hungfen class

**Above:** The Bangladesh Navy has no amphibious warfare ships, but there are many small boats for use along the coast and on rivers. This section of sappers are on river patrol; the uniforms show their British background, but the weapons are Soviet-manufactured AK-47s.

**Below:** Bangladeshi soldiers jump ashore during amphibious training. The country occupies the largest delta in the world, crossed by the Ganges, Brahmaputra and Meghna rivers. The armed forces are inevitably involved in disaster relief.

## BRUNEI

THE small but very rich Sulanate of Brunei Darussalem lies on the north coast of the island of Borneo. For many years its foreign affairs and defence were the responsibility of the British, but Brunei now exercises full sovereignty and its defence is the responsibility of the unified Royal Brunei Armed Forces. The maritime element is designated the "Naval Flotilla" and its tasks are to patrol the state's coastal waters and extensive rivers. It has 530 officers and ratings, with a further 120 in a riverine "Special Combat Squadron". The naval base is at Muara and virtually all the vessels have been built in the United Kingdom or Singapore.

There are three patrol boats of the Waspada class (150tons) which are armed with two Exocet SSMs and a number of machine-guns. These will be reinforced in the mid-1990s by a new class of 1,000ton off-shore patrol boats. There are another six smaller boats and some light landing craft.

There are currently no maritime aircraft, but four CN-235 light aircraft were ordered from Indonesia in 1989 and will be operated by the air wing.

### EQUIPMENT

**Patrol Boats:**
Waspada class

**Below:** *Waspada*, name-ship of a class of three guided-missile patrol boats built in Singapore for Brunei's Naval Flotilla. The two Exocet launchers give these boats heavy hitting power, even so there are plans to buy three vessels.

**Above:** *Ali Haider*, one of two ex-British Leopard class frigates operated by Bangladesh. They have a heavy gun armament of two twin 4.5in (114mm) but no ASW weapons.

**Below:** *Umar Farooq* is a former British Salisbury class air-direction frigate. She suffered major mechanical damage in 1985, but has now been returned to service.

## CAMBODIA

CAMBODIA has been the scene of almost constant conflict for many years and was under the control of Vietnamese armed forces until very recently. The Cambodian Army is by far the biggest force, but there is a small navy based at Kompong Som which is responsible for patrolling the country's coastline and rivers.

Information on the naval force is sparse. Some US- or French-supplied boats may still exist from previous regimes, but if they do they are old and of limited use. The main units are believed to be some Soviet patrol craft delivered in the early 1980s, including three Stenka class light patrol craft (210tons) and three Turya class patrol hydrofoils.

## CHINA

NOT until Mao's Communists gained power did the creation of a powerful navy become a priority for China, one that has been acted upon and sustained ever since, even through the Cultural Revolution. The navy has three missions: to help to establish and maintain China's position as a world power, to control the seas bordering China's eastern and southern coasts, and to pursue the aim of finally overcoming the Nationalists on the island of Taiwan.

The Chinese moved in a methodical and sensible way. At first they purchased Soviet ships, then they constructed Soviet designs in their own yards. Later, they developed their own designs and then, once they had achieved rapprochement with the West, they bought Western equipment and expertise. The result today is that they not only have a modern and well-equipped fleet, but are also one of the world's major exporters of warships. Today's Chinese Navy is approximately 200,000 strong, with a further 40,000 in the naval air arm, 43,000 in the marine corps and some one million in the paramilitary naval militia.

It is organized into three fleet areas, which are subdivided into afloat forces and coastal defence districts. The South Sea Fleet has its HQ at Zhanjiang and covers the coast from the border with Vietnam to approximately 23deg N. Its area of responsibility includes the South China Sea and the troublesome neighbour of Vietnam, as well as the disputed Spratley and Paracel Islands. The East Sea Fleet has its HQ at Shanghai and extends north from the junction with the South Sea Fleet to the border between Jiangsu and Shandong provides at 35deg N. Its area includes the island of Taiwan and the mouth of the mighty Yangtse River. The North Sea Fleet's area (HQ Quingdao) is northwards from the junction with the East Sea Fleet to the border with North Korea.

The main element of the fleet is a large force of approximately 20 destroyers and 40 frigates, of which the only remaining Soviet-built ships are two Zhangzhun class (Soviet Gordiyy class) destroyers. Completed in the USSR in 1941 and transferred to China in 1954, these ancient vessels have no ASW sensors or armament and now have little operational value, despite having been fitted with four Chinese HY-2 SSMs. The main element of the destroyer force is the Luda class with 15 known to be in service. They displace 3,960tons and although the weapons fit varies between ships most seem to have six SSMs, four 5in (130mm) DP guns, a number of 2.25in (57mm) or 1.5in (37mm) AA guns, and various light ASW weapons. They were to have been modernized in the late 1980s with US equipment, but the 1989 US arms embargo stopped this.

The four oldest frigates of the Chengdu class were built in Chinese yards to the Soviet Riga class design in the late 1950s and have been altered in service by replacing the torpedo tubes with a twin CSS-N-1 missile launcher. There are also five ships of the Jiangnan class, which are Chinese-modified versions of the Riga design but

**Below:** Three Shanghai class patrol boats operating off the coast of southern China. Weapons are a twin 1in (25mm) AA (nearest camera) and a twin 1.45in (37mm) AA aft.

without the missiles. These were followed by the first real Chinese design, the Jiangdong class, a 1,900ton frigate armed with two HQ-61 SAM launchers and, like all subsequent Chinese frigates up to the present, powered by two French SEMT-Pielstick diesels. These two ships were completed in the early 1970s, but their missile systems did not attain service status until about 10 years later.

The main element of the frigate force is a series of progressive designs designated the Jianghu class. The Jianghu-I and -II designs, of which some 24 have been built, have identical hulls and differ only in their weapons and sensor fits. Both have two twin HY-2 SSM launchers, but the Jianghu-I has two single 3.9in (100mm) DP guns whereas the Jianghu-II has two 3.9in (100mm) twin mounts. The Jianghu-I has 12 1.5in (37mm) AA guns, while the Jianghu-II omits two twin 1.5in (37mm) guns presumably to compensate for the extra topweight of the twin 3.9in (100mm) mounts. The Jianghu-III has the same hull and propulsion, but is armed with eight C-801 SSM launchers mounted on a long shelter deck. This design is fitted with fin stabilizers and has much improved sensors and control equipment. Jianghu-IV is yet further improved, principally by the installation of a helicopter hangar and flight-deck.

Only the latest Luda destroyers are powered by gas-turbines, all the rest having diesel engines with no mixed power plants. ASW sensors and weapons are rudimentary and would be unlikely to be effective against modern high-performance submarines.

Finally, only the very latest Jianghu-IV class been built with helicopter facilities, while plans to convert some of the Ludas to take a helicopter have been delayed by the arms embargo. Surface and air sensors, and fire control systems are fairly unsophisticated and some of the older frigates have little more than an optical gun control system. Thus, although all these frigates and destroyers are well laid out and elegant there are significant differences from Western designs. It should not be doubted, however, that the Chinese Navy has every intention of catching up with the most modern designs of other navies.

The Chinese Navy is faced with a huge coastal patrol task and thus not surprisingly has nearly 1,000 patrol boats. One of the major elements of this force are some 120 Huangfeng class guided-missile boats, copies of the Soviet Osa-I class armed with four HY-1 SSMs. There are also about 75 Hoku class boats, rather smaller Chinese-designed boats armed with two HY-1 or four C-801 SSMs. The Huchuan class torpedo boats are an interesting design, some having hydrofoils forward but none in the stern, while others appear identical except for omission of the hydrofoils. There are many minor patrol boats, including over 300 Shanghai-II class and 60 Hainan class.

As would be expected of the navy of a country which claims Taiwan there is a large amphibious warfare fleet. The largest units are 15 WWII-vintage ex-US Navy LSTs and four of the Chinese-designed Yukan class built in the late 1970s. There is also a host of minor landing craft.

**Below:** The Chinese Navy's training ship *Zheng He* (5,500tons) in transit across the Pacific for an official visit to the US Navy base at Pearl Harbor in November 1989.

**Below:** A Chinese ES3B submarine, a locally-built copy of the basic Soviet Romeo class. Some 84 of these are in service, armed with Soviet Type 53 torpedoes.

**Above:** The first Romeos entered Chinese service in 1960; the last in 1984. These worn-looking Romeos are at Qing Dao in November 1986.

**Below:** A very smart honour guard welcomes the first US Navy ship to visit Qing Dao on 5 November 1986. The rifle is a Type 59.

The Chinese received a few elderly Soviet submarines in the early 1950s, but were determined from an early stage to establish their own construction capability. In 1956 they were supplied with the parts for five Soviet Whiskey class subarmines which they assembled at a new yard at Jiangnan. Thereafter, the submarines were built completely in China, with 15 constructed in the 1960s. Next, the USSR supplied parts for three Romeo class and to date no less than 87 have been built, plus eight more for export (four to Egypt and four to North Korea).

The first indigenous Chinese submarine design was the Ming class (Type ES5C/D) in the 1970s, relatively large boats with a displacement of 2,113tons submerged. They have an Albacore-type hull, but do not seem to have been too successful; one suffered a serious fire and was subsequently scrapped. The problems appear to have been rectified and production of a modified design (Type ES5E) restarted in 1987 at the rather slow rate of one hull per year.

The same hull appears to have been used for the modified Romeo class cruise-missile submarine (Type ES5G). This submarine has six missile bins in neat housings either side of the fin, but launching is only possible when surfaced — a serious tactical drawback in today's conditions. The missile is the C-801 Ying-ji, a sea-skimming cruise-missile with a 22nm range and a distinct visual resemblance to the French Exocet.

Development of nuclear-powered attack submarines started in the mid-1960s and the first Han class SSN was laid down in 1971 and completed in 1974. Since then three have been completed, with another three on order. "Xia" is a Western nickname for the first class of Chinese SSBNs, which represent a remarkable national achievement and illustrate the intention of the People's Republic to take its rightful place among the Superpowers. Prior to the spectacular break between the two countries the USSR provided China with plans for its Golf-II class, diesel-electric powered, ballistic missile submarine. The plans were modified slightly by the Chinese to meet their needs and then one submarine was built which was launched in 1964. The Chinese boat was fitted with two tubes for the CSS-N-3 missile, the first known launch being in 1982.

Meanwhile the Chinese nuclear warhead, propulsion, missile and submarine development programmes were forging ahead. The first Han class SSN had been launched in 1974; in 1978 the first Xia class hull was laid down at Huladao and launched in April 1981. It is of typical SSBN layout, with a large turtleback abaft the sail which houses 12 CSS-N-3 missiles. The first Xia class SSBN became operational in 1988. The PRC's submarine deterrent cannot be credible until a minimum of two more SSBNs have been completed, but having shown the determination and capability to get this far, it is highly unlikely that the PRC will fail to construct a sufficient number of SSBNs.

The Naval Air Arm is under the operational control of the navy and consists of some 40,000 men and about 800 aircraft. A few helicopters serve afloat on frigates and research ships, but the vast bulk of the air force is shore-based and there are no known plans for any aircraft carriers. There are about 600 fighters and 150 bombers, of which about 100 are the copies of the Ilyushin Il-28 with the remainder Tupolev Tu-16 copies. The naval air force has long operated 12 Soviet Beriev Be-6 amphibians, but these are now being supplemented by the locally-designed Harbin Shuihong 5 ASW amphibian, a very elegant, four-engined machine which was unveiled for the first time in 1985.

There is a small, but growing number of naval helicopters. Largest is the French-designed Super Frelon; armed and equipped for ASW missions, 13 were supplied by France and more are being built in China as the Zhi-8. In addition, up to 50 Zhi-9s are being built, a copy of the SA.365 Dauphin. Other more advanced Western helicopters were also under consideration when the arms embargo was declared in response to the events in Tianamen Square.

The marine force is large, although estimates of its size vary from as little as 6,000 to as many as 40,000. It appears to be modelled on the Soviet naval infantry and is equipped with amphibious tanks and armoured personnel carriers (APCs). In addition, there is a Coastal Defence Force tasked with the protection of important coastal facilities such as naval bases and offshore islands. It consists of a large number of artillery units armed with guns and CSS-C-2 (Silkworm) anti-ship missiles.

### EQUIPMENT

**Submarines:**
Soviet Romeo class
Ming class
Han class
Xia class
**Destroyers:**
Luda class
Zhangzhun (Soviet Gordiyy) class
**Frigates:**
Jianghu-I, II, III & IV classes
Jiangdong class
Jiangnan (modified Soviet Riga) class
Chengdu (Soviet Riga) class
**Patrol Boats:**
Huangfeng (Soviet Osa-I) class
Hoko class
Huchuan class
Hainan class
Shanghai-II class
**Amphibious Warfare:**
*Yukan* class
*Shan* (ex-US LST-1) class
**Naval Aircraft:**
CAC Jian-5 (MiG-17)
CAC Jian-6 (MiG-19)
CAC Jian-7 (MiG-21)
CAC Jian 8 (Modified MiG-21F)
XAC H-5 (Il-28)
XAC Hong-6 (Tu-16)
Beriev Be-6
Harbin Shuihong SH-5
CAMC Zhi-8 (Super Frelon)
HAMC Zhi-9 (Aerospatiale AS.365 Dauphin)
**Marines:**
Several divisions

**Above:** An alert crew mans an EDS-25A ASW rocket launcher (PRC-built adaptation of the Soviet RBU-1200), one of which is being fired from the Hainan class patrol boat to port.

### HONG KONG

A British colony of 244 islands, until control reverts to China, Hong Kong maintains its own 3,000 strong marine police/naval force as well as benefiting from the protection afforded by three RN corvettes permanently stationed there. There are 15 King Lai class (Damen-III) patrol boats built in Kowloon and each armed with a light machine-gun. There are approximately 40 other craft, including nine Fairey Marine Spear class, 10 86ton boats of the Damen design, and seven 78ft (23.7m) craft from Vosper Thornycroft which are designated *Sea Cat* class.

**Below:** *Sea Panther* (PL3 ) a command/patrol boat of the Marine District of the Royal Hong Kong Police Force, one of the busiest marine police forces anywhere.

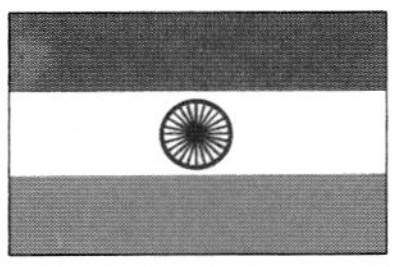

## INDIA

THE Royal Indian Navy was formed by the British as an adjunct of the Royal Navy for Imperial defence tasks. At the end of WWII it numbered some 400 ships and approximately 26,000 men, but by the time of independence in 1947 it had been reduced to a mere 11,000 men, four sloops, two frigates and one corvette. From that low-point it has expanded steadily until today it is one of the strongest navies in the world and, by a very considerable margin, the strongest indigenous navy in the strategically vital Indian Ocean.

India has fought five wars since 1947, three against Pakistan and two against China, but only against Pakistan has the navy been able to play a significant role. In the 1965 war the Pakistan Navy was able to carry out raids against the western coast of India, which led to a restructuring of the Indian Navy. As a result it did very much better in the 1971 war, with the Western Naval Command successfully bombarding Karachi, while in the Bay of Bengal a task force centred on the aircraft carrier *Vikrant* bottled up the Pakistan fleet. This prevented resuplly or evacuation of the beleaguered garrison and was one of the major factors which led to Pakistan's loss of its eastern provinces, which became the independent state of Bangladesh.

Another significant incident in the 1971 war was the deployment of the US Navy's nuclear carrier USS *Enterprise* to the Indian Ocean. This was seen as a threatening gesture from a Superpower, which the Indian Navy has never forgotten and which has been a major factor in the expansion programme.

In the early days after independence the navy retained a strong British influence and used predominantly British ships, equipment and methods. In the 1970s, however, the Soviet influence began to grow, with the supply of ships, sensors and armament. Today, the Indian Navy operates a mixture of ships and submarines, but there is no clearly predominant external influence, and with its own ever-stronger design and construction base it is clear that the Indian Navy is now its own master.

Afloat there are two major fleet commands, based on the carrier groups: the Western Fleet being based on Bombay and the Eastern Fleet on Visakhapatnam. There are also two functional commands, one for submarines (Visakhapatnam), the other for naval air (Goa). Ashore the major headquarters are at Bombay (HQ Western Command), Cochin (HQ Southern Command) and Visakhnapatnam (HQ Eastern Command).

Today the Indian Navy has a front-line strength of two aircraft carriers, five destroyers, 19 frigates, numerous smaller vessels and auxiliaries, and 16 submarines. This force is designed for two principal missions. First is the ever-present threat of war with Pakistan; second is a concern over the many actual and potential conflicts along the periphery of the Indian Ocean. The navy sees its responsibilities covering the entire area, extending from the mouth of the Red Sea in the west to the Straits of Malakka in the east, and from its own coastline south to the Antarctic. Indeed, there exists a scarcely-concealed wish to be the predominant naval power in the Indian Ocean.

**Above:** The Indian Navy carrier *Viraat* (ex-British *Hermes*). With her Sea Harrier V/STOL aircraft and Sea King helicopters she is now a major strategic force in the Indian Ocean.

**Below:** *Ranvir* is one of five Kashin class destroyers built in the USSR for India between 1980 and 1988. Their weapons and equipment differ from the Soviet units.

**Above:** The corvette *Kukri*, lead-ship of a new class of 12. Built in India they are armed with a 3in (76mm) gun and two twin SS-N-2 launchers forward, with two 1.12in (30mm) Gatling CIWS and two SA-N-5 launchers aft. There is a flight-deck for a HAL Chetak ASW helicopter.

**Left:** Indian marine commandos carrying out a training exercise in clandestine raiding. They are armed with Indian-produced versions of the FN 0.30in (7.62mm) FAL rifle, 0.35in (9mm) Sterling SMG and the 0.30in (7.62mm) Bren LMG. The commando force is of recent origin and is expanding rapidly as part of India's move to play a dominant role in the Indian Ocean area.

The surface fleet is based on two aircraft carriers, currently the elderly ex-British light fleet carriers, *Vikrant* and *Viraat*. These each operate air groups of eight Sea Harrier V/STOL fighters and eight Sea King ASW helicopters. A new carrier is under construction in India, which is scheduled to enter service in 1997. The design is based on that of the French nuclear-powered carrier *Charles de Gaulle* which is currently under construction in France, but the Indian carrier will be conventionally powered. At least one more is likely to be built.

There are five Rajput class destroyers, built in the Soviet Union to a specially modified Kashin class design, which includes a helicopter hangar and revised armament. There are also six Nilgiri class frigates, built in India between 1966 and 1977, whose design is based upon that of the very successful British Leander class. These were progressively developed to meet Indian needs, but the latest frigates, the Godavari class, use an enlarged version of the Leander hull, but with much improved armament and a very much larger hangar which can house two Sea King helicopters. There are six Soviet Petya class acquired in the 1970s and two older British frigates remain in service as training ships.

A 22 strong force of minesweepers is operated, mostly Soviet designs, and the navy is seeking to acquire minehunters for the fleet shortly.

The surface fleet is completed by a large number of corvettes and fast patrol boats. Virtually all of these have been constructed in the USSR, but the new Khukri class corvettes and some of the Soviet-designed Tarantul class are being built in India; some new patrol boats have also come from Korea. Amphibious warfare ships comprise eight Soviet Polnocny-C landing ships and two Indian-designed and built Magar class LCTs, with a further six to follow. Finally, there is the usual plethora of auxiliaries, including two German-built fleet oilers, with a new Indian-designed class under construction.

The Indian submarine fleet started with Soviet Foxtrot class boats, eight of which were supplied between 1970 and 1974. The Foxtrot has a good reputation as a simple, rugged and reliable boat, and was quite sufficient for the Indian Navy's needs at that time. After a gap of some years four Type 209 submarines were ordered, of which the first two were built in Germany. The second pair are being built in Bombay to establish an Indian submarine-construction capability. However, construction has proved more difficult than expected and there are serious delays; as a result, 10 Soviet Kilo class (3,000 tons), diesel-electric submarines were ordered to fill the gap. The first was delivered in 1986 and seven had been delivered by the beginning of 1991. It is believed that the Indian Navy may seek a licence to construct further Kilo class boats in India.

The Type 209 and Kilo programmes have already given the Indian Navy the largest and most modern submarine fleet in the Indian Ocean. In 1988 a Soviet Charlie class SSGN entered service on loan from the Soviet Navy, the first nuclear-powered submarine to be operated by any developing navy, indicating not only a high level of sophistication in Indian Navy training and technological expertise, but also a major extension of its maritime ambitions. Mysteriously, this was returned early in 1991.

The Naval Air Force comprises some 50 fixed-wing aircraft and 70 helicopters. The carrier-borne component is based on the Sea Harrier FRS Mk 51 V/STOL fighter, with 18 delivered out of a current order of 24, possibly with more to follow. Afloat ASW is provided by helicopters, with both Soviet and British types being operated from the carriers, destroyers and frigates. Long-range maritime reconnaissance is conducted by five Soviet-built Tupolev Tu-142M Bear-F (a further three are on order) and three Ilyushin Il-38 May aircraft. Nine Britten-Norman Islanders provide coastal patrols. The remainder of the naval air force is a mixture of light helicopters, communications aircraft, search-and-rescue helicopters and training aircraft.

There has long been a requirement for marines, but only recently have such troops been formed. There is currently one regiment (approximately 1,000 men), with a second regiment being formed.

The Indian Navy clearly plans to dominate the Indian Ocean with a modern and well-balanced fleet. India also clearly aims to be independent of outside suppliers as is shown by the construction of their own aircraft carriers, frigates and submarines. Further, the acquisition of the nuclear-powered SSGN, coupled with the establishment of a submarine-construction capability in Bombay and the already known missile and nuclear-warhead capability, suggest that the long-term plans almost certainly include a force of SSBNs armed with SLBMs. Such a strategic force would be supported by domestically-designed and built SSNs and SSKs.

## EQUIPMENT

**Aircraft Carriers:**
Viraat (British Hermes) class
Vikrant (British Majestic) class
**Submarines:**
Shishumar (German SSK-1500) class
Sindhugosh (Soviet Kilo) class
Kursura (Soviet Foxtrot) class
**Destroyers:**
Rajput (modified Soviet Kashin) class
**Frigates:**
Godavari class
Nilgiri (modified British Leander) class
Arnala (Soviet Petya) class
**Patrol Boats:**
Prachand (Soviet Osa-II) class
Abhay (Soviet Pauk) class
Sukanya (Korean Neptune) class
**Corvettes:**
Khukri class
Veer (Soviet Tarantul-I) class
Vibhuti (modified Soviet Tarantul-I) class
Vijaydurg (Soviet Nanuchka-II) class
**Amphibious Warfare:**
Magar class
Ghorpad (Soviet Polnocny-C) class
Vasco da Gama class
**Mine Warfare:**
Bulsar (British Ham) class
Pondicherry (Soviet Natya-I) class
Mahe (Soviet Yevgenya) class
**Naval Aircraft:**
BAe Sea Harrier FRS.51
Westland Sea King Mk42
Kamov Ka-25 Hormone
Kamov Ka-27 Helix
HAL Chetak (Aerospatiale SA.316B Alouette III)
Ilyushin Il-38 May
Tupolev Tu-142M Bear-F
HAL Dornier 228
Britten-Norman BN.42B/T Maritime Defender
**Marines:**
Two regiments

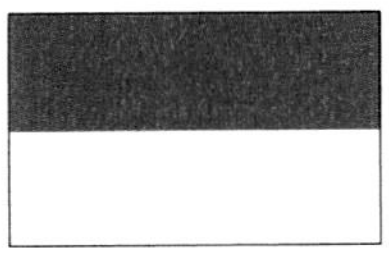

## INDONESIA

**Above:** The Indonesian Navy's *Ahmad Yani*, a former Dutch Van Speijk class frigate, built to the British Leander design.

**Below:** *Ajak* is one of the Indonesian Navy's four Lürssen PB-57 patrol boats. Note the two stern-mounted, aft-firing torpedo tubes.

THE Dutch East Indies was a sprawling mass of some 1,000 islands, ranging in size from huge territories such as Sumatra and Borneo to tiny atolls. It became independent from the Netherlands in 1949 and since then Indonesia has sought to become one of the dominant powers in the area.

The navy is divided into the Western and Eastern Fleets, with their HQs at Djakarta and Surabaya respectively. There is also an important body called the Military Sea Communications Command which controls inter-island communications. Total naval manpower is about 30,000, with a further 1,000 in naval aviation and 12,000 marines organized into twelve battalions and a combat support regiment.

There are 17 frigates from five sources, the oldest of which are the four Samadikun class which were once US Navy Claud Jones class destroyer-escorts. They are armed with light guns and torpedoes, but are of little value other than as patrol ships.

In the late 1970s Indonesia ordered three Fatahilah class frigates from Wilton-Fijenoord in The Netherlands. Displacing 1,450tons, and described variously as either corvettes or frigates, their main armament is four Exocet launchers and a 4.7in (120mm) DP gun; just one of the three, *Nala*, is fitted with a flight-deck and hangar for a Wasp helicopter. During the same period Indonesia bought a training frigate from Yugoslavia. With a displacement of 1,850tons, the *Hajar Dewantara* is armed with four Exocet launchers and a number of light guns. It also operates an MBB Bo-105 helicopter and the ship obviously could be used for operational tasks in wartime.

After these new-builds the Indonesian Navy bought two classes of second-hand frigates in the mid-1980s. The first were three British Tribal class frigates which were built in the early 1960s and transferred after a major refit. Designed for use in tropical waters and equipped for both surface and ASW roles these handy ships should last for some years. They have a tiny helicopter deck and Indonesia bought Wasp helicopters to go with them.

The others were six Van Speijk class frigates from The Netherlands, acquired in the period 1986-90. These ships were made in The Netherlands to a design based on that of the British Leander class. They were commissioned into the RNethN in the late 1960s and were modified in service so that their present armament consists of four Harpoon SSM launchers, two Sea Cat SAM launchers, a single 3in (76mm) DP gun and six ASW torpedo tubes. They operate Westland Wasp helicopters and are fitted with predominantly Dutch electronic systems.

There is currently a plan to build a large class of new frigates to replace all the current types. Known as the FSG-90 project, the intention is for the first to be built abroad, following which the remainder would be built in Indonesia.

There are 22 patrol boats of five classes, a remarkably small number for the huge sea area to be covered. In the early 1980s the navy produced a plan to purchase no less than 47 Boeing Jetfoil hydrofoils in two versions, one armed and the other for troop transport. Displacing 115tons and with a top speed of 46kts five were actually delivered but only one ever entered service; the craft proved fragile and expensive to operate and the project is now dead.

Indonesia bought two of the "Tripartite" type glass-reinforced plastic (GRP) minehunters (568tons) from The Netherlands in 1988 and plans to build 10 more at home. They operate as the Pulau Rengat class. There is a large number of amphibious warfare ships, which includes 10 old US Navy LSTs and six new-build Teluk Semangka class LSTs constructed in South Korea.

At one time the Indonesian Navy operated 14 Soviet Whiskey class diesel-electric submarines, but only one of these remains in service. The only other submarines are two of the widely used German Type 209s, which were delivered in 1981 and refitted in 1989.

The principal responsibility of the naval air force is coastal surveillance, and for this it is equipped with a variety of light aircraft types from several different sources. There are 12 Australian N228 and six N22SL Searchmasters, while helicopter types include British Westland Wasps, German Bo-105s and locally-built AS.332 Super Pumas. Longer range surveillance is undertaken by the air force which operates three modified Boeing 737 airliners fitted with sideways-looking radar and other equipment for the maritime recce role. There are also three C-130H-MP aircraft and six smaller ITPN- Casa CN-235s.

### EQUIPMENT

**Submarines:**
Cakra (German Type 209) class
Pasopati (Soviet Whiskey) class
**Frigates:**
Hajar Dewantara class
Fatahilah class
Ahmad Yani (Dutch Van Speijk) class
Martha Khristina Tiyahahu (ex-British Tribal) class
Samadikun (US Claud Jones) class
**Patrol Boats:**
Mandua class
Andau (German Lürssen PB-57) class
Sibaru (Australian Attack) class
**Amphibious Warfare:**
Teluk Semangka class
Teluk Langsa (US LST 542) class
**Mine Warfare:**
Pulau Rengat (Dutch Tripartite) class
**Naval Aircraft:**
ASTA N22B/SL Searchmaster
Aerospatiale SA.316 Alouette III
IPTN NBo-105
Westland Wasp HAS.1
IPTN NAS.332 Super Puma
**Marines:**
A regiment and 12 battalions

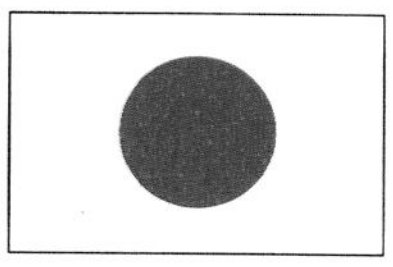

## JAPAN

JAPAN'S naval force is designated the Kaiso Jeitai, or Maritime Self-Defence Force (MSDF). There is also a large civilian organization, the Kaijo Hoancho (Maritime Safety Agency), which in time of war would come under control of the MSDF.

Today's MSDF consists of some 34,000 men, with a further 12,000 in the air component and 12,000 in the Maritime Safety Agency. The MSDF fleet is organized into four surface flotillas, each consisting of some six to eight destroyers or frigates: two flotillas are home ported at Yokosuka and one each at Sasebo and Maizuru. The submarine force is organized into two flotillas, one at Kure, the other at Yokosuka. Remaining ships are allocated to 10 regions.

The MSDF is faced by several problems. First, is the proximity of the very powerful Soviet Far Eastern Fleet and its bases along the Soviet Pacific coast. Second, is the proximity of the Chinese fleet, which is growing rapidly in both size and capability, having recently commissioned its first nuclear-powered, ballistic missile submarine (SSBN). Thirdly, there is the total dependence of Japan upon sea trade.

The surface fleet consists of a large number of modern, well-designed and effective units, all built in Japan and equipped, predominantly, with United States' missiles and helicopters, Italian guns and Japanese electronics. There are no less than 39 destroyers in service with more building. A great variety of classes exists; the oldest of these are several classes built in the 1960s: the Minegumo (three ships), Yamagumo (six ships), Takatsuki (four ships) and Amatsukaze (one ship) classes.

The more modern destroyers start with the Tachikaze class built in the 1970s, three 4,800ton displacement ships equipped with four launchers, each with a magazine of 10 Standard SAM or Harpoon anti-ship missiles. There are no less than 12 of the next group, the 3,800ton Hatsuyuki class, which are heavily-armed, fast and operate a Sea King ASW helicopter. Next are two of the rather larger (5,600tons) Hatakaze class, again very well-armed and equipped, but with a surprising feature of a helicopter deck but no hangar, somewhat on the style of the US Navy's Arleigh Burke class.

The most recent class to enter service is the Asagiri class, eight ships of 4,300tons displacement, with a medium-sized flight-deck and a hangar for one Sea King helicopter. Currently under construction is the first of the Yukikaze class which are classified as destroyers, although their displacement of 8,900tons makes them larger than most cruisers. They are specifically designed to take the US Navy's AEGIS system and the design is essentially an enlarged and improved version of, again, the US Navy's Arleigh Burke class.

Finally, there are two classes of very large helicopter-carrying destroyers: two Haruna class (6,550tons) and two of the improved Shirane class (6,800tons). Both have a very compact superstructure which includes a large aircraft hangar, and a long flight-deck which takes up about one-third of the overall length of the ships, enabling them to operate three Sea King helicopters.

The MSDF also operates 18 frigates, a term which covers ships designed specifically for the escort role and displacing less than about 2,500tons. They are well armed and equipped with up-to-date electronic equipment and sensors, but none is equipped to handle helicopters. There are six of the latest Abukuma class (2,550tons), one of the Ishikari class (1,450tons) and two of the similar but slightly larger Yubari class (1,760tons). Oldest escorts are the 11 strong Chikugo class (1,800tons).

The surface fleet is completed by just five fast torpedo boats, which are to be replaced by six new boats in the mid-1990s. Such small numbers suggest that this is a category of warship which is not regarded too seriously in the MSDF. Finally, there is a large group of mine warfare vessels and 10 landing craft.

The MSDF would never be allowed to operate nuclear-powered submarines, but they have some of the finest diesel-electric submarines currently in service. Oldest among them is the Uzushio class of 3,600 tons submerged displacement, with a tear-drop hull and a high underwater performance. These five boats were built in the 1970s and one has already been transferred to the training role. The 10 submarines of the Yuushio class were built in the 1980s as enlarged and more capable versions of the Uzushio class, displacing 2,600tons. Latest to join the fleet is the first boat of the Haruna class, with at least four more to follow. Displacing 2,750tons they are armed with Sub-Harpoon missiles and Japanese GRX-2 torpedoes.

The main element of the naval air arm is the land-based ASW force with some 70 P-3C Orions, six P-2J Neptunes and seven US-1As. Of the land-based helicopters there are six S-80M1s; while there are nearly 80 Sea Kings and two Seahawks, with dozens more on order, based at sea.

Thus, the MSDF can be seen to be a very modern and well-equipped naval force, whose real combat strength lies in its destroyers and submarines. As expected, all vessels are technologically advanced.

### EQUIPMENT

**Submarines:**
Harusho class
Yuushio class
Uzushio class
**Destroyers:**
Shirane class
Haruna class
Asagiri class
Hatakaze class
Hatsuyuki class
Tachikaze class
Amatsukaze class
Takatsuki class
Yamagumo class
Minegumo class
**Frigates:**
Abukuma class
Yubari class
Ishikari class
Chikugo class
Isuzu class
**Amphibious Warfare:**
Miura class
Atsumi class
**Naval Aircraft:**
Kawasaki P-2J (Lockheed P-2 Neptune)
Kawasaki P-3C (Lockheed P-3 Orion)
Mitsubishi HSS-2A/B (Sikorsky SH-3 Sea King)
Kawasaki KV-107A (Boeing Vertol CH-46)
Mitsubishi S-80M1 (Sikorsky MH-53E Sea Dragon)
Mitsubishi SH-60J (Sikorsky SH-60 Seahawk)
Shin Meiwa US-1A (SAR)

**Left:** There are 39 modern and highly capable destroyers in service with the JMSDF. This ship, *Natsugumo*, is one of three in the Minegumo class, built from 1967 to 1970.

**Right:** Four JMSDF destroyers lie alongside a wharf in Pearl Harbor, Hawaii in 1988. All belong to the Hatsuyuki class, a group of 12 well-equipped ships built in the early 1980s.

## KOREA (NORTH)

COMMUNIST North Korea is obsessed with secrecy and it is difficult to obtain information on its armed forces. It is reasonably certain, however, that its navy is not as powerful as that of its neighbour to the south and that the greater part of its strength is devoted to a large number of outdated designs.

The navy is organized into two command areas, one on the west coast with its HQ at Nampo, the other on the east coast with its HQ at Wonsan. There are no known marines and all the aircraft in service are operated by the air force.

The fleet has just three frigates in two different classes. All are designed and built locally but fitted with Soviet weapons and equipment. The sole Soho class ship (2,000tons) was completed in 1983 and is armed with four Soviet SS-N-2 Styx launchers and a 3.9in (100mm) gun. The two Najin class frigates are older, having been completed in the mid-1970s. Slightly smaller than the Soho they have two SS-N-2 launchers and two 3.9in (100mm) guns. All three are considered to be poor designs, relatively unsuccessful in service and of limited tactical value.

The major strength of the surface fleet lies in the 300-plus small patrol boats and craft. Some were supplied by the USSR and a few by China, but the majority have been constructed in North Korean yards. There are also four medium-sized LCTs and some 100 small assault landing craft, a force clearly designed for a short-range "hook" around the De-Militarized Zone (DMZ) which dates from the 1950's civil war.

The 21 submarines all date back to the 1970s. There are 17 Romeo class boats (of which four were built in China and the remainder in North Korea) and four remaining Whiskey class submarines which were supplied by the USSR in 1974. Finally, there are approximately 20 Korean-designed and built midget submarines which are no doubt intended to deliver sabatoeurs and/or special forces into South Korea for a destabilization campaign.

### EQUIPMENT

**Submarines:**
Chinese Romeo class
Soviet Whiskey class
**Frigates:**
Soho class
Najin class
**Corvettes:**
Sariwan class

## KOREA (SOUTH)

**Left:** *Kum Kok*, a US-built minesweeper provided to the South Korean Navy in 1959. The North Korean Navy has a major minelaying capability and would not hesitate to use them in any conflict with the Republic of Korea.

THE modern South Korean Navy is large and well-balanced. They have moved away from their reliance on the USA and an increasing number of indigenious designs and builds have joined the fleet. With the ever-present threat of attack from the north, the navy's primary defensive mission is in no doubt. Naval headquarters is at Chinhae.

Currently, the navy has some 35,000 personnel and there are also 25,000 marines who garrison islands and guard the Han River estuary. The major units in the fleet are 10 very old ex-USN destroyers which date from WWII. The oldest of these is *Chung Mu* (2,850tons), a Fletcher class ship completed in 1943, which is armed with a mix of 5in (127mm) and 1.6in (40mm) guns, ASW mortars and torpedo tubes; her operational value is low. The others are of slightly more use, having all been updated in the US Navy's Fleet Refit And Modernization (FRAM) programme before they were handed over and then undergoing later refits in Korea when they received new sensors and Harpoon SSMs. Despite this even these ships are showing their years and at least nine of a replacement design are due to be built in Korea between 1992 and 1999.

A large number of frigates are operated, all of them modern and home-built. There are three classes currently being produced; the largest is the Ulsan class (2,180tons), of which seven are in service with up to eight more planned; next comes the Donghae class (1,300tons) with 22 in service and four under construction; the smallest is the HDC 800 class (950tons) of which at least two are being built. All of these ships are armed with Harpoon SSMs, 3in (76mm) DP guns, 1.6in (40mm) Bofors, 1.12in (30mm) Emerlec AA cannon and ASW torpedo tubes, the numbers of each depending on the size of the hull.

There are 82 patrol boats, only a few of which were built abroad in the USA. The best of these is the fast, gas-turbine powered PSMM-5 class mounting four Harpoon SSMs, a 3in (76mm) GP gun, two 1.12in (30mm) Emerlec AA cannon and two light MGs in a 268ton hull. Most North Korean patrol boats can lay mines and therefore South Korea has eight small, US-built minesweepers and is building a class of 10 minehunters based on the Italian Lerici design, of which two are already in service.

A large amphibious force of seven ex-US Navy LSTs and a similar number of LSMs equips the marines. Surprisingly, although Korean yards have produced some excellent LSTs for foreign navies, the South Korea Navy has yet to buy any replacements for its now elderly fleet.

In the early 1980s an under-surface element was added to the fleet when the Hyundai Shipyard built three small (175tons), Korean-designed Tolgorae class submarines. These are to be followed by 12 larger submarines; six of them IKL Type 1400s which are currently on order from Germany. The first three are being built there and the rest in Korea; the other six will be a new Korean design.

Finally, there is the Republic of Korea Coast Guard which operates some 50 patrol ships. Most of these are for inshore protection duties, but the larger ones are quite capable warships. The HDC 1150 class, for example, displaces 1,200tons and is armed with a 3in (76mm) DP gun, a 1.6in (40mm) AA gun and two 0.8in (20mm) Mk 15 Vulcan Phalanx CIWS.

### EQUIPMENT

**Submarines:**
Tolgorae class
**Destroyers:**
Taejon (US Gearing FRAM I) class
Chung Buk (US Gearing II) class
Dae Gu (US Allen M Sumner FRAM II) class
Chung Mu (US Fletcher) class
**Frigates:**
Ulsan class
Donghae class
**Patrol Boats:**
PSMM-5 class
**Amphibious Warfare:**
Un Bong (US LST 1 and LST 542) class
**Marines:**
Two divisions, one brigade

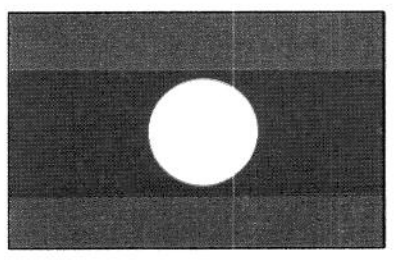

## LAOS

LANDLOCKED Laos has no coastline but does have many rivers, including the mighty Mekong. A force of some 46 riverine craft patrol these inland waters. They are thought to have come from the USSR during the 1980s.

## MALAYSIA

THE Federation of Malaysia consists of the mainland territory of West Malaysia and the East Malaysian territories of Sabah (formerly North Borneo) and Sarawak. Not only do each of the territories have a lengthy coastline, but they are separated by some 1,000nm of the South China Sea. In addition, the Straits of Melakka are one of the world's great maritime "choke points" which have a considerable amount of traffic passing through them, not least the tankers plying between the Middle East oilfields, China and Japan.

The Royal Malaysian Navy (RMN) is small but notable for its efficiency. In the past it has obtained its warships from a variety of sources including the United Kingdom, Germany, Sweden, France, Korea and Italy, but, as with many other developing countries, there is a growing tendency to build new ships in its own yards.

There are three commands, two of which cover geographical areas; the first is designated Malayan Peninsula (HQ at Lumut), while the second is designated Borneo (HQ at Labuan). The third command is afloat and designated "Fleet". An unusual feature of the RMN's organization is that the main training base is in a foreign country — Singapore.

The largest type of ship is the frigate, of which four are in service. The most modern two are *Kasturi*, and *Lekir*, both German-built Type FS-1500 designs from Howaldtswerke at Kiel. They have no hangar but do have a deck for a light helicopter. They are armed with four Exocet launchers, a 3.9in (100mm) Creusot-Loire Compact DP gun, a 2.25in (57mm) Bofors DP gun, four 1.12in (30mm) Emerlec AA guns and a Bofors ASW rocket launcher. The ships are similar to the four Almirante Padilla class frigates built for Colombia's navy. The older *Hang Tuah* was built in the 1960s for the Ghanaian Navy, which intended to use her as a combined warship and yacht for President Nkrumah. Nkrumah was expelled from office before the ship coud be delivered and the builders were stuck with a one-off type which they persuaded the Royal Navy to take on as HMS *Mermaid*. In turn, the RN sold her to Malaysia in 1977. A curious design, she has a relatively light armament of two 4in (102mm) DP guns, four 1.12in (30mm) Emerlec and two 1.6in (40mm) Bofors AA guns, plus one Limbo ASW mortar. The similarly aged *Rahmat* is also of British construction. She is somewhat smaller than *Hang Tuah* but with a similar armament and a rather better sensor fit.

Like many other navies the RMN now finds itself responsible for patrolling the country's 200nm economic zone. Although virtually any ship can carry out this task two corvettes have been procured specifically. These Musytari class vessels displace 1,300tons; the first-of-class was built in Korea, but the second was built in Malaysia and any further ships will be too. They are armed with a 3.9in (100mm) DP gun and two 1.12in (30mm) Emerlec AA guns. They have a large helicopter flight-deck but no hangar.

There are 34 patrol boats in four classes, each of which was built in a different country. The latest are four boats of the Handalan class which were laid down in Sweden in the late 1970s and are armed with four Exocet missile launchers. These guided-missile boats complement the four boats of the Perdana class built in France in the early 1970s and armed with a 2.25in (57mm) gun and two Exocet launchers. The largest group consists of 20 Vosper-designed patrol boats, all of which were delivered in the 1960s. These light craft displace 109tons and are armed with one or two 1.6in (40mm) Bofors guns. They are in need of replacement but most have been modernized. There are also six newer and slightly larger boats of the Jerong class which were made in a local yard at Butterworth to a Lürssen design. These are armed with two calibres of Bofors gun.

Recent additions to the fleet are four Italian Lerici class minehunters delivered in 1986. They are made of glass-reinforced plastic and have some different elements than their Italian counterparts (armament, engine and sonar). They are used for both patrol and mine warfare duties. The principal units in the amphibious warfare role are two former US Navy LSTs of the Sri Indera Sakti class. These 4,300ton ships are capable of acting as flagships, cadet training ships, depot ships for deployed groups of small units (eg, minehunters or patrol boats), or as transports of tanks, wheeled vehicles and troops. They also have a large flight-deck for helicopters. They are assisted by more purpose-built amphibious vessels; there are 20 landing craft bought from Australia, five of them LCM (6) class designs and 15 LCP class craft built by De Havilland Marine. There are also 9 RCP class landing craft built in Malaysia to a Lürssen design, each of which can carry 35 combat troops.

The semi-autonomous Malaysian State of Sabah also operates several naval vessels, some on detachment from the navy and marine police. It has six patrol boats and a landing craft.

The Malaysians have a small naval air wing which operates a force of some six Westland Wasp ASW light helicopters. Other duties are carried out by the air force which operates a C-130 Hercules on maritime patrol. There is no marine corps.

### EQUIPMENT

**Frigates:**
Kasturi (German FS-1500) class
Rahmat class
Hang Tuah (ex-HMS British *Mermaid*) class
**Patrol Boats:**
Handalan (Swedish *Spica-M*) class
Perdana (French Combattante-II) class
**Corvettes:**
Musytari class
**Amphibious Warfare:**
Sri Indera Sakti class
**Mine Warfare:**
Mahamiru (Italian Lerici) class

**Above:** *Handalan* is a Spica-M class patrol boat, one of four built in Sweden for the Royal Malaysian Navy during the late 1970s.

**Below:** The Malaysian patrol boat *Ganyang* was built in France. The two Exocet launchers amidships fire one on each quarter.

## MALDIVE ISLANDS

THE Republic of the Maldives is located south of Sri Lanka in the Indian Ocean and consists of some 2,000 small islands. The tiny maritime force is equipped, in the main, with British patrol boats, several of them transferred by the RAF in the 1970s. The exceptions are three ex-Taiwanese fishing boats which were confiscated in 1976 for poaching. There are three 29.5ft (9m) craft, four 64ft (19.5m) landing craft, one 69ft (21m) Tracker used for protecting fishing grounds, one 1300 class tender and one RTTL Mk2 class target-towing launch.

## MYANMAR

THE Republic of Myanmar (formerly Burma) has coastlines on the Bay of Bengal and the Andaman Sea. It has naval and marine forces of some 7,000 personnel operating a mixture of corvettes, patrol vessels and auxiliaries. The corvettes are a former USN escort (ex-USS *Farmington*) and a USN minesweeper (ex-USS *Creddock*); both are of WWII vintage. The more modern vessels are nine patrol boats, six of which (PGM 43 class) were built in the USA in 1959-61, the remainder (PGM 412 class) in Burma during the early 1980s. Displacing 141tons and 128tons respectively they are lightly armed with machine guns and AA guns of 0.8in (20mm) and 1.6in (40mm). They are complemented by a force of riverine craft 20 strong. There are two each of the Burmese-built 301 class and Nawarat class, six of the American PBR Mk II class and 10 of the Yugoslav Y301 class. There are also a number of auxiliaries (again, many supplied by Yugoslavia) and small landing craft.

**Above:** The Pakistan Navy's destroyer *Badr*, with her sister *Khaibar* astern. Four of these former US Navy Brooke class frigates were acquired on a 5-year lease in 1989, but may well be purchased in the longer term.

**Below:** Pakistan's *Taimur* is one of many ex-US Navy Gearing class destroyers now serving with various navies around the world. The helicopter facility is fully operational, but is apparently little used.

**Above:** *Ghazi* is one of four French-built Daphne class submarines serving with the Pakistan Navy. *Hangor* of this class sank an Indian Navy frigate during the 1971 war.

## PAKISTAN

PAKISTAN, was created as an independent state in 1947 as home for India's large Moslem minority. Today it is an Islamic Republic. The mighty Indus River flows through it and into the Arabian Sea in Sind province, where the largest city and main naval base, Karachi, is situated along the country's 650 miles (1,047km) of coastline.

The Pakistan Navy was formed from elements of the Royal Indian Navy and from them it inherited that force's British traditions. Today it has approximately 11,000 officers and men plus 5,000 reservists. Pakistan's main potential enemy remains India (although events in the Persian Gulf area cannot be disregarded) and the navy has considerable battle experience as a result of its conflicts with the much larger Indian Navy.

A marine force also exists to guard sensitive coastal installations; crack commandos form an integral part of the force.

The fleet's flagship is *Babur*, formerly the British County class ship HMS *London*. Displacing 6,200tons she was classified by the Royal Navy as a destroyer, but is designated a cruiser in Pakistan Navy service. Her Sea Slug SAM facilities have all been removed, enabling a very large flight-deck to be installed. Currently one Alouette III helicopter is in use but there is clearly space for a larger complement. There is a strange mixture of armament, which includes four 4.5in (114mm) DP guns and two Sea Cat SAM launchers from the original British installation, plus a US Mk 15 Vulcan Phalanx CIWS and 12 Soviet ZSU-23 0.9in (23mm) AA cannon.

There are also eight destroyers, oldest of which are four ships of the Alamgir class, survivors of six former Gearing class ships acquired from the US Navy in 1977-83. Again the armament is an odd mix, with Harpoon SSMs, 5in (127mm) Mk 30 DP guns, an ASROC launcher and Vulcan CIWS from the USA, a 0.9in (23mm) cannon from the USSR and a French Alouette helicopter. The other four are former USN Brooke class ships that were designated frigates in US service but are now classified by Pakistan as destroyers, presumably because of their SAM armament, and named Khaiber class. These ships form 25 Destroyer Squadron.

The fleet now has six frigates, two of which were acquired recently from the Royal Navy. These Leander class ships were among the last of their class to be built and were transferred virtually unaltered. (Pakistan is known to be keen to buy more as they are sold-off by the British.) The remainder are four ex-USN Garcia class (now in the Badr class).

The rest of the surface fleet consists of 24 patrol boats which have been acquired from China, eight of them high-speed, guided-missile boats (four Huangfeng class with four CSS-N-1 SSMs and four Hoku class with one CSS-N-1). The remainder are 12 slower patrol boats (four Hainan and eight Shanghai-II class) and four Huchuan class torpedo-armed hydrofoils.

The Pakistan Navy has long placed great emphasis on submarine operations and in the 1971 war against India their submarine *Hangor* (S-131) sank the Indian destroyer *Kukri* — one of the few such sinkings since the end of WWII. There are currently four Hangor class submarines (1,043tons), all were built in France as standard French Daphne class boats and fit Harpoon missiles. There are also two of the larger Hashmat class (French Agosta class). These were originally ordered by South Africa but were bought by Pakistan when that purchase was prevented by the UN arms embargo. The Pakistan Navy also operates some Italian-built midget submarines (SX 404 class) which can carry a dozen special forces raiders.

Finally, there is a small naval aviation force. The largest aircraft are four Breguet Atlantiques for long-range maritime patrol and ASW missions plus eight Fokker aircraft also used for patrols. There are also six Sea King and four Alouette III helicopters.

Future plans include the acquistion of more modern destroyers, four more conventional submarines (possibly Chinese Romeo or Ming class) and six Kaman SH-2F shipborne ASW helicopters. There are also reliable reports that the navy has the long-term aim of operating nuclear-propelled submarines (SSN).

### EQUIPMENT

**Cruiser:**
Babur (British County) class
**Submarines:**
Hangor (French Daphne) class
Hashmat (French Agosta) class
**Destroyers:**
Alamgir (US Gearing FRAM I) class
Khaiber (US Brooke) class
**Frigates:**
Badr (US Garcia) class
Zulfiquar (British Leander) class
**Patrol Boats:**
Hainan class
Hoku class
Huangfeng (Soviet Osa-I) class
**Naval Aircraft:**
Aerospatiale SA.316/319 Alouette III
Breguet BR.1150 Atlantique
Fokker F-27-200
Westland Sea King Mk 45

## THE PHILIPPINES

THE Philippines is a huge, sprawling network of more than 7,000 islands containing 61 million people. It is very poor, internal communications between the islands are a constant problem and the nation has been wracked by insurrections since obtaining independence from the United States in 1946. The navy's missions are to protect the country from seaward attack, to thwart any attempts by insurgents to use the sea and to combat piracy.

The navy has nearly 15,000 men plus 9,000 marines and a 2,000 strong coastguard. It possesses a large number of small vessels almost all of which are very old and in a bad state of repair; indeed, many may not be seaworthy. Most have been purchased from the USA and a good many were acquired when they arrived in Philippine waters having escaped from South Vietnam when it fell to the Communists in 1975. The principal naval bases are at Cebu, Sangley Point, Poro Point, Zamboanga and, the biggest of all, Subic Bay, which is run by the USN.

The largest ships in the fleet are three frigates, one of 1,850tons displacement and two of 1,620tons. The two were commissioned into the US Navy in 1943 as Cannon class, sold to Japan in 1955 and then sold to the Philippines in 1978! Their armament is antiquated, consisting of three 3in (76mm) DP guns, six 1.6in (40mm) AA guns and a number of machine-guns, depth charge projectors and a Hedgehog ASW mortar. The biggest ship is the *Rajah Lakandula*, an ex-US Savage class vessel which was transferred to Vietnam in 1971 and joined the Philippines Navy in 1975. It is only very lightly armed.

There are 10 ships of around 1,000tons displacement serving as corvettes, many of them having come via South Vietnam. Two are ex-USN Auk class minesweepers, one is an ex-USN Admirable class minesweeper, while the remaining seven are a mixture of ex-USN PCE 827 and PCER 848 classes.

There are a number of smaller patrol boats, most of them elderly ex-USN vessels except for a new class of 50tons craft from Australia of which it is hoped to buy about 35 in due course. In addition, there are approximately 40 ex-USN landing-ships and landing-craft, although only about 10 are actually operational, plus a small number of auxiliary ships.

There is a very small naval air arm equipped with 10 Britten-Norman Defenders (built in the Philippines) and 10 MBB Bo-105 helicopters.

### EQUIPMENT

**Frigates:**
Datu Sikatuna (US Cannon) class
**Corvettes:**
Rizal (US Auk) class
Migule Malvar (US PCE 827 and PCER 848) class
**Amphibious Warfare:**
Agusan del Sur (US LST 1 and LST 542) class
**Naval Aircraft:**
Britten-Norman BN.42 Maritime Defender
MBB Bo-105
**Marines:**
Ten battalions

**Left:** The Philippine archipelago comprises a huge network of islands. The navy thus operates a large number of amphibious warfare vessels for use by its marine forces, some of whom are seen here storming ashore on a regularly held training exercise.

## SINGAPORE

### EQUIPMENT

**Patrol Boats:**
Victory (German Lürssen MGB-62) class
Sea Wolf (German Lürssen FPB-45) class
**Amphibious Warfare:**
Endurance(US LST-542) class

THE small island state of Singapore, a former British colony, is located at one of the great maritime crossroads on the Asian sea lanes. Its fine harbour has helped make it one of the richest countries in the region and the envy of larger neighbours. Modern Singapore is noted for its efficiency and its navy is no exception; it is composed of up-to-date ships, the great majority of which have been constructed in local yards and are maintained to the very highest levels. The navy has some 4,500 men and its main base is at Pulau Brani, a small island off the southern coast of Singapore.

The main combat element of the Singapore Navy is its patrol boat fleet. The largest and most modern are six Victory class (600tons) guided-missile boats designed by Lürssen in Germany. The first-of-class was built in Germany, the rest in Singapore. They are armed with eight Harpoon SSMs, a 3in (76mm) DP gun, a Mk 15 CIWS and six torpedo tubes. They are being used to replace six older Lürssen boats (Sea Wolf class) to be transferred to the Reserve.

In addition, there are six Vosper Thorneycroft patrol boats which displace 130tons, three Type A and three Type B. They are armed with a mixture of Bofors and Oerlikon guns. Twelve Swift class patrol craft entered service in the early 1980s, providing the navy with further useful capability. There are two ex-USN Redwing class minesweepers, several landing craft, and some large amphibious warfare ships, known as Endurance class, which are ex-USN LST 542 class dating from WWII.

**Below:** The efficient Singapore Navy operates a small number of ex-US Navy landing ships, including *Excellence* seen here in Penang.

**Bottom:** *Victory*, lead-ship of the latest class of patrol boats to join the Singapore Navy. Her armament is eight Harpoon SSMs, torpedoes and CIWS.

## SRI LANKA

SRI LANKA, formerly the British possession of Ceylon, has a remarkably small navy considering that it is an island occupying a major strategic position in the Indian Ocean. The navy has a strength of some 8,000 men with its HQ in the old Royal Navy base at Trincomalee; other bases are at Colombo, Karainagar, Tangala and Welisara.

The main element of the navy consists of eight patrol boats: six Sooraya class, which were built in China as Shanghai-II class, and two Sri Lankan Jayesegara class. There are dozens of small patrol craft, all of them armed with at least one machine-gun. There are no marines and air support is provided by the air force.

**Above:** *Jayesegara* (P601) and her sister-ship *Sagarawardene* are the largest vessels in the Sri Lankan Navy. Built in Colombo Dockyard they are armed with Chinese 1in (25mm) cannon.

## TAIWAN

THE state of Taiwan (or the Republic of China) consists of the main island itself together with 85 others in outlying groups. Home to the nationalist, anti-Communist Kuomintang since 1949 Taiwan has had to develop a strong indigenous arms industry because of hostility from mainland China. In recent years relations between the two Chinas have begun to mellow slightly.

The Republic of China Navy (ROCN) is some 30,000 strong and operates a large force of destroyers and frigates, together with numerous amphibious warfare ships and several submarines. The navy's prime mission is the defence of the republic's waters against incursions by mainland forces, a task which includes the defence of the Pescadores islands which lie just off the coast of the mainland.

There are 24 former USN WWII-era destroyers which were transferred to the ROCN in the 1970s. Originally of the Gearing and Allen M. Sumner classes all have been modified in recent years to a variety of standards, of which the most important are the Wu Chin-I, II and III conversions. These vary in detail, but entailed a great deal of work involving the replacement of old weapons and sensors with new and much more effective items. For example, the Wu Chin-III hulls are armed with two triple and one double Standard missile launchers, a 3in (76mm) DP gun, a Mk 15 CIWS, an ASROC launcher and six torpedo tubes. They also have had a flight-deck and hangar installed to enable them to operate a Hughes 500 ASW helicopter.

There is a considerable programme for the construction of modern frigates with eight local versions of the USN's Oliver Hazard Perry class under construction (Kuang Hwa class), together with at least four of an updated and lengthened version of the same class. It was also planned to buy 16 South Korean Ulsan class frigates but this was changed to 12 French FL 3000 class in 1989, although the PRC government is exerting strong pressure on France to stop this sale. The frigates already in service are one Tai Yuan class (ex-USS *Rudderow*) and nine Tien Shan class (ex-USN Lawrence and Crosley classes).

There is a very large number of smaller patrol boats and fast attack craft (70-plus), together with well over 20 major landing ships. The fast attack types are all armed with missiles and the most numerous is the 50 strong Tzu Chang class.

The submarine force has two old ex-USN Guppy-II boats re-named Hai Shih class which are now used mostly for training. Pride of the force, however, are the Hai Lung class, two Dutch submarines of a modified Zwaardvis design which were delivered despite strong protests from the PRC. A request, however, for two more was not agreed and negotiations are now taking place to order up to six German Type 2000 submarines.

The landing ships are complemented by over 30 LSTs which are needed because Taiwan has one of the world's largest forces of marines — some 30-40,000 men in two divisions equipped with a range of armour and artillery.

The large air force provides most types of support for the ROCN, but there is a small naval air component responsible for the provision of shipborne helicopters and maritime reconnaissance (MR). The marines themselves also operate some light helicopters. The naval MR mission is undertaken by the 32 Grumman S-2E Trackers on strength. All are being updated to include totally new electronics and sensors, and the piston engines will be replaced by turboprops. The standard shipborne helicopter is the Hughes 500 MD ASW.

### EQUIPMENT

**Submarines:**
Hai Shih (US Guppy-II) class
Hai Lung (Dutch Zwaardvis) class
**Destroyers:**
Wu Chin-III (US Gearing) class
Wu Chin-II (US Gearing) class
Wu Chin-I (US Gearing, Allen M. Sumner and Fletcher) class
**Frigates:**
Kuang Hwa-I class
**Patrol Boats:**
Tzu Chang class
**Corvettes:**
Ping Jin (US Auk) class
**Amphibious Warfare:**
Chung Chi (US LST-1 and LST-542) class
**Naval Aircraft:**
Grumman S-2E/G Tracker
Hughes 500 MD Defender
**Marines:**
Two divisions

**Above:** *Sui Yang* is one of 24 elderly, ex-US Navy destroyers serving with the ROCN. The great majority have been given major armament and sensor updates to extend their lives, but new ships are now being built.

**Below:** The pride of the ROCN are the two Dutch-built Hai Lung (Sea Dragon) class submarines which are among the most efficient diesel-electric submarines in service in any of the world's navies today.

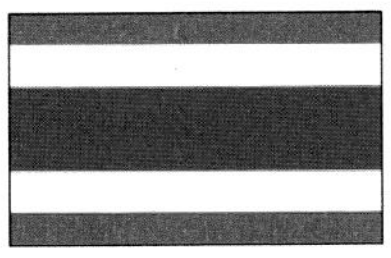

## THAILAND

THE Kingdom of Thailand is a large country with some 2,000 miles (3,220km) of coastline along the Andaman Sea and Gulf of Thailand. After WWII it joined the South-East Asia Treaty Organization (SEATO) and cooperated closely with the United States. The vast majority of its warships are of US origin, although some British and Italian types have also been bought. Recently, however, there has been a trend towards the placement of orders for small ships with Thai shipyards, while major orders have been placed in China for frigates (and possibly for submarines), and there is also talk of a helicopter-carrier being built in Germany.

The navy has a manpower strength of some 21,000 men with a further 24,000 in the marine corps. Naval HQ is at Bangkok and there are bases along the South China Sea coast at Paknam, Phanga Sattahip and Songkla; a special riverine unit on the Mekong is situated at Nakhon Phanom.

The largest unit in the fleet is currently the frigate *Makut Rajakumarn* (1,900tons) which was built in the UK in the early 1970s. She is armed with two 4.5in (114mm) DP guns, two 1.6in (40mm) Bofors AA guns, plus six torpedo tubes and depth charges. There are plans to replace the aft 4.5in (114mm) gun with Harpoon launchers and to add Sea Sparrow SAMs and a Mk 15 CIWS. Six new Chinese frigates will be added to the fleet in the early 1990s: two Jianghu-IV class and four Jianghu-II class. These will be similar to Chinese ships of the same classes, but will have German (instead of French) diesels and will have some American weapons systems fitted in Thailand after delivery. There are a further five ex-USN frigates currently serving which will be decommissioned once the new vessels arrive, as well as two ships of the Ratanakosin class which are a curious "in-between" design. They displace 960tons and have a heavy armament of eight Harpoons, an Albatros SAM launcher, a 3in (76mm) DP gun, twin Breda 1.6in (40mm) and two 0.8in (20mm) AA guns, and a six-tube torpedo launcher. Despite all this, these well-designed and businesslike ships are classified by the Thais as corvettes, whereas most navies would grade them as frigates.

There are quite a considerable number of patrol boats/craft of different classes, amphibious vessels and some small minesweepers in the fleet too. As with almost all Asian navies the Thais operate some ex-USN LST 542 class amphibious warfare ships re-designated Chang class. They are also building a class of French LSTs under licence, two of which have been completed with another one to follow. One curiosity is that the Thai Navy still has in service the training ship *Maeklong* which was constructed in Japan in 1937 and is now almost certainly the only pre-war Japanese warship left afloat.

The 24,000-man marine corps is large and is organized into a division headquarters and six infantry regiments. These are supported by an artillery regiment, an amphibious assault battalion and a reconnaissance battalion.

Finally, there is a comparatively large naval aviation component, with a significant maritime reconnaissance element. There are eight Grumman S-2F Trackers, five Fokker F-27s, 10 Australian-built Nomad Searchmasters and two Cessna Skymasters. Unusually, the Thai Navy operates amphibian aircraft in the SAR role, including two Canadair CL-215 and two Grumman HU-16. It is planned to acquire a naval fighter wing of 12-18 Shenyang A-5M or McDonnell-Douglas Superskyhawks.

**Above:** A Dutch-built Fokker F.27 of the Royal Thai Navy's naval air arm, fitted to launch US Harpoon ASMs. The F.27 is used for maritime patrol duties by many countries.

**Below:** The Royal Thai Navy frigate *Khirirat*, which has an armament of one 3in (76mm) gun, one 1.6in (40mm) and two 0.8in (20mm) cannon, and six 12.7in (324mm) torpedo tubes.

### EQUIPMENT

**Frigates:**
Makut Rajakumarn (British Yarrow) class
Tapi (US PF 103) class
Pin Kiao (US Cannon) class
Tahchin (US Tacoma) class
**Patrol Boats:**
Ratcharit (Italian BMB 2309) class
Prabrarpak class
**Corvettes:**
Ratanakosin (PFMM Mk 16) class
**Amphibious Warfare:**
Sichang (French PS 700) class
Chang (US LST 542) class
**Mine Warfare:**
Bangrachan (German M 48) class
**Naval Aircraft:**
Grumman S-2F Tracker
Fokker F-27-200
Nomad N-24A Searchmaster
Canadair CL-215
Grumman HU-16 Albatross
Bell 214 ST
**Marines:**
One division (six infantry, one artillery regiments)

**Above:** *Khirirat*'s OTO Melara 3in (76mm) Compact Dual-Purpose gun, seen mounted forward, is one of hundreds of these successful Italian guns used around the world.

**Below:** The Royal Thai Navy operates a large number of patrol boats. This is *Thai Muang*, one of six Sattahip (PSMM Mk5) class boats built in Thailand between 1982 and 1986.

**Above:** *Sukhothai* is classified as a corvette despite her heavy armament, which includes one 3in (76mm) DP, two 1.6in (40mm) AA, two 0.8in (20mm) cannon, six 12.7in (324mm) torpedo tubes, an eight-cell SAM launcher and eight Harpoon SSMs.

## VIETNAM

AFTER the Communist victory and the unification of their country the new Vietnamese government acquired a number of former South Vietnamese ships, most of them of US origin. Since that time Vietnam has been friendly with the USSR and has acquired additional Soviet naval vessels. For their part, the Soviets until recently maintained a naval base in the former US facility at Cam Ranh Bay.

In 1991 the Vietnamese Navy had some 7,000 men organized into four naval zones, with the main HQ in Hanoi and bases at Haiphong, Da Nang, Cam Ranh Bay and Ho Chi Minh City. The tasks of the navy are to control coastal waters and to patrol the country's 200-mile (322km) economic zone. It is also involved in a variety of disputes, especially over the control of some small islands in the South China Sea.

The largest warships are seven frigates. Two of these are of WWII-vintage (ex-USN), of which one, *Phan Ngu Lao*, has had two Soviet SS-N-2 Styx launchers fitted. Much more modern and of far greater tactical value are five Soviet Petya class frigates which displace 1,150tons and have four 3in (76mm) guns, three torpedo tubes and four RBU-2500 ASW rocket launchers. There are 11 minesweepers, six from the USSR (four Yurka and two Yevgenya) and five from Poland (K-8 class), plus there are two former USN minesweepers which have had their sweeping gear removed.

Of the lighter forces there are about eight Soviet Osa-II guided-missile patrol boats and some 16 Shershen torpedo boats. A host of other smaller Soviet types exist too, among them the Zhuk and SO-1 classes, plus Chinese Shanghai-II class boats and East German Bremse class. Three Soviet Polnocny-B class ships and three former USN LSTs constitute the amphibious warfare fleet, essential to provide the large force of marines (naval infantry), some 27,000 strong, with proper support. Aviation is provided by the air force which has a number of Mi-4 SAR helicopters.

### EQUIPMENT

**Frigates:**
Soviet Petya class
Phan Ngu Lao (US Barnegat) class
Dai Ky (US Savage) class
**Patrol Boats:**
Soviet Shershen class
Soviet Osa-II class
**Corvettes:**
US Admirable class
**Amphibious Warfare:**
Soviet Polnocny-B class
US LST 1 and LST 543 class
**Mine Warfare:**
Soviet Yurka class
Polish K-8 class

# OCEANIA

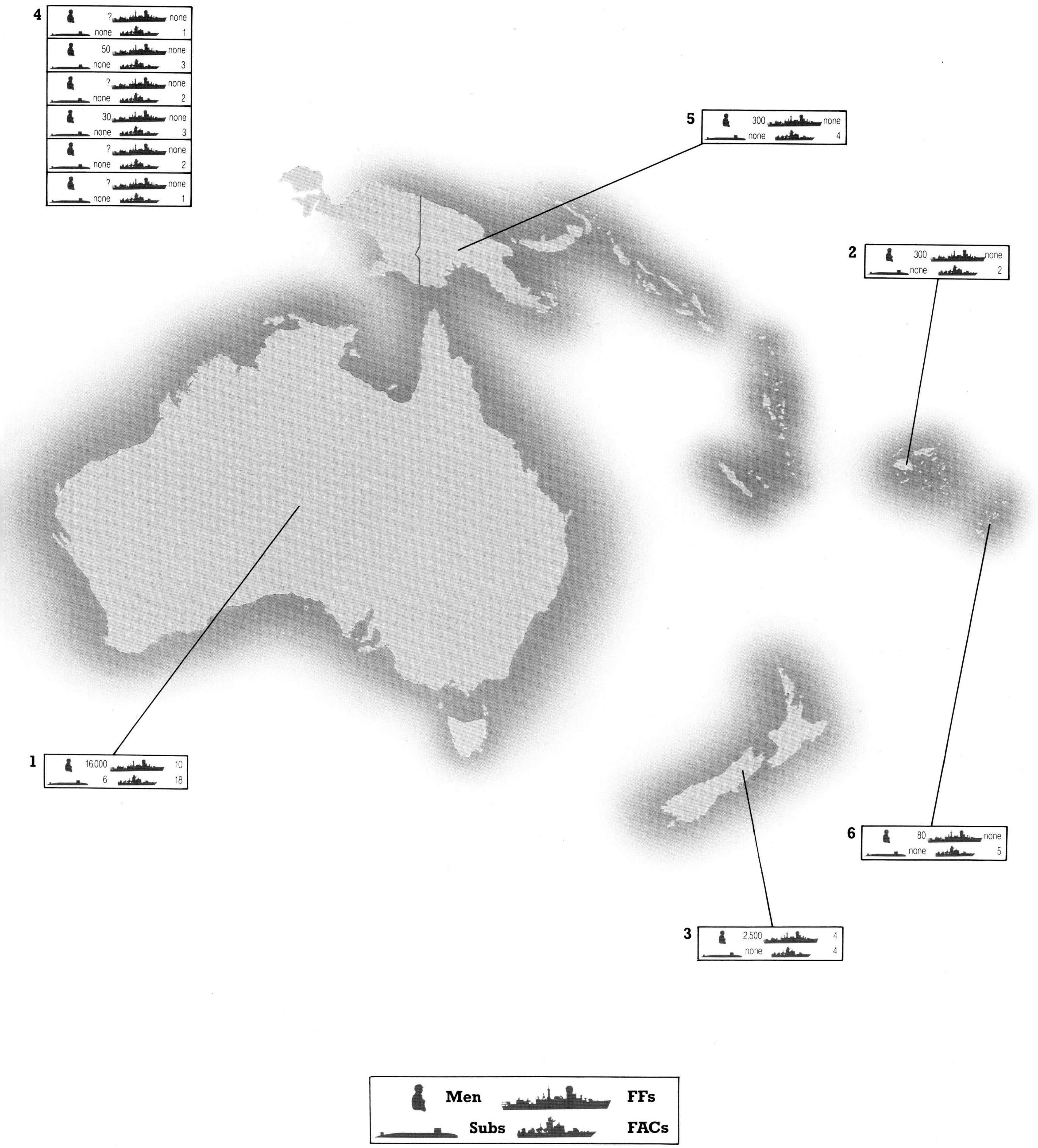
4
? none
none 1
50 none
none 3
? none
none 2
30 none
none 3
? none
none 2
? none
none 1
5
300 none
none 4
2
300 none
none 2
1
16,000 10
6 18
6
80 none
none 5
3
2,500 4
none 4
Men
FFs
Subs
FACs

## AUSTRALIA

MODERN Australia occupies an important strategic position in one of the world's major economic regions, the "Pacific Rim". The Royal Australian Navy (RAN) was raised at the turn of the century and has from that time onwards operated a small but very efficient force of cruisers, destroyers and submarines, which have distinguished themselves in two world wars, the Korean War and, most recently, during the international blockade of Iraq in 1990-91.

During the 1960s the RAN gradually shook-off RN influence and began to turn more to the USN for ideas and ships; the first major purchase being three Charles F Adams class destroyers which were redesignated Perth class.

The task of today's 16,000 strong RAN is to defend Australia's very extensive coastline and to exert naval influence in the Indian and Pacific Oceans. The RAN also assists the many small former British colonies and Australian Trustee territories scattered across the southern and central Pacific, places such as Christmas Island, Cocos-Keeling Islands and Norfolk Island. Their major allies in this mammoth task are the US and Royal New Zealand Navies, RN influence in the area now being minimal. The major operational command is Maritime Command, with its HQ and main operating base at Sydney and a second base at Cockburn Sound in Western Australia. There are subsidiary bases at Cairns in Queensland and Darwin in the far north of Northern Territory.

The fleet's largest warships are the three ex-USN Perth class destroyers which displace 4,720tons and are armed with Harpoon SSMs, Standard SAMs, two 5in (127mm) DP guns and six torpedo tubes. They were modernized once in the mid-1970s and again in the late 1980s. In addition there are 10 frigates: five of the 3,962ton displacement Adelaide class, all built in Australia, with a sixth due to be commissioned in 1994. Virtually identical to the USN's Oliver Hazard Perry class they are armed with Harpoon and Standard missiles. The five River class ships were built in Australia in the 1960s to a design based upon that of the British Rothesay class. Armed with two 4.5in (114mm) guns, Sea Cat SAM launchers and six torpedo tubes they are now somewhat elderly (a sixth member of the class was stricken in 1985 to become a source of spares for the others).

Because of the River and Perth classes' age the decision was taken in the early 1980s to replace them; the Royal New Zealand Navy (RNZN) had a similar problem and so the two neighbours got together to run an international competition. The winner of the ANZAC design requirement was the German MEKO 200ANZ. Eight have been ordered for the RAN and two for the RNZN, with first delivery in 1996. The MEKO design by Blohm und Voss is based upon a standard hull with modular inserts which enables customers to vary numerous features, such as armament, sensors, engines, ancillaries and general equipment, without adding significantly to the overall cost as happens with traditional designs. All the ships will be built in Australia, and Australian and New Zealand manufacturers will be given some 80 per cent of the work (by value).

With an extensive coastline the RAN needs a large number of patrol boats; in fact, they have relatively few. There are 15 Fremantle class boats, each armed with a 1.6in (40mm) Bofors, a 3.2in (81mm) mortar and two machine-guns. These were built in the early 1980s in Australian yards to a British design and are powerful and effective boats considering their small (230tons) displacement. Three older Attack class patrol boats also remain in service, the last survivors of a class of 18 built in the 1960s.

**Above:** HMAS *Tobruk*, a ro-ro logistic landing ship, can carry an infantry battalion and a squadron of Leopard battle tanks.

**Below:** HMAS *Darwin*, an Australian-built version of the Oliver Hazard Perry class, returns to Sydney in triumph from its part in the Gulf blockade of Iraq.

**Right:** HMAS *Geraldton*, based in Western Australia, is a patrol boat of the PCF 420 design by Brooke Marine Ltd which is known as the Fremantle class in RAN service.

The amphibious warfare capability is limited (with no dedicated naval infantry/marines), consisting of an Australian-built version of the British Sir Bedivere class landing ship, logistics (LSL) design which is named *Tobruk*, plus six smaller Balikpapan class utility landing craft. The RAN has, however, developed an unusual design of minehunter, the Rushcutter class, which is based on a glass-fibre catamaran hull. It combines with the Bay class minehunters.

The RAN's submarine force has for many years comprised six Oxley class boats which were built in Scotland in the 1960s and 1970s to the British Oberon design. These have been updated but will need to be replaced in the late 1990s. The RAN put the project out to international competition and, to the surprise of the naval world, the winner was the Swedish firm of Kockums; their Type 471 design will be designated the Collins class in RAN service. Kockums have built submarines for the Swedish navy for many years, but this was their first known attempt to sell abroad, and has proved successful with eight ordered so far.

Following the demise of the aircraft carrier HMAS *Melbourne* all the remaining naval fixed-wing aircraft were transferred to the RAAF, except for two EW trainers. The RAN Fleet Air Arm now operates helicopters, primarily Sikorsky designs, with nine Sea Kings, three Wessex and a number of smaller types currently in service. The mainstay of the force is intended to be the Sikorsky S-70B2, an RAN version of the USN's SH-60B ASW helicopter; 16 have been ordered, of which five have been delivered by early 1991.

**Right:** HMAS *Rushcutter* (M80) is one of two minehunters built by Carrington Slipways which entered service in the late-1980s. Problems with its MWS 80 weapon system have led to new trials with the Krupp Atlas MWS 80-4 and the Thomson Sintra Ibis V Mk2 systems and there may be changes.

**Left:** Four of the RAN's six Oberon class submarines, which were acquired between 1967 and 1978, are seen here putting to sea: (top to bottom) *Otama, Onslow, Otway* and *Oxley*. Its two diesel engines give a dived speed of 17kts and it carries 20 SSMs and torpedoes. The large hump on the bows houses the passive array for the Krupp Atlas CSU-3-41 sonar. The first of the Kockums-designed Collins class should commission in the mid-1990s.

### EQUIPMENT

**Submarines:**
Oxley (British Oberon) class
**Destroyers:**
Perth (US Charles F Adams) class
**Frigates:**
Adelaide (US Oliver Hazard Perry) class
River (improved British Rothesay) class
**Patrol Boats:**
Fremantle class
Attack class
**Amphibious Warfare:**
Tobruk (improved British Sir Bedivere) class
**Mine Warfare:**
Rushcutter class
Bay class
**Naval Aircraft:**
Westland Sea King Mk 50
Westland Wessex Mk 31B
Sikorsky S-70B2 Seahawk

## FIJI

THE South Pacific Ocean state of Fiji — independent from Britain since 1970 — has a tiny navy with some 300 men which operates from Suva.

There are two Kikau class minesweepers (ex-USN Redwing class) which have had their minesweeping gear removed, and one of which has had a small helicopter flight-deck installed. There are also two former oilfield support craft, now designated Rapture class. All have token machine-gun armament. Plans for ASI-135s have come to nought.

The navy operates two helicopters; one Aerospatiale AS.355 Ecuriel and a leased Agusta-Bell.206 JetRanger.

**Above:** Virtually the entire strength of the Fijian naval arm; from left to right: *Lautoka* (102) and *Levuka* (101) of the Rapture class, both former oil rig support craft; and *Kiro* (206) and *Kikau* (204), coastal minesweepers. (*Kiro* has been stricken since this picture was taken).

## NEW ZEALAND

THE major portion of New Zealand consists of North and South islands in the South Pacific Ocean, but there are other islands too, including Stewart and Chatham. New Zealand also has several dependent states: Cook Islands, Niue, and Tokelau. (These sometimes operate small boats; Cook Islands, for instance, has an ASI-315, *Te Kukupa*.)

Like Australia, New Zealand depended for years upon the RN for its maritime protection. The Royal New Zealand Navy (RNZN) was not actually formed as a separate service until October 1941 when two of its first major units were the former RN cruisers HMS *Ajax* and HMS *Achilles*.

The RNZN continued to man at least one cruiser and a number of destroyers for some years after the war, but today the largest units are four British-built Leander class frigates. The navy is very small, consisting of 2,500 regulars and about 500 reserves. The main headquarters and the fleet base is at Auckland on North Island.

Of the four Leander class frigates, *Waikato* dates from the 1960s, having been one of the two built specifically for the RNZN, and is now used mainly for training. Because of her age she is scheduled to be stricken in about 1995. The other three were built originally for the RN and after many years service were purchased by the RNZN in the early 1980s. *Southland* is armed with the Ikara ASW missile system and is due to strike in 1994, but the other two, *Wellington* and *Canterbury*, are of the so-called "broad-beamed Leander" type. These were refitted after delivery to New Zealand and are due to serve to about 2005. *Southland* and *Waikato* are due to be replaced by two MEKO 200 frigates which are being constructed in Australia to a design by the German company of Blohm und Voss. They are now scheduled to enter service in 1997.

The remainder of the RNZN consists of a number of small patrol/training boats, some auxiliaries and a 12,300ton fleet oiler. In the late 1970s plans were developed for a submarine force, but these were shelved before any orders had been placed.

There is no separate fleet air arm, all aircraft being provided and maintained by the RNZAF. However, the seven Westland Wasp ASW helicopters which operate from the Leander class frigates are flown by RNZN aircrews, even though the onboard support is provided by six-man RNZAF maintenance crews. The RNZAF also operates six Lockheed P-3C Orions on maritime patrol duties, while one role for the 24 A-4 Skyhawks is that of maritime attack.

**Above:** *HMNZS Wellington* (shown here in the Hauraki Gulf) and her sister *Canterbury* are "broad-beamed Leanders" and are the most recent purchases for the RNZN.

### EQUIPMENT

**Frigates:**
Southland (British Leander) class
Waikato (British Leander) class
Wellington (British Leander) class

**Patrol Boats:**
Moa class
Pukaki class

## PACIFIC ISLANDS

THE Pacific Islands is an expression which refers to the range of islands that are often arranged ethnographically into Melanesia (Solomon Islands, Vanuatu et al), Micronesia (Marshall Islands, Kiribati et al) and Polynesia.

A great many of the islands in this group remain dependent states of larger powers, the principal examples of the latter being the USA, France, New Zealand and the United Kingdom. Many other islands, however, have become fully sovereign, independent nations during the latter half of this century and they conduct their own defence affairs.

**Below:** Australian-built ASI-315 class patrol boats serve with several Pacific navies. Displacing 165tons, it is armed with 0.8in (20mm) cannon and 0.5in (12.7mm) MGs and has a crew of 17.

## KIRIBATI

FORMERLY known as the Gilbert Islands it gained its independence from the UK in 1979. The republic has 33 islands in the central Pacific Ocean, including the famous Tarawa atoll of WWII fame. It operates one 55ft (17m) glass-reinforced plastic patrol craft.

## MARSHALL ISLANDS

A GROUP of self-governing islands, the Marshalls relies principally on the United States for its defence. It does however have a 50-man maritime authority which acts as its own naval force and is equipped with several vessels; among these are one Pacific Forum ASI-135, one US Cape class boat, *Ionmeto II*, and one supply ship, *Ionmeto*.

## MICRONESIA

THE Federated States of Miconesia also rely on the USA for major defence needs, but they do operate their own patrols with a fleet of two ASI-135s, *Palikir* and *Micronesia*.

## SOLOMON ISLANDS

THEY became independent from the UK in 1978, although part of the chain (Bougainville) forms an island belonging to Papua New Guinea which lies to the west. The small naval force operates three patrol boats: *Savo*, a P-150 class; *Tulagi*, a 27ton Carpentaria class; and a new ASI-315 type. There are two 88.5ft (27m) landing craft, *Ligomo* and *Ulusaghe*.

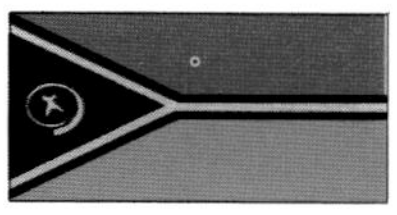

## VANUATU

UNTIL 1980 the New Hebrides were jointly controlled by the UK and France, thereafter as an independent nation the many islands of the republic are known as Vanuatu. It has one patrol boat, *Mala*, converted from a motor yacht and has just acquired an Australian ASI-315, *Tukoro*.

## WESTERN SAMOA

SELF-GOVERNING since 1962, the nation has nine islands in the south-central Pacific Ocean. Its small marine force has one Australian ASI-315, *Nafanua*, with a second on order.

## PAPUA NEW GUINEA

THE large island of New Guinea is divided into two, with the Indonesian territory of Irian Jaya at the western end and the former Australian territory of New Guinea at the eastern end. When this territory was given independence it united with a number of adjacent smaller island groups plus part of the Solomon Islands which included Bougainville. It established its capital at Port Moresby.

There is a small defence force totalling some 3,500 men, of which just 300 are in the navy. The naval headquarters is at Port Moresby, with a subsidiary base at Lombrum. The primary task of the navy is to patrol coastal waters and to provide inter-island transport for the military. There is a minor insurrection on the island of Bougainville, which was blockaded for a while, but there is no external threat.

As with other territories in the region the principal vessels are of the standard 165ton ASI-315 type built by Australian Shipbuilding Pty at South Coogie in Western Australia. Four are operated as Tarangau class, having been provided by Australia over the period 1987-89.

The Papua New Guinea Navy also operates two ex-Australian 503ton landing-craft (Bura class), four 725ton Burfoam class utility landing craft built in Singapore in the early 1980s, and seven Kokuba class personnel craft.

## TONGA

THE Kingdom of Tonga consists of 169 islands in three groups lying east of Fiji in the South Pacific. It gained its independence from Britain in 1970 and like many such island states maintains a small marine element.

The principal units manned by the 82 men in the division operate three of the ubiquitous Australian ASI-315 165ton patrol boats armed with three 0.5in (12.7mm) machine-guns. There are also two smaller patrol boats and a 116ton landing craft.

# EUROPE

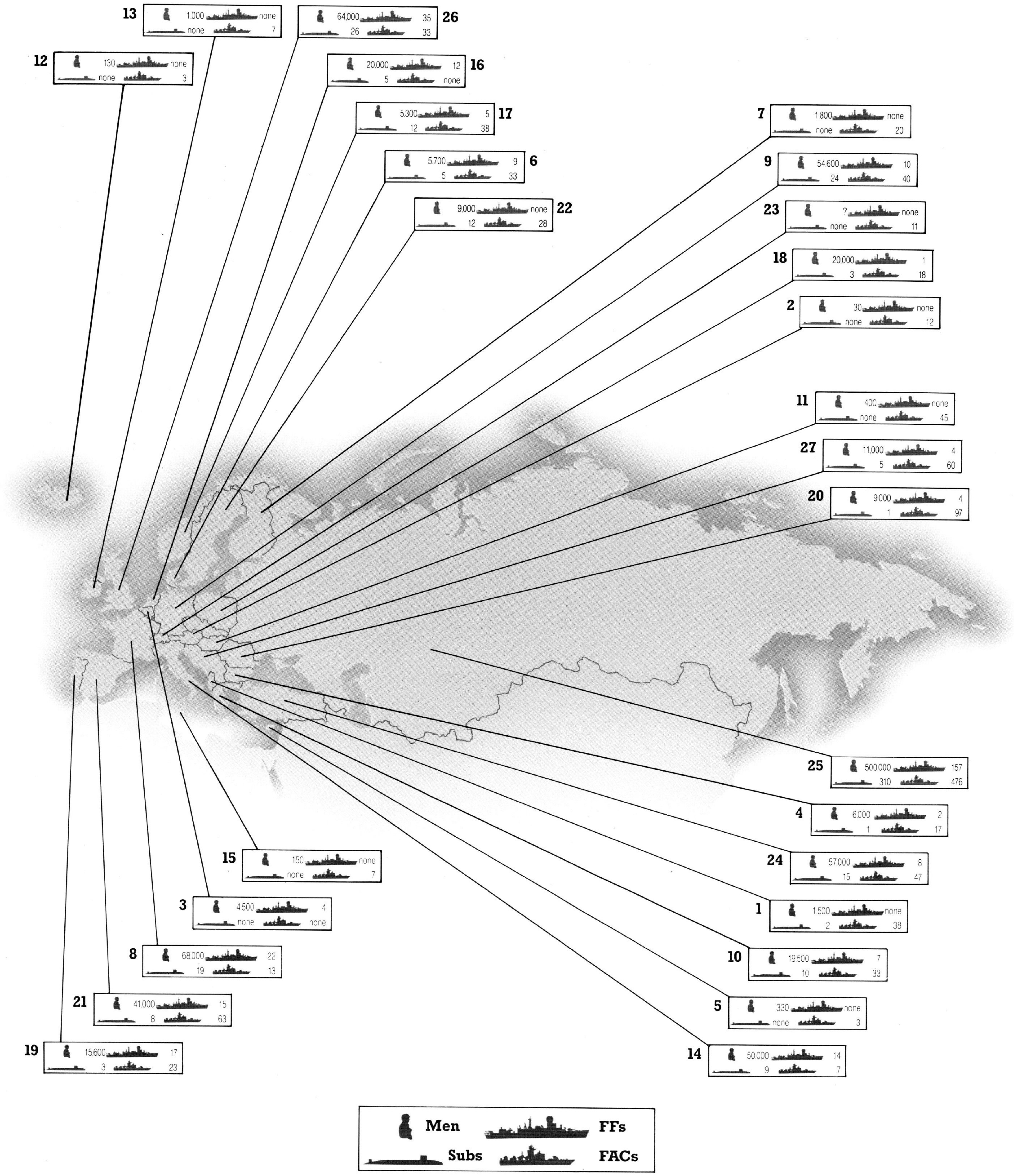
13 1,000 none none 7
26 64,000 35 26 33
12 130 none none 3
16 20,000 12 5 none
17 5,300 5 12 38
6 5,700 9 5 33
22 9,000 none 12 28
7 1,800 none none 20
9 54,600 10 24 40
23 ? none none 11
18 20,000 1 3 18
2 30 none none 12
11 400 none none 45
27 11,000 4 5 60
20 9,000 4 1 97
25 500,000 157 310 476
4 6,000 2 1 17
24 57,000 8 15 47
1 1,500 none 2 38
10 19,500 7 10 33
5 330 none none 3
14 50,000 14 9 7
15 150 none none 7
3 4,500 4 none none
8 68,000 22 19 13
21 41,000 15 8 63
19 15,600 17 3 23
Men
FFs
Subs
FACs

## ALBANIA

THE modern Albanian Navy consists of some 1,500 men (1,000 of whom are conscripts) with bases at Durres, Pasha Liman, Sazan Island and Valona. Its equipment was obtained from the USSR between 1946 and 1961 and from China between 1961 and 1978. So far as is known, Albania has obtained neither new equipment nor spares for existing equipment since the break with China and thus the state of the navy's ships must be poor.

There are nearly 40 patrol boats. These include two elderly Soviet Kronstadt class (330tons) — the survivors of a class of four — which are armed with a single 3.35in (85mm) DP gun, a twin 1.45in (37mm) AA mount, six 0.5in (12.7mm) machine-guns, depth-charges and mines; and six Chinese Shanghai-II class (135tons) patrol boats. The bulk of the fleet consists of 30 Chinese Huchuan class (46tons) hydrofoil torpedo boats which are known to have been supplied, but how many are serviceable is open to question. In addition to these there are two elderly Soviet minesweepers and a small number of auxiliaries.

The most capable warships in the navy are a number of Soviet-supplied Whiskey class submarines. Four of these were supplied by the USSR but one is now a hulk cannibalized for spares for the others. It is thought that only two of these, at most, are operational.

Albania has neither marines nor a naval aviation service. There are six battalions of coastal defence artillery, which, following the pattern in most countries, are army-manned but under naval operational control.

### EQUIPMENT

**Submarines:**
Soviet Whiskey class
**Patrol Boats:**
Soviet Kronstadt class
Chinese Shanghai-II class
Chinese Huchuan class
**Mine Warfare:**
Soviet T-43 class
Soviet T-301 class

## AUSTRIA

THE Austrian river patrol craft operate on the Danube as part of the unified defence force. The largest two are *Niederösterreich* and *Oberst Brecht* at 97ft (29m) and 40ft (12m) respectively. Each has a 0.30in (12.7mm) MG and an 3.3in (84mm) PAR 66 Carl Gustav anti-tank mortar. In addition, there are 10 M-Boot 80 patrol craft.

**Left:** Austria operates a small riverine flotilla. This is *Niederosterreich*, the largest of the patrol craft, which is armed with a 0.8in (20mm) automatic cannon atop the armoured bridge, two 0.5in (12.7mm) and two 0.30in (7.62mm) MGs and a 3.35in (84mm) Carl Gustav mortar to give good firepower.

## BELGIUM

TODAY'S Royal Belgian Navy is some 4,500 strong — the majority regulars — with its main bases at Ostende and Zeebrugge. The principal combat elements are the four Wielingen class frigates which were designed and built in Belgium in a remarkable national undertaking. The Belgian naval staff requirement was for a class which would "provide, in close cooperation with Allied naval forces, protection of the Allied and national merchant shipping in the North Sea, the English Channel and its western approraches." The units were to have a full ASW capability, with limited air-defence and anti-surface weapons, and were to be constructed in Belgian yards.

This formidable requirement was met on schedule and all four ships were commissioned during 1978. They displace some 2,400tons and are armed with four Exocet SSM launchers, a single French 3.9in (100mm) DP gun, a Sea Sparrow SAM launcher, a 14.75in (375mm) ASW rocket-launcher and two L5 ASW torpedo tubes. The only major deficiencies are the lack of an ASW helicopter and of a CIWS; nothing can now be done about the former, but Sea Sparrow has been updated to compensate for the lack of a CIWS — plans for Goalkeeper having been abandoned. These four ships will probably have to last for a good few years as the Belgian government has reduced defence spending drastically since the ending of the Cold War.

Belgium has long taken the threat of naval mine warfare seriously and her largest single contribution to NATO forces has been with mine counter-measure vessels (MCMV). The oldest vessels are four Belgian-built US Adjutant class (390tons) minesweepers delivered in 1955/56, and seven Herstal class (190tons) inshore minesweepers — the latter were con-

**Left:** *Narcis*, one of 10 Tripartite mine-hunters acquired by the Belgian Navy between 1985 and 1990. Some deployed to The Gulf.

**Below:** *Wandelaar*, one of four Wielingen class frigates designed and built in Belgium in 1974-77. Budget cuts currently frustrate modernization plans.

structed in Belgium in the late 1950s to a modified British Ham class design and their primary mission is to clear the Schelde estuary of mines in time of war. Also delivered in the late 1950s were six ex-USN Dash class ocean-going MCMVs with a displacement of 780tons; they are now equipped as minehunters but are reaching the end of their useful lives.

The most modern design in service is the Tripartite Minehunter type designed and produced in conjunction with France and The Netherlands. There are 10 of these 595ton vessels carrying a sophisticated and comprehensive range of minehunting equipment. They are normally armed with a single 0.8in (20mm) AA cannon, but this can be supplemented by two 0.5in (12.7mm) machine-guns.

The Belgians have also constructed two Zinnia class (2,600tons) command and logistic support ships for their MCMVs. These are fitted out with the latest technology for command facilities, carry fuel and other supplies for MCMVs, and have a telescopic hangar and flight-deck for an Alouette III helicopter. This is a very sensible design to meet a genuine requirement, and it was noticeable in the 1990 Gulf War that the UK had to press hydrographic survey ships into service as temporary MCMV command ships which obviously did not have the additional logistic support capability offered by the Zinnia class.

The Belgian contribution to the mine clearance force in the Gulf at the end of the Iran-Iraq War was one Zinnia class command ship, and one Tripartite and two Dash class MCMVs.

The balance of the Belgian Navy is very small; there are no amphibious warfare ships, no submarines and no replenishment auxiliaries (apart from the two Zinnia class). Naval aviation is limited to three Alouette IIIs for deployment on the Zinnia class vessels. The Belgian Air Force operates five Sea King helicopters on SAR duties, but there are no maritime patrol aircraft.

### EQUIPMENT

**Frigates:**
Wielingen class
**Mine Warfare:**
Aster (Tripartite) class
J E Van Haverbeke (US Dash) class
Heist (US Adjutant) class
Herstal (modified British Ham) class
**Naval Aircraft:**
Aerospatiale SA.316B Alouette III

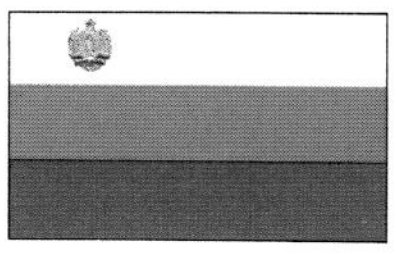

## BULGARIA

THE Bulgarian Navy is about 6,000 strong, half of them conscripts. The main naval HQ is at Varna and there are other bases at Atiya, Sozopol and Balchik. The HQ of the Danube flotilla is at Vildin, well to the west and near the Yugoslav border.

The navy operates a large number of patrol boats, but also has a number of frigates, corvettes and replenishment oilers which have undertaken deployments to the Mediterranean. There are two Soviet frigates in service: *Smeli* (Koni class) and *Bodri* (Riga class). *Smeli* was acquired in 1990 and replaces another, older vessel of the same name. It displaces nearly 2,000tons and carries considerable armament, including SA-N-4 Gecko twin launcher SAM and four 3in (76mm) guns. *Bodri*, the last of its class of three, was transferred in 1985 and has reasonably modern equipment.

The corvettes number four, all ex-Soviet vessels: two Poti class, one Pauk-I class and one Tarantul-II class. The latter is the most recent transfer and more may follow to replace the now elderly Poti class.

The patrol boat fleet comprises the usual mixture of Soviet export types: three Osa-I and three Osa-II missile-armed fast attack craft, four Shershen class and seven Zhuk class. There are 14 minesweepers: two T-43 class (580tons, ocean type), four Sonya class (450tons, coastal type), six Vanya class (245tons, coastal type) and two Yevgenya class (90tons, inshore type). There is also a limited amphibious warfare potential with two Polnocny-A medium landing ships and 18 Vydra class landing craft.

The Bulgarian Navy has operated submarines for many years. She originally had a pair of Soviet Whiskey class but these were replaced by newer Romeo class boats in the early 1970s. Only one Romeo class remains operational, *Pobeda*, and another two have been placed in reserve for training duty. A Kilo class may soon be acquired.

There are two Bulgarian designed and built replenishment oilers of the Mesar class. When the first of these 3,500ton ships joined the navy in 1979 it disclosed a shipbuilding capacity which had not been appreciated in the West up to that time. The two ships, *Mesar* and *Dimitri A Dimitrov* enable the Bulgarian Navy to deploy a group to the Mediterrean. In 1980 they made their first such "blue water" deployment with two Riga class frigates.

The naval aviation branch operates some 12 land-based Mil Mi-14 Haze-A.

**Above:** The small, Black Sea, Bulgarian navy operates the sail-training ship *Kaliakra* which has been in service since 1984.

### EQUIPMENT

**Submarines:**
Pobeda (Soviet Romeo) class
**Frigates:**
Smeli (Soviet Koni) class
Bodri (Soviet Riga) class
**Patrol Boats:**
Soviet Osa-I & -II classes
Soviet Shershen class
Soviet Zhuk class
**Corvettes:**
Soviet Poti class
Soviet Pauk-I class
Soviet Tarantul-II class
**Amphibious Warfare:**
Soviet Polnocny-A class
Soviet Vydra class
**Mine Warfare:**
Soviet Sonya class
Soviet T-43 class
Soviet Vanya class
Soviet Yevgenya class
**Naval Aircraft:**
Mil Mi-14 Haze
**Marines:**
Three companies

## CYPRUS

THE Republic of Cyprus has a naval command within its national guard which operates *Salamis*, a French-built coastal patrol craft armed with a 1.6in (40mm) Breda AA gun and a 0.30in (7.62mm) machine gun. The marine police have two French Type 32L patrol boats, *Aphrodite* and *Kimon*. There are a further three boats on order from Yugoslavia which will carry 0.8in (20mm) Oerlikon and ISBRS.

The Turkish Republic of Northern Cyprus has three coastal patrol craft transferred from the Turkish coastguard, and there is a Turkish craft, *Caner Gonyeli*, which is permanently based at Girne.

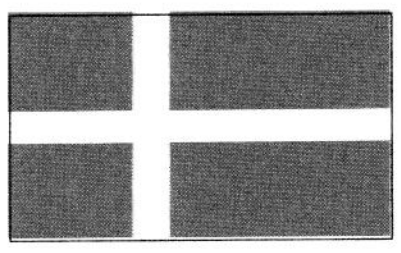

## DENMARK

THE Royal Danish Navy has a manpower strength of some 5,680, of whom about 18 per cent are conscripts. The main bases are at the capital, Kopenhavn (Copenhagen), Korsør, and Frederikshavn in the north. For such a small country, a very high proportion of her ships have been designed and built in domestic yards. Denmark is responsible for the defence of the self-governing Faroe Islands and is herself situated on the strategically important "Belts" controlling (with Sweden) the exit from the Baltic to the North Sea.

With the scrapping of the two large Peder Skram class frigates in 1991 the largest surface warships are the three frigates of the Nils Juel class. These 1,320ton vessels are armed with eight Harpoon SSMs, a single OTO Melara 3in (76mm) DP gun, a NATO Sea Sparrow SAM launcher, four 0.8in (20mm) AA cannon and a depth-charge rack. Various armaments and sensors are not fitted, reducing ASW ability.

To protect Denmark's extensive fishery interests the navy has developed some "fishery protection frigates". The four ships of the 1,970ton Hvidbjørnen class have a reinforced bow for operations in northern waters, a 3in (76mm) DP gun plus a flight-deck and hangar for a Westland Lynx Mk 80 helicopter. The original class were built in 1963, thus one improved Hvidbjørnen class (1,970tons) entered service in1976 and in the meantime a replacement design was ordered. The result is the Thetis class, the first vessels of which have entered service, with a purpose-built design flexibility which enables them to develop into fully-armed frigates. This concept emerged from the StanFlex 2000 programme; it is of steel construction, has one OTO Melara 3in (76mm) DP gun, two 0.8in (20mm) cannon and a large hangar and flight-deck for a Lynx.

For operations in the Baltic there is a need for high-speed patrol boats. The Søløven class torpedo boats (114tons) are normally kept in reserve, giving way to the 10 Willemoes class guided-missile boats which were built in Denmark in the late 1970s and based on the Swedish Spica class design. A third combat type is the Daphne class (170tons) anti-submarine patrol boats designed and built in Denmark but paid for by the USA. Of limited value against submarines in open waters they could well give a good account of themselves in the constricted waters of The Belt. In addition there are two large patrol craft of the Maagen class (190tons) and three Agdlek class which are ice-strengthened for operations off Greenland.

There is a small group of mine warfare vessels and the Royal Danish Navy is unusual in being one of the very few navies to have more minelayers than minesweepers, a consequence of its NATO task of closing The Belts to Soviet shipping. There are four large minelayers of the Falster class (1,880tons); built to a NATO design in the early 1960s, each can carry 400 mines and is armed with four 3in (76mm) 50 Mk 33 guns and four 0.8in (20mm) Oerlikons. All are about to undergo a major refit to enable them to serve through into the next century. Also, there are two coastal minelayers of the Lindormen class (575tons) whose mission is to lay controlled minefields. The minesweeping force comprises three Sund class coastal minesweepers (ex-USN Bluebird class).

The Danes were among the first in Europe to operate submarines. Currently, they have five; the oldest are the three Tumleren class (German Type 207) which were bought from Norway where they served as the Kobben class. The remaining two are Improved Type 205 designs built in Denmark in the 1960s as the Narhvalen class. All have been refurbished to enable them to serve into the next century.

In the mid-1980s the Royal Danish Navy found itself facing the imminent obsolescence of several classes. Expensive to replace them all the Danes have come up with a novel solution: the StanFlex 300 multi-function combat vessel. This is a revolutionary idea in warship construction and practice. (The StanFlex 2000 is a derivative of it.)

In this concept a standard hull has been designed with certain common facilities and services which can accommodate different modules or pallets, according to the required role. The common hull is of foam-core, glass-reinforced plastic construction with three engines in a CODOG layout. The two diesels power the outboard propellers, while the gas-turbine is brought in to power the centreline propeller. The command, control and communications ($c^3$) system and the associated database are also common, with the programmes required for the individual weapons and the four roles stored in the software.

As a result, these ships can perform four roles: surveillance, minelayer, mine counter-measures and missile patrol boat. In addition, the hull and superstructure have been designed to minimize radar, infra-red and noise signatures, and key areas have Kevlar armour protection. The hull is subdivided by six watertight bulkheads and great thought has been devoted to damage control measures. Four of this Flyvefisken class have entered service and three more will be delivered by the end of 1992. A firm order for another six has alreadybeen placed and if the remaining three can be financed the eventual total will be 16.

Naval aviation operates nine Lynx ASW helicopters for shipboard duties. The air force operates three Aerospace SMA-3 Gulfstream III aircraft in the maritime reconnaissance role and eight Sikorsky S-61 A-1 Sea Kings for SAR.

There is no marine force but the navy is supported in its role by some 5,200 men and women in the Home Guard who operate 37 patrol craft and a number of smaller vessels.

### EQUIPMENT

**Submarines:**
Narhvalen (German Type 205) class
Tumleren (German Type 207) class
**Frigates:**
Nil Juel class
Hvidbjørnen and Modified Hvidbjørnen classes
Thetis (StanFlex 2000) class
**Patrol Boats:**
Willemoes class
Agdlek class
Maagen class
Flyvefisken (StanFlex 300) class
**Mine Warfare:**
Falster class
Lindormen class
Sund (US Bluebird) class
**Naval Aircraft:**
Westland Lynx Mk 80

**Below:** *Hvidbjørnen*, the nameship of a class of four fishery protection frigates. Now elderly, these vessels carry a crew of 70 and have sufficient range for patrol duties, a vital factor given the outlying Faroe Islands.

**Below:** Designed for Baltic operations, the patrol boat *Sehested* (P-547) belongs to the Willemoes class. well-armed, they have four Harpoon SSMs, a 3in (76mm) gun and Type 61 torpedoes from Sweden.

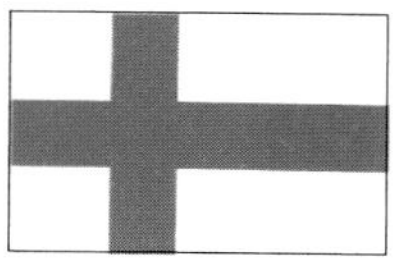

## FINLAND

DURING the Winter War (1939-40), Finnish minesweepers and submarines threatened Soviet naval adventures. The eventual peace treaty of 1944 remains in force today. Among other conditions, it bans the Finnish Navy from possessing torpedo boats and submarines, and has imposed a ceiling of 10,000tons and 4,500 men.

Post-WWII Finland has maintained small but notably efficient defence forces equipped with a mixture of Western, Soviet and indigenous equipment. The navy has to defend a very long Baltic Sea coastline and numerous small islands (30,000) which cannot be fortified in peacetime; every aspect of its work is dominated by the huge Soviet Baltic Fleet lying just the other side of the Gulf of Finland.

The navy has a strength of some 1,800 men, of whom a little over 1,000 are conscripts. There is a base at Helsinki and the main one at Türkü. The warships of the navy are grouped into four functional squadrons, one each for gunboats, guided-missile patrol boats, patrol boats and mine warfare vessels. In addition, there is a 600-man Frontier Guard coastguard which operates eight large patrol craft and more than 50 smaller, coastal ones.

The principal warships in today's navy are two very interesting corvettes of the Turunmaa class (770tons) which were both completed in 1968. These are sleek-looking vessels with a very low superstructure; their CODOG propulsion plant consists of three diesels and a gas-turbine which gives them a maximum speed of 35kts. Armament comprises a single 4.7in (120mm) Bofors DP mounted on the foredeck, two 1.6in (40mm) Bofors and two twin Soviet 0.9in (23mm) AA guns, two RBU-1200 ASW rocket launchers and two depth-charge racks. They were designed and built in Finland, and were completely refitted in 1984-86 by Wärtsilä in Helsinki.

There is a powerful guided-missile patrol boat element, eight strong. There are four Tuima class (Soviet Osa-II) armed with four SS-N-2B Styx missiles and four 1.12in (30mm) AA cannon. These were purchased in 1975 and the Finns have since added some Western electronic equipment, including a navigational radar. In 1978 they strengthened this element by ordering a prototype of a Finnish-designed boat and subsequently ordered three more. These Helsinki class boats (280tons) are armed with four stern-mounted, Swedish Saab RBS-15 anti-ship missiles (with two missiles per launcher), a Bofors 2.25in (57mm) DP gun on the foredeck and four Soviet 0.9in (23mm) AA machine-guns; there are also rails for laying mines. Eight new Rauma class boats, to a modified Helsinki-II design with a revised hull shape, are now under construction with the first one built and in service. They are armed with the same type of Saab missiles, but the 2.25in (57mm) gun is replaced by a turret-mounted Bofors 1.6in (40mm) gun, and a French Matra Sadral air-defence missile system is installed.

**Above:** Built by Wärtsilä, Helsinki, *Kotka* is a guided-missile boat of the Helsinki class. Finnish boats cannot be armed with torpedoes due to the 1944 treaty.

**Below:** Camouflaged *Rymättylä* of the Rihtniemi class is a converted minesweeper which can now lay mines but whose main role is now A/S patrol.

There are 11 patrol boats. The three Ruissalo class and two Rihtniemi class are generally similar: both were formerly convertible minesweeper/gunboats but are now used solely as gunboats. They are armed with two twin, turret-mounted 0.9in (23mm) cannon and two RBU-1200 ASW rocket launchers and their two Mercedes-Benz diesels give them a top speed of 18kts. The six Nuoli class patrol boats (64tons) are much faster with Soviet M50 diesels which give them a maximum speed of 40kts. They are armed with one Bofors 1.6in (40mm) and two Oerlikon 0.8in (20mm); but whereas in most other navies such boats would also have two torpedo tubes, these boats, due to the provisions of the treaty with the USSR, have none. There is a new class of patrol boat at the design stage.

The Finns have placed a considerable emphasis on mine warfare. The largest and most heavily armed warship in the Finnish Navy is the *Pohjanmaa* (1,100tons) which doubles as a minelayer and peacetime training ship. She is armed with one Bofors 4.7in (120mm) and two 1.6in (40mm) guns, plus eight Soviet 0.9in (23mm) AA guns, and two RBU-1200 ASW launchers. Her minerails (capacity for 120 mines) are used in peace as mounts for two training containers which are easily removable when it is necessary to use her in her primary role. A second multi-purpose ship has recently been commissioned, the *Hameenmaa* (1,000tons), which has bow and stern doors to enable her to be used as either a ro-ro logistics ship or as a minelayer. There are also six minesweepers (Kuha class) and seven smaller ones (Kiiski class) originally designed as unmanned drones but now operating as manned vessels.

The coastguard has an air wing with two Mi-8 Hip, two ASW-equipped Super Puma, and three Agusta-Bell JetRanger helicopters. The army is responsible for coastal artillery, which includes large numbers of guns (some mounted in tank turrets emplaced in concrete) and some RBS-15 anti-ship missiles mounted on trucks.

### EQUIPMENT

**Patrol Boats:**
Tuima (Soviet Osa-II) class
Helsinki class
Rauma class
Ruissalo class
Rihtniemi class
Nuoli class
**Corvettes:**
Turunmaa class
**Mine Warfare:**
Pohjanmaa class
Hameenmaa class
Kuha class
Kiiski class
**Naval Aircraft:**
Aerospatiale AS.332B Super Puma
Agusta-Bell AB.206B JetRanger
Mil Mi-8 Hip

## FRANCE

THE French Navy is one of the great naval forces of the world; despite a number of historical setbacks it has always recovered its position. It has long been the close rival of Britain's Royal Navy; indeed, it seems highly probable that if the French growth and the decline of the Royal Navy continue at their present rates the French Navy will become the single most powerful western European navy.

The current French strategic considerations obviously centre upon the defence of Metropolitan France. The Marine Nationale contributes to this by maintaining a submarine-based strategic nuclear deterrent and also by providing naval forces in the three areas of responsibility: the Mediterranean, the North Atlantic and the English Channel. In all three areas there is the closest possible cooperation with NATO.

France has a number of colonial territories remaining and also maintains defence ties with some of her former colonies. The navy thus has responsibilities in the Caribbean, and the Indian and Pacific Oceans. The latter, in particular, has been a very active area for the French Navy; French Polynesia, New Caledonia and Walllis & Futura are all locally autonomous parts of France and are defended as such by the French military.

The current force comprises 54,500 men and women on active duty, with a further 11,000 in the naval air arm. There are four theatre commands: Atlantic Theatre (CECLANT), Mediterranean Theatre (CECMED), Indian Ocean (ALINDIEN), and Naval Forces Pacific (ALPACI). There are also a number of functional commands: Atlantic Fleet, Mediterranean Fleet, Submarines, Naval Air, Maritime Patrol Air and Aircraft Carriers. Most significant of all, however, is Force Ocean Strategique (FOST), the strategic submarine command.

The principal naval bases in France are Brest, Cherbourg, Lorient and Toulon; those overseas are Fort de France (Martinique), Nouméa (New Caledonia), Papeete (Tahiti) and Saint Denis (La Réunion). Within France the Atlantic Command has its HQ in Brest and Mediterranean has its HQ in Toulon; there is also a subordinated Channel Command with its HQ in Cherbourg.

The French Navy replaced its five wartime carriers with two of the French-designed Clemenceau class (32,700tons). *Clemenceau* and *Foch* were laid down in the 1950s and incorporated all the advances in carrier practice made in the early post-war period.

They have served the French Navy well, operating in the Pacific in support of the remaining French colonial territories and of the nuclear test programme, as well as supporting operations closer to home: for example, off Lebanon and in the Gulf War. They are of conventional design, with an 8 deg angled deck. Both ships are now reaching the end of their useful lives and are due to be paid off.

The French have undertaken a number of very ambitious naval programmes over the past 40 years, none more so than the new, nuclear-propelled aircraft carriers. The first, *Charles de Gaulle* (36,000tons), will join the fleet in 1998 and the second in 2002. The hull design is based upon that of the Clemenceau class; it has very similar dimensions but with major developments to reflect the latest advances in carrier practice, including a substantial missile armament. In an unusual step, a 20ton scale model exists for hydrodynamic testing.

The K15 nuclear-propulsion plant, two of which will power each carrier, is the latest in a series of very successful French designs; these include the smallest operational marine reactor in the world installed in the Rubis and Amethyste class submarines. It will give the carriers virtually unlimited range and will provide the French with the most powerful surface warfare capability of any European navy in the early years of the next century.

Another interesting design is the *Jeanne d'Arc* (12,400tons) which is employed in peacetime as a cadet training ship but which in wartime would be used as an ASW helicopter carrier or amphibious transport. The hull design was based on that of the air-defence cruiser *Colbert*, but the after part of the superstructure is devoted to a large flight-deck, 203ft (62m) in length and 69ft (21m) wide, with a single centre-line lift at the after end. *Jeanne d'Arc* has a significant surface armament with six Exocet launchers and four 3.9in (100mm) guns; her air-defence armament, however, is negligible and she would have to depend entirely on other ships in the group during an actual sea battle.

*Colbert* (11,300tons) itself was constructed in the 1950s as an anti-aircraft cruiser. She was armed with 16 5in (127mm) DP guns and 20 2.25in (57mm) Bofors AA guns, all in twin mounts. This was a dated concept, however, and in the early 1970s she was completely rebuilt and her armament changed radically. She is now fitted with a heavy anti-aircraft armament consisting of a single, twin-arm ECAN Masurca SAM launcher on the quarterdeck (48 missiles), two 3.9in (100mm) DP guns and 12 2.25in(57mm) AA guns. She also has an anti-ship capability with four MM38 Exocet launchers. She is fitted with sophisticated command facilities and her normal employment is as flagship of the Mediterranean Fleet.

The oldest destroyer still in service is the Type T-53 *Duperre* (3,740tons), due to strike in 1992. *Aconit* (3,870tons), a Type F-65, was completed in 1973 and was the first with the now characteristic French destroyer hull-form. There are no facilities for a helicopter and she too will not serve out the century.

Slightly more modern are the two large (7,000tons) destroyers of the Suffren class which are instantly recognizable by the massive radome covering the DRBI-23 3-D radar. Armament comprises the ECAN Masurca SAM system, four Exocet SSM launchers, two 3.9in (100mm) DP guns, four 0.8in (20mm) AA, a Malafon ASW missile

**Below:** French carrier *Clemenceau*, one of two built in the 1960s. They are now at the end of their operational lives and will be replaced by nuclear-powered carriers.

**Below:** *Jeanne d'Arc* offers France good wartime capabilities as a helicopter carrier for ASW or amphibious missions. She is seen here on a visit to New York, USA.

system and two catapult launchers for L5 ASW torpedoes. These fine ships are excellent weapons platforms as they roll and pitch only very slightly. They have spent most of their service in the Mediterranean, although at least one has been deployed to the Persian Gulf. Both underwent major refits in the mid-1980s and are due to serve until 1998 (*Suffren*) and 2000 (*Duquesne*).

Next to join the fleet were the three ships of the Tourville class (5,885tons), *Tourville*, *Duguay-Trouin* and *De Grasse*. Developed from the Aconit class they have a very similar hull-form to the Suffren class and are equally good seaboats. They are armed with six Exocet launchers, the Crotale SAM system, two 3.9in (100mm) DP guns, two 0.8in (20mm) AA cannon and a Malafon ASW missile system — but unlike the Suffren class they have full facilities for helicopters and normally carry two Lynx. All normally serve in the Atlantic, taking it in turn to be the flagship, and are scheduled to serve until 2000-2003.

The Type F-70 was the next class. There are two types which successfully use a common hull for the two different roles of ASW and air-defence, a goal which has eluded many other navies. First to appear was the seven strong Georges Leygues class of ASW ships; the first-of-class was commissioned in 1979 and the seventh and last, *Latouche-Tréville*, in 1990. Displacing over 4,000tons their armament is generally similar to that of the Tourville class. The only shortcoming in the original design was that the bridge was too low; this led to problems in heavy seas and the final three have the bridge one deck higher.

The second type is the slightly larger Cassard class which has two vessels, *Cassard* and *Jean Bart*, with armament, sensors and C³ facilities optimized for the air-defence role. The principal air-defence weapon is the Standard missile fired from Mk 13 launchers, the whole installation plus the related fire control system having been removed from two earlier destroyers, *Bouvet* and *Kersaint*. There are also two Sadral point-defence missile systems, one 3.9in (100mm) DP gun, two 0.8in (20mm) cannon, two ASW torpedo launchers and one Lynx helicopter. The 3-D radar is not given a separate mast but is mounted atop the exhaust stack, to give a unique look.

The French regard frigates as valuable all-round warships capable of fulfilling a number of missions; among the most important of these is patrolling and showing the flag in the numerous remaining overseas territories. The oldest type still in service is the Commandant Rivière class (2,170tons), with the four ships left due to leave service by 1993. One modified Commandant Rivière class frigate will remain in service for some years yet. This ship, *Balny* (2,150tons), trialled the first French CODAG propulsion system, a very compact installation which allows her to carry 100tons of

**Above:** *Duguay-Trouin*, a Tourville class destroyer, was built in the 1970s and is one of a long line of successful large, French destroyers since the 1930s.

**Below:** The Georges Leygues (F-70) class destroyer *Dupleix* is a handsome and capable design. There are two versions: one for ASW (seven built) and one for air-defence (two).

**Below:** The French dock landing ship *Foudre* entered service in 1990. She can carry one mechanized battalion of the Force Action Rapide (FAR), plus 1,080tons.

**Below:** *Jean Bart*, one of the two air-defence versions of the F-70 design. Note the Mk 13 launcher forward of the hangar for Standard SM-1 SAMs; the missile magazine is below.

extra fuel to give her the exceptional cruising range (on diesels alone) of 13,000nm at a steady speed of 10kts.

The successor to the Commandant Rivière was the d'Estienne d'Orville class (1,170tons). They are designated "avisos" and intended for ASW operations in coastal waters; 23 were built originally and today there are 17 grouped in five three-ship divisions, with others in different theatres. The single 3.9in (100mm) gun is mounted forward and a Bofors 14.75in (375mm) ASW rocket launcher is on the after deckhouse roof. When deployed on colonial duties they mount an MM 38 Exocet on either side of the funnel, conferring some independent offensive capability These handy little ships will serve until early next century.

The latest class to enter service takes a slightly different approach. The *Floréal* (3,000tons) is intended for ocean surveillance missions in low-risk theatres, economic exclusion zone patrols and fishery protection. The first of six, it is built to commercial standards and its armament comprises four MM 38 Exocets, one 3.9in (100mm) DP gun, two Sadral point-defence SAM systems, two 0.8in (20mm) AA cannon and one light helicopter. With a range of 9,000nm at 15kts and an endurance of 50 days (compared to 15 days for the d'Estienne d'Orville class), plus a high degree of crew comfort, they are capable of very protracted operations. It is hoped to have all six commissioned by 1993/94. There is a further frigate type under construction, three light frigates of the Lafayette class, which will enter service from 1994 to 1997.

There are a number of patrol boats (less than 20) for various tasks such as fishery protection, SAR and economic zone patrols. One, *Albatros*, is based permanently at La Réunion for patrols in the southern Indian Ocean, especially off the remote island of Kerguelen. The biggest class is that of the P-400 fast-attack type, with 10 examples in existence. These are modern (1986-88); the first in service was the *L' Audacieuse*.

The French have always paid considerable attention to mine warfare Three elderly, former USN Aggressive class minesweepers will remain in service for a few years more, but the backbone of the MCM force are 10 Eridan class or Tripartite minehunters, six of which are based at Brest and four at Toulon.

There are also five Circe class (508tons) single-role minehunters with the task of locating and destroying mines laid as deep as 197ft (60m). A new and very sophisticated type of ocean-going minesweeper is now under construction. Designated Bâtiment Anti-Mines Océanique (BAMO), this new Narvik class has a catamaran hull made of GRP and will displace 900tons. There are six already on order with more to follow.

France has a small but very capable amphibious warfare capability. The *Foudre* is a large (11,880tons) dock landing ship which joined the fleet in 1990. There are three other smaller dock landing ships (the Ouragan class and one Bougainville class), as well as five Champlain class (1,386tons) medium landing ships, 12 ocean-going landing craft and 26 smaller types. There is also a full range of auxiliaries which give France a full bluewater capability.

The first European navy to develop its own submarines, the French have consistently operated a highly-effective submarine arm. The oldest boats in service today are the patrol submarines. There are five Daphne class (two at Lorient, three at Toulon) which were launched between 1959 and 1967. With a submerged displacement of 1,038tons they were initially popular and attracted a number of export orders, but a series of losses marred their reputation for some years. Next came the Agosta class (1,750tons) which appears likely to be the final diesel-electric class for the French Navy. French yards have built four of these submarines for the French Navy and two for the Pakistan Navy, while Bazan in Spain has built four for the Spanish Navy.

Design work had started on a French nuclear submarine in the 1950s and a hull was laid down in 1958. The project was cancelled in 1959 and work on the hull suspended. President de Gaulle decided in the late-1950s that France needed an independent nuclear deterrent and although land- and air-based systems were developed, the major resources and expenditure were devoted to the sea-based element. Unlike any other navy, political pressure forced the French Navy to develop their first nuclear-propelled submarine for use as a ballistic-missile launcher rather than as an attack submarine. This was a very tall order, requiring the simultaneous development and integration of a number of very advanced technologies: nuclear propulsion, missiles, missile guidance, missile launch from a submerged submarine and very precise navigation and position-fixing; but, in the event, and to the very great credit of French industry, it all worked.

The first SSBN, *Le Redoutable*, was laid down in 1964 and launched in 1967. It became operational in 1971 — a truly

**Above:** The French Navy's Rubis class, nuclear-powered, attack submarines displace 2,670tons submerged and are the smallest SSNs anywhere.

**Below:** *Commandant Bouan*, one of the d'Estienne d'Orves class frigates designed for coastal ASW and for general patrol, is the most modern.

remarkable French national effort — and has been followed by four more similar SSBNs and a modified design, the single boat L' Inflexible class. The first submarine of the new "SNLE-NG" or Le Triomphant class was laid down in 1989 and will enter service in 1994, to be followed by two more before the turn of the century.

Having created an SSBN force the French Navy turned to the development of a nuclear-propelled attack submarine. The result is four Rubis class and an improved version, the Amethyste class, of which the first is scheduled to appear in late-1991. These are the smallest operational SSNs yet constructed by any navy.

There are some 11,000 officers and men in French naval aviation, making it the fourth largest naval air force after the USA, USSR and PRC. The principal front-line aircraft is the Super Etendard strike fighter (61 in service), supported by the Etendard IVP photo-reconnaissance aircraft (12). The current fighter is the Vought F-8E (FN) Crusader (23 remain in service of the 42 delivered in 1963) with most in the process of yet another refurbishment to fit them for service until the advent of the Rafale. Carrier-borne ASW is provided by the Alizé, another very old type which has been in service for some 30 years; 22 aircraft have been modernized to give them a few more years of service.

Naval helicopters for shipborne ASW duties comprise 17 very large Super Frelons, 38 medium-sized Lynx and 13 light Alouette IIIs. The French Navy is also responsible for shore-based maritime surveillance and operates 30 Atlantique and five Gardian aircraft. It also has some 150 aircraft for support and training tasks.

The two new nuclear carriers will require a complete updating of the navy's aircraft. The Super Etendard will operate from the new carriers, at least until about 2000, when they should be replaced by the Avion de Combat Maritime (ACM); the F-8E Crusaders require replacement even earlier. An airborne early warning type is also urgently needed, as a replacement for the Alize in the ASW role. It is known that the French admirals want the Grumman E-2C Hawkeye, although other sources suggest that rebuilt Grumman S-2E Trackers are being considered with new French radar and turboprop engines.

The title "marines" in France is accorded to 12 army regiments which have nothing at all to do with the navy, this being a traditional title for regiments raised to serve overseas in France's colonial territories. The 2,600 strong Fusilier-Marins are proper naval marines and they are organized into four assault groups, one attack swimmer unit and a headquarters.

**Above:** The ACM (*Avion de Combat Marine*) will be based on Dassault's Rafale flight demonstrator. It is a twin-engine, double-swept delta wing fighter.

**Above:** Super Etendards will continue to operate until the ACM enters service later in the 1990s.

**Below:** The latest patrol boat class is the P-400 (Super PATRA), of which *L'Audacieuse* (P-682) was the first.

## EQUIPMENT

**Aircraft Carriers:**
Clemenceau class
Jeanne d'Arc class
**Cruisers:**
Colbert class
**Submarines:**
L' Inflexible class (SSBN)
Le Redoutable class (SSBN)
Rubis class (SSN)
Agosta class
Daphne class
**Destroyers:**
Cassard (F-70 AA) class
Georges Leygues (F-70 ASW) class
Tourville (F-67) class
Suffren class
Aconit class
**Frigates:**
Floreal class
d'Estienne d'Orville class
Commandant Rivière class
**Patrol Boats:**
Grebe class
L' Audacieuse (Super PATRA-400) class
Sterne class
Trident (PATRA) class
Albatros class
Combattante class
**Amphibious Warfare:**
Foudre class
Bougainville class
Ouragan class
Champlain class
EDIC class
**Mine Warfare:**
Eridan (Tripartite) class
Circé class
US Aggressive class
**Naval Aircraft:**
Aerospatiale SA.319 Alouette III
Aerospatiale SA.321 Super Frelon
Aerospatiale SA.365F Dauphin 2
Breguet BR.1050 Alizé
Breguet Gardian
Dassault-Breguet BR.1150 Atlantique Mk1/Mk2(NG)
Dassault Etendard IVP
Dassault-Breguet Falcon 10
Dassault Super Etendard
Vought F-8E (FN) Crusader
Westland Lynx Mk2/4
**Marines:**
Four assault groups
One attack swimmer unit

## GERMANY

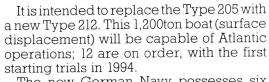

TWICE this century Germany has created a navy to challenge the supremacy of Britain's Royal Navy and twice it has been utterly destroyed as a consequence. Each time, however, it came close to achieving its objectives.

In 1954 the pressures of the Cold War led NATO to take the decision to re-arm the Federal Republic of Germany (FRG) and the Soviets responded by doing the same in-their zone. Thus, two German navies were raised, the Bundesmarine in the west and the Volksmarine in the east, which developed as part of their respective alliances. Both had limited roles and even the more advanced of the two, the Bundesmarine, was certainly not a blue water navy.

At the time of unification in 1990 the Bundesmarine had 38,600 men and the Volksmarine 14,000. These two forces are now combined into one and will be reduced as part of the overall post-Cold War force reductions affecting all European navies. Naval headquarters is at Glücksburg, near Flensburg. North Sea naval bases include Borkum, Bremerhaven, Emden and Wilhelmshaven; those on the Baltic are Drankse-Bug, Eckenförde, Flensburg, Kiel, Olpenitz, Peenemunde, Sassnitz, Warnemünde and Wolgast.

The main strategic interests of the new German Navy lie in the Baltic Sea, the North Sea and the English Channel, although there is an increasing interest in operations in the North Atlantic and the Mediterranean. To meet these requirements the Bundesmarine operated a fleet based on six destroyers, seven frigates, five corvettes, 40 fast patrol boats and over 60 minewarfare vessels; the Volksmarine had commitments only within the Baltic and operated three small frigates, 23 corvettes, some 40 patrol boats/craft, and 44 minewarfare vessels.

It is natural that a navy with such a record in submarine warfare should have a strong underwater force. The designers were limited to 350tons and they drew on experience gained with the wartime submarines (which proved of great value) and prepared the requirement with great care.

The first post-war design, the Type 201, was made of a special anti-magnetic steel. This, it was quickly discovered, suffered from serious corrosion and the last nine boats of the class were therefore rebuilt under the new designation, Type 205. Built in the 1960s, six of these boats remain in service, of which *U-1* has been converted to trial a new oxygen/hydrogen fuel-cell closed-cycle propulsion system.

In 1962 the upper limit for tonnage was raised to 450tons and the Bundesmarine embarked on the design of an improved class, the Type 206. A single-hull boat, it has the main ballast tanks at the fore and after ends of the submarine. Eighteen were built (*U13-U30*) and remain in service with 12 of them undergoing a modernization programme to Type 206A standard.

It is intended to replace the Type 205 with a new Type 212. This 1,200ton boat (surface displacement) will be capable of Atlantic operations; 12 are on order, with the first starting trials in 1994.

The new German Navy possesses six destroyers. The oldest are the three remaining Hamburg class (4,700tons) built in the mid-1960s armed with four Exocet launchers, three 3.9in (100mm) guns (two forward, one aft), eight 1.6in (40mm) AA guns, four ASW torpedo tubes, two Bofors 14.75in (375mm) ASW rocket launchers, depth-charge racks and up to 80 mines. As with all German-designed warships they have a very high top speed (35kts) and exceptionally comprehensive damage-control arrangements.

Following the Hamburg class, the navy bought its next destroyers from the USA: three Lütjens class (Type 103B) built to a modified Charles F Adams design. The prime role of these ships is air-defence, for which a Mk 13 missile launcher is mounted with a normal armament of Standard MR-1 missiles. The same launcher is also capable of firing Harpoon SSMs and a total of 40 Standard/Harpoons can be accommodated in the magazine. There is currently no close-in air-defence system, but it is planned to fit RAM launchers in the near future. There are two single 5in (127mm) guns, six tubes for Mk 46 ASW torpedoes and a launcher for ASROC ASW missiles. These ships will serve into the next century.

The navy's anti-submarine force consists of eight modern frigates of the Bremen class (3,800tons), a design developed from that of the Dutch Kortenaer. These excellent ships are armed with eight Harpoon SSMs, a

**Left:** *U-14*, one of 18 Type 206 submarines built in the early 1970s which have recently been given a major equipment update.

**Right:** A Hamburg class destroyer taking part in a NATO exercise in the North Atlantic. Of the four built three remain in service.

**Below:** *Halle*, a Soviet-designed Koni class frigate, is one ship retained from those inherited upon German reunification.

NATO Sea Sparrow SAM system, a 3in (76mm) OTO Melara DP gun, and four ASW torpedo tubes. They also carry two Lynx helicopters for which there is a large hangar aft; unlike the Kortenaer design, this extends to the full width of the hull.

A new class of frigate is on order to replace the Hamburg class destroyers. These Deutschland class (Type 123) ships will displace 4,275tons and will be armed with a mix of Exocets, vertical launch Sea Sparrow, RAM point-defence SAM system, as well as a single 3in (76mm) gun, ASW torpedo tubes and two ASW helicopters. Four are on order for delivery between 1994 and 1996.

The navy has retained two Koni class frigates from the Volksmarine. The latter was essentially a coastal defence force with a powerful amphibious element; *Rostock* and *Halle* were its main units and are now in partial reserve. They displace 1,900tons and carry four 3in (76mm) guns as their main armament.

The Bundesmarine was relatively light on corvettes, setting greater store by its large fleet of fast patrol boats. This element of the fleet has been boosted by acquisitions from the Volksmarine. There were already five ships of the Thetis class (Type 420) in service but these are now somewhat aged. Five Parchim class out of 16, one Tarantul-I class out of five and one Balcom 10 class out of three have been retained for use in the unified navy from those vessels serving formerly with the Volksmarine.

The fast patrol boat or light force element is now quite extensive. There are 20 Tiger class (Type 148) which were commissioned between 1972 and 1975; capable of 36kts, they are armed with four Exocet missiles, a single OTO Melara 3in (76mm) DP gun and either a 1.6in (40mm) AA gun or eight mines. There are also 20 Type 143 boats, 10 of the standard Albatros type and 10 of the improved Gepard class (Type 143A). Both have the same hull, a steel frame with wooden planking, 300ton displacement and four Exocet missile launchers; but the basic Type143 has two OTO Melara 3in (76mm) DP guns and two torpedo tubes, while the Type 143A has a RAM point-defence missile system, minerails and only one 3in (76mm) gun. The 10 Albatros class are being refitted to the same standard as the Gepard class whereupon they will be redesignated Type 143B. These boats serve in four 10-boat squadrons, all operating in the Baltic. Nothing has been retained from the Volksmarine.

The Bundesmarine devoted large resources to its mine warfare fleet and today it operates seven minesweeper squadrons. There are eight Ariadne class (Type 393, 205tons) and 10 Frauenlob class (Type 394, 246 tons) inshore minesweepers, the only difference lying in the type of sweep-current generators fitted. In addition there are 12 Lindau class (Type 331A/B minehunters of 402tons), six improved Schleswig (Type 351) conversions, four Schütze class (Type 340-341) coastal minesweepers, and six Kondor-II class ex-Volksmarine vessels. Among the latest minesweepers are the Type 343 (620tons) or Hameln class which are capable of magnetic, acoustic and mechanical minesweeping. Ten are in service to replace the Schütze, and will combine eventually with 10 of the very similar Frankenthal class Type 332 minehunter (650tons) before the end of the century. An unusual concept is the drone-operating system for clearing magnetic mines in which remotely-controlled, magnetic minesweeping launches act, essentially, as floating solenoids. In groups of three these Seehund vessels are directed by a Type 351 control ship; there are six such Troikas, as these units are called.

**Above:** The FGN built up a minesweeping force to cope with the Warsaw Pact threat; this is a Type 340 minesweeper/minelayer.

**Below:** A former East German Parchim class corvette enters Kiel harbour in 1991 under a new flag and with a new pennant number.

Amphibious warfare capability consists of 20 Type 520 utility LCTs, based on the US Navy's LCU-1646 design, and 17 Type 521 LCMs based on the US Navy's LCM (8). All were built in the 1960s and many others, of both types, have been placed in reserve, sold, or converted to other uses. The Volksmarine vessels have not been retained, neither have the large naval infantry forces which used them.

In addition to this comprehensive navy, there is a large support force of survey ships, underway replenishment ships, ammunition ships and repair ships, plus three purpose-built intelligence collectors.

Naval operations in the Baltic and North Seas would be impossible without effective air cover from units dedicated to the fleet support role and so the naval aviation branch, Marineflieger, is a large one. It has four wings with 6,700 men and nearly 200 fixed-wing aircraft and helicopters. The Panavia Tornado accounts for half the numbers, but there are 19 Breguet Atlantique aircraft serving in the maritime reconnaissance and Elint roles, 19 Lynx helicopters used on the Type 122 frigates and there are also 22 land-based Sea King helicopters for SAR.

## EQUIPMENT

**Submarines:**
Type 205 class
Type 206 class
**Destroyers:**
Lütjens (modified US Charles F Adams) class
Hamburg class
**Frigates:**
Bremen (Type 122, modified Dutch Kortenaer) class
Rostock (Soviet Koni) class
**Patrol Boats:**
Gepard (Type 143A) class
Albatros (Type 143) class
Tiger (Type 148) class
**Corvettes:**
Thetis class
Parchim class
Tarantul-I class
Balcom 10 class
**Mine Warfare:**
Ariadne class
Schutze class
Hameln (Type 343) class
Schleswig (Type 351) class
Lindau (Type 331) class
Frauenlob (Type 394) class
Kondor-II class
**Naval Aircraft:**
Panavia Tornado
Breguet BR.1150 Atlantique
Westland Lynx Mk 88
Westland Sea King Mk 41

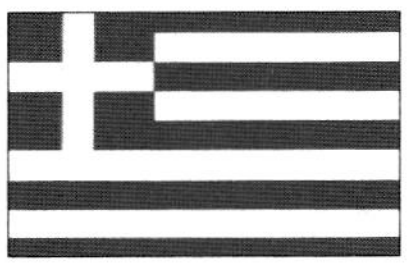

## GREECE

SINCE the defeat of the Turkish-Egyptian fleet at the Battle of Navarino (20 October 1827), the Hellenic Navy's primary mission has been to maintain parity with the Turkish Navy. The region of greatest interest is the eastern Mediterranean and the Aegean, an area which includes Cyprus and numerous Greek-owned islands close to the Turkish coast.

Today the Greek Navy has two principal tasks: one is to be part of NATO's southern region and the other is, as ever, to watch the Turks. The navy is quite large with some 19,500 officers and ratings (about 60 per cent are conscripts). The main bases are at Salamis, Patras and Soudha Bay, and there are three naval districts: Aegean, Ionian and Northern Greece.

The current main surface combatants are 12 former US Navy destroyers, all dating from WWII. There are six former US Navy (ex-Gearing class) destroyers (3,500tons) which were completed in 1945-46 and transferred to Greece between 1972 and 1981. All were modernized under the FRAM I programme when in US service and have been given further updates by the Greeks since. Four of the six have four Harpoon SSMs, four 5in (127mm) guns, one 3in (76mm) OTO Melara DP (on what used to be the DASH helicopter deck), an ASROC launcher, six ASW torpedo tubes and a depth-charge rack; the other two lack the Harpoon launchers.

A seventh former Gearing class ship, HS *Themistocles* (3,500tons), was originally a radar picket but has been rebuilt extensively. She retains the original six 5in (127mm) guns, Hedgehog ASW mortars and six torpedo tubes and has had two 0.8in (20mm) and two 0.5in (12.7mm) AA weapons added. More importantly, however, she has had a helicopter deck and hangar fitted which enables her to operate an Agusta-Bell AB.212 ASW helicopter. Another destroyer, HS *Miaoulis* (3,320tons), is formerly of the US Navy's Allen M Sumner class. She has had an almost identical rebuild. Finally, there are four ex-US Navy Fletcher class destroyers held in reserve.

The frigate force is much more modern. There are two Dutch Kortenaer class ships redesignated Elli class (3,786tons) which were bought in 1981 and actually taken from production for the Royal Netherlands Navy (RNethN) in order to satisfy the Greek timetable. They are very similar to the ships in Dutch service except that their hangar has been lengthened by 7.2ft (2.2m) in order to accommodate the AB.212. The SAM missile is the Aspide, the Italian version of the Sea Sparrow, and the after 3in (76mm) gun has been replaced by a 0.8in (20mm) Mk 15 Vulcan Phalanx CIWS. Currently on order are four German MEKO-200 frigates which will be known as the Ydra class. One is under construction at the Blohm und Voss yard in Germany, while the other three will be built in Greece between 1992 and 2000.

**Above:** The Greek frigate *Limnos* of the Dutch Kortenaer class. Note the two 3in (76mm) turrets, one on the foredeck the other positioned on top of the hangar roof aft.

The German armed tender *Weser* (2,740tons) was bought in 1976 and renamed the HS *Aegeon*. The Hellenic Navy has changed her armament to two 3in (76mm) OTO Melara DPs, four 1.6in (40mm) AA and 70 mines, and now employs her as a frigate. The frigate fleet is completed by four Aetos class (1,750tons) vessels (ex-USN Cannon class) with a very limited capability which will be replaced soon by new ships. An interesting development is the construction of two new frigates/corvettes to the Osprey design based on the British Thornycroft "short-fat" hull concept. Two have been completed and there are plans for eight more.

There are 16 guided-missile patrol boats of three classes: four Combattante-II, 10 Combattante-III and two Kelefstis Stamou. The latter are poorly armed, but the Combattante's have excellent systems, including Exocet and Penguin SSMs.

There are also two gun-armed patrol boats of the Ormi class (ex-USN Asheville class), five Esperos class (ex-German Jaguar Type 141) torpedo boats, four re-engined Nasty class boats from Norway, three Dilos class craft and three other pursuit patrol craft. Mine warfare ships include two minelayers and 14 small minesweepers: 11 are ex-USN (LSM 1 and MSC 294 classes) while five were built in the USA for the Belgian Navy in the early 1950s (ex-Adjutant class) and passed on to Greece in 1969. There are no known plans for new construction to replace any of these.

All the amphibious warfare ships and craft are elderly and were donated by the US Navy, except for two which were built in the 1960s and came from Germany plus two in the late 1940s from Britain. Five new large LSTs are currently being completed — the Jason class (4,400tons) — which can carry 300 troops or a number of tanks/wheeled vehicles and have facilities for two Sea King helicopters.

During the 1960s the Hellenic Navy found itself with a few rather elderly ex-USN submarines and decided to expand by placing orders for a number of the then relatively untried German Type 209 submarines from Howaldtswerke at Kiel. This was, in fact, the first of many foreign orders for this type and eight entered service between 1971 and 1980 as the Glavkos class. In the early 1990s four are being upgraded, which will include fitting them with Sub-Harpoon missile launchers. The submarine force now consists of ten boats: eight Type 209s plus the elderly ex-USN Guppy-III and Guppy-IIA, both of which are used for training.

The navy has sole responsibility for operating the shipborne helicopters; currently, these include four Alouette III and 16 Agusta-Bell 212. The air force is responsible for all other support from land bases and this now includes 14 recently-modernized Grumman HU-16B Albatross amphibians for maritime reconnaissance manned by mixed navy/air force crews. There are no marines but the army has two commando regiments, each of six battalions, and a raider battalion for possible use in the Aegean.

### EQUIPMENT

**Submarines:**
Papanikolis (ex-US Guppy-IIA) class
Katsonis (ex-US Guppy-III) class
Glavkos (German Type 209) class

**Destroyers:**
Kanaris (ex-US Gearing FRAM I) class
Themistocles (ex-US Gearing FRAM II) class
Miaoulis (ex-US Allen M Sumner) class
Aspis (ex-US Fletcher) class

**Frigates:**
Elli (Dutch Kortenaer) class
Aegeon (ex-German Rhein) class
Aetos (ex-US Cannon) class

**Patrol Boats:**
Kelefstis Stamou class
Ipopliarchos Arliotis (French Combattante-II) class
Antipliarchos Lascos (French Combattante-III) class
Ormi (ex-US Asheville) class
Esperos (ex-German Jaguar Type 141) class

**Amphibious Warfare:**
Ipopliarchos Grigoropolous (ex-US LSM-1) class
Syros (ex-US LST 1/LST5111) class
Oinoussai (ex-US Terrebonne Parish) class
Jason class

**Naval Aircraft:**
Aerospatiale SA.319B Alouette III
Agusta-Bell AB.212

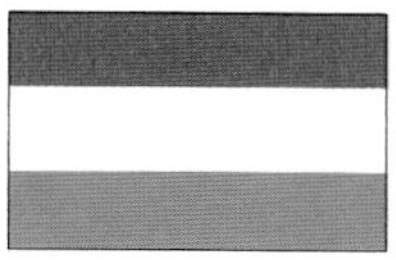

## HUNGARY

HUNGARY has no access to the sea, but the Danube flows through the country and the army operates a small riverine force manned by an independent maritime brigade of 400 men. Their craft include minesweepers, patrol boats, landing-craft and troop transports. Although most are held in reserve, there are more than 40 AN-2 class mine warfare/patrol craft armed with two 0.5in (12.7mm) machine-guns. There are six Újpest class river minesweepers (ex-Yugoslav Nestin class) armed with five 0.8in (20mm) Hispano machine-guns and carrying 24 mines.

## ICELAND

ICELAND was a Danish possession for many centuries, but, until WWII, it lay well outside normal European political and military events. The USA established bases there in 1941 and maintains them today. Iceland became a member of NATO in 1949, but, as she possesses no armed forces of her own, she has never been part of the integrated military command structure.

The only Icelandic maritime requirement has been for fishery protection vessels, the first of which was purchased in the early 1930s. The most extraordinary event in the country's recent history was the Anglo-Icelandic "Cod War" in 1972-73 which was the result of a dispute between the two countries over fishing rights.

Today, the coastguard or Landhelgisgaeslan operates two Aegir class (1,500tons) and one Odin class (1,000tons) fishery-protection ships. All were built in Denmark and are armed with a single 2.25in (57mm) low-angle gun. The coastguard also operates one Fokker F-27 maritime patrol aircraft, one Hughes 500MDH Defender and one Aerospatiale SA.365N Dauphin helicopter.

**Above:** The Icelandic coastguard patrol ship *Tyr*, one of the two Danish-built Aegir class vessels used to protect the fishing grounds.

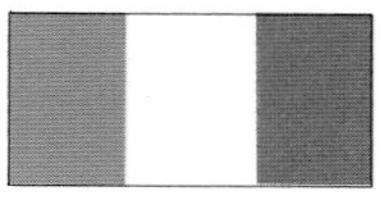

## IRELAND

IRELAND gained its independence from Britain in 1921 and subsequently declared itself a republic. It remained neutral during WWII and has maintained that position throughout the Cold War, firmly declining several invitations to join NATO.

Although still very small, the Irish Navy has expanded considerably over the past 20 years and has a volunteer force of 1,000 officers and ratings. Its tasks are the defence of Irish coastal waters, fishery protection and the prevention of gun-running by various terrorists groups. Its main base is on Haulbowline Island in Cork.

The oldest of the major units currently in service is the *Deirdre* (966tons), a patrol vessel and the first ship of the navy's to be built in Ireland (in 1971/72). She is armed with one 1.6in (40mm) Bofors and two 0.5in (12.7mm) weapons. She was followed by three improved versions, the Emer or P21 class (1,003tons), with a raised forecastle to improve seakeeping, better electronics and two GAM-B01 0.8in (20mm) guns in place of the 0.5in (12.7mm) weaponry.

Next came *Eithne* (1,915tons); she is the largest warship built so far in an Irish yard. She is fitted with a flight-deck and hangar for a Dauphin 2 helicopter and her armament comprises one 2.25in (57mm) Bofors DP gun and two 0.8in (20mm) Rheinmetall cannon. A second unit was delayed and then the yard closed for financial reasons.

The Irish Navy then took the opportunity presented by the British sale of some of its three-year old Peacock class patrol boats (712tons), buying two and commissioning them in 1988 as the *Orla* and *Clara*. They are armed with a 3in (76mm) OTO Melara DP gun and four 0.30in (7.62mm) machine-guns, but have no helicopter facilities.

### EQUIPMENT

**Patrol Boats:**
Deirdre (P 20) class
Emer (P 21) class
Eithne (P 31) class
Orla (ex-British Peacock) class

**Above:** The 2.25in (57mm) Bofors aboard the Irish patrol ship *Eithne* fires at 235rpm, putting more HE into a target in 30 sec than any other gun of less than 3.9in (100mm) calibre.

**Below:** *Eithne* is one of seven patrol ships operated by the Irish Navy. Displacing 1,915tons, she has a hangar and flight-deck aft for an SA.365 Dauphin helicopter.

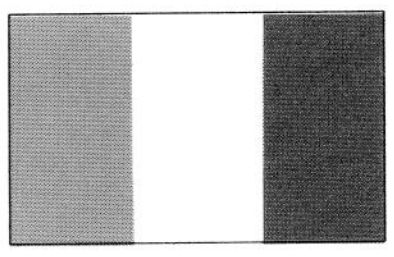

## ITALY

THE National Navy was formed in 1861 when the various Italian states unified. Italy had a strong desire to be the dominant power in the Mediterranean and built up a strong navy in WWI, followed by one in WWII which possessed a large number of modern, well-armed, well-designed and extremely fast ships. In the event, both were less successful than had been hoped and suffered serious losses.

After WWII the Italian Navy found itself closely allied to the US Navy on NATO's southern flank, with its first priority being to counter Soviet naval expansion in the Mediterranean. There is also a requirement, increasingly emphasized in recent years, to support its government's political aims in the Mediterranean and North Africa/Middle East and, in particular, to take part in peacekeeping and disaster relief operations.

The navy is currently some 48,000 strong and there are five major commands which cover the fleet: Upper Tyrrhenian Sea, Lower Tyrrhenian Sea, Adriatic Sea, Ionian Sea and Straits of Otranto. The main bases are at Ancona, Augusta, Brindisi, Cagliari, La Maddalena, La Spezia, Messina, Taranto and Venice.

The pride of the fleet is the new aircraft carrier *Giuseppe Garibaldi* (13,240tons). During the 1950s and 1960s the Italian Navy built some excellent cruisers and destroyers fitted with large flight-decks. It was not until 1978, however, that political agreement was obtained to construct a ship with a full-length flight-deck; although, as with the British 'through-deck cruisers'', the design purported to be a cruiser with an increased air capability rather than a "proper" aircraft carrier.

The *Giuseppe Garibaldi* is an exceptionally neat design with an unangled flight deck, a ski-jump and two lifts. Her intended role is as an ASW carrier, for which she can carry up to 16 Sea King helicopters (her normal load is 12) — a slightly smaller number of the new EH.101 helicopters will be carried too. An order for McDonnell-Douglas/BAe AV-8B Harrier IIs has been placed and they will be operated by the navy in combination with the helicopters.

The Italians have a firm commitment to disaster relief work and a capability for such operations has been designed into this ship. She has a heavy armament for her size and role. It consists of four SSM launchers,

**Below:** Italian carrier *Giuseppe Garibaldi* carrying out trials with Royal Navy Sea Harriers; in the end, AV-8Bs were bought.

**Below:** *Alpino* is the name-ship of a two-ship class of frigates (the other is *Carabiniere*) which are now near the end of their lives.

two SAM launchers and six AA guns, together with (most unusually for a Western aircraft carrier) six torpedo tubes. A second ship is planned which may displace some 1,000tons more.

Two cruisers remain in service, both with large flight-decks and hangars. The *Andrea Doria* (7,300tons) is the surviving lead ship of the class, *Caio Duilio* having retired in 1990. It was built to accommodate three AB.212 ASW helicotpers, with a heavy armament of one Mk 10 launcher for Standard SM-1 ER SAMs, eight 3in (76mm) AA guns and six ASW torpedo tubes. The other cruiser is the *Vittorio Veneto* (9,500tons), completed in 1969, which has a spacious flight-deck with a large hangar below and operates six AB.212 ASW helicopters. This is combined with a large weapons fit which includes a Mk 20 launcher for ASROC and Standard SAMs, four Otomat-Teseo SSM launchers, eight OTO Melara 3in (76mm) DP guns, six 1.6in (40mm) AA guns and six torpedo tubes. This exceptionally capable ship was the fleet flagship until the commissioning of the *Giuseppe Garibaldi*.

Continuing their pre-war custom the Italian Navy operates some large, well-armed and very fast destroyers. The oldest in service is the *Impavido*, the lead ship of a class (3,851tons) about to be replaced by the Animoso class. In the early 1970s two ships of the Audace class (3,950tons) appeared; recently they have been completely modernized and now mount an astonishing variety of weapons. There are three different missile systems: eight Otomat-Teseo SSM launchers, a Mk 13 launcher for 40 medium-range Standard SM-1 MR missiles and an Albatros point-defence SAM system. There are no less than five guns: one 5in (127mm) OTO Melara Compact DP on the foredeck and four 3in (76mm) OTO Melara Super Rapids in the waist. Then there are two separate torpedo systems: six 12.75in (324mm) tubes for Mk 46 torpedoes and four 21in (533mm) tubes mounted in the stern which fire AS-184 wire-guided torpedoes into the wake. On top of all this, the ships have a large flight-deck and hangar which will accommodate two AB.212 or one SH-3D ASW helicopter. This heavy weapons fit, their good habitability and seakeeping qualities, high maximum speed of 33kts and range of 400nm at 25kts make these very formidable ships.

The two ships of the improved Impavido design, the Animoso class (5,250tons), enter service in 1992. Their armament is identical to that of the Audace class, except that there are only three 3in (76mm) guns and no 21in (533mm) torpedo tubes, while the helicopter facilities are large enough to take two EH.101s. The superstructure is made of steel, with Kevlar armour to protect the most vulnerable areas; propulsion is by diesel or gas turbine (CODOG), unlike the Audace class which have steam propulsion.

There are 14 frigates in three classes. The oldest are two Alpino class (2,689tons) which were completed in 1967 and are due to be stricken in 1997. They mount six 3in (76mm) guns, six 12.75in (324mm) torpedo tubes and have a flight-deck and hangar for one AB.212 ASW helicopter. The four Lupo class (2,525tons) and eight Maestrale, or "Improved Lupo" class (3,200tons), provide a very strong frigate element for the fleet. Both are armed with Otomat SSMs (eight inthe Lupo class, four in the Maestrale class), NATO Sea Sparrow SAMs, one 5in (127mm) and four 1.6in (40mm) guns, and six 12.75in (324mm) torpedo tubes.

The Maestrale class is slightly larger, has better sea-keeping qualities and has an

**Left:** *Lupo*, lead-ship of a class of four frigates. Ten have been sold abroad to Venezuela and Peru. An Iraqi order has not been delivered for financial reasons and still lie moored in port.

**Left:** *Audace*, now 20 years old, remains an imposing sight. Her sister-ship is *Ardito* and together these two destroyers continue to give good service.

**Above:** The *Vittorio Veneto's* long flight-deck and large hangar enable her to operate six AB.212 ASW helicopters, while still having heavy armament.

**Right:** *Zeffiro*, a Maestrale class frigate. The gun is a 5in (127mm) OTO Melara Lightweight and the eight-cell launcher is an Albatros SAM system.

**Left:** Minerva class *Urania* (F-552), one of the first four of these new corvettes which is based at Augusta in Sicily. A well-armed class it may yet be expanded further.

additional pair of 21in (533mm) torpedo tubes as well as accommodation for two rather than one AB.212 ASW helicopters. These are very useful ships and 14 of the Lupo class have been sold to foreign customers.

The navy also operates three classes of corvette, some 15 ships in total: eight Minerva class, four De Cristofaro class and three Albatros class. The last two classes date from the 1950s and 1960s, but the Minerva class is very modern with the latest ship, *Sibilla*, commissioned in 1991. In addition, there is a modern patrol force with four Cassiopea class boats and seven Sparviero class guided-missile hydrofoils. The mine warfare vessels number approximately 20, with several ex-USN ships and the indigenous Lerici class minehunters and Agave class minesweepers.

The two ships of the San Giorgio class (7,665tons) are a most interesting design of ro-ro ship with a full-length flight-deck. They are intended primarily for amphibious warfare operations, for which they can carry 400 troops and their vehicles accommodated in a large hangar below the flight-deck. There is a docking-well, holding three large LCMs, and a bow ramp; three slightly smaller LCVPs are carried on davits on the upper deck. There is also extensive stowage for refrigerated stores, dry stores and aviation fuel. The aircraft are stowed on the flight deck; the normal complement being five helicopters, either the Boeing CH-47 Chinook or Sikorsky SH-3Ds. The ships' secondary role is peacetime disaster-relief and the second ship, *San Marco*, was partially funded by the Ministry of Civil Protection and her hospital facilities are more extensive than those on *San Giorgio*.

Italy did not restart submarine construction in the post-war period until 1965, when the first of the Toti class (593tons) was laid down. Four of these small boats were built, of which three remain in service. The second post-war class was the larger and more heavily armed Sauro class (1,637tons). Two were ordered in 1967 and after some delays joined the fleet in 1976 and 1977; two more were completed in 1981-82. They are of conventional design, and are being given a mid-life refit between 1990 and 1995 which will include replacement of the batteries and some of the machinery, and improvements to the living accommodation. Reliability will be increased too.

The first two of the Pelosi class (also known as the "Improved Sauro class") now in service are longer, while the second two will be longer still. When all four boats are operational in the early 1990s the navy will have achieved its goal of 12 submarines, all Italian-designed and built. All three types are equipped with six 21in (533mm) torpedo tubes. For the future, the Italian Navy is planning to build at least two of a yet further improved and larger version of the Sauro class, to be designated the Type S90. This will have a submerged displacement of

**Above:** *Nazario Sauro* (S-518), name-boat of a class of four diesel-electric submarines. Italy builds all its own submarines but has not achieved any export orders to date.

**Below:** Marines of the *San Marco* battalion, a unit with an excellent reputation for soldiering which did particularly well in the 1982 deployment to Beirut during the civil war.

**Right:** The Agusta-developed anti-submarine version of the licence-built AB.212 carries torpedoes, depth bombs and Marte/Sea Killer missiles.

2,490tons and will replace the ageing Toti class to give the navy a balanced fleet of large and very modern attack submarines.

The naval air arm or Marinavia has a strength of some 1,500 men. For the most part it operates helicopters. The 25 SH-3D Sea Kings are used for ASW and are based either aboard *Giuseppe Garibaldi* or ashore. A further 27 AB.212 helicopters (navalized versions of the Bell UH-1) operate from the cruisers, destroyers and frigates. This design, which has sold well abroad, is one of the few ship-borne helicopter to use skids rather than a wheeled undercarriage. The navy will shortly take delivery of its AV-8B Harriers and the Agusta/Westland EH.101 ASW helicopter. There are TAV-8B trainers in service, pilots have trained with the USMC and a unit will be based at the port of Taranto.

There is a small but notably efficient marine unit, the San Marco battalion, some 750 strong which is highly-mechanized and has played a successful role in a number of peacekeeping operations. There is also a highly-skilled specialist unit of underwater swimmers and commandos (COMSUBIN) based at La Spezia and following in the footsteps of Italian units from WWII.

### EQUIPMENT

**Aircraft Carriers:**
Giuseppe Garibaldi class
**Cruisers:**
Vittorio Veneto class
Andrea Doria class
**Submarines:**
Toti class
Sauro class
Pelosi class
**Destroyers:**
Animoso class
Audace class
Impavido class
**Frigates:**
Maestrale class
Lupo class
**Patrol Boats:**
Sparviero class
Cassiopea class
Bambu (ex-US Adjutant class minesweeper) class
**Corvettes:**
Minerva class
De Cristofaro class
**Amphibious Warfare:**
San Giorgio class
**Mine Warfare:**
Lerici-I & II classes
Salmone (ex-US Agressive) class
Castagno (ex-US Adjutant) class
**Naval Aircraft:**
Agusta-Bell AB.212
Agusta SH-3D Sea King
McDonnell-Douglas AV-8B Harrier II Plus
**Marines:**
One battalion
One commando unit

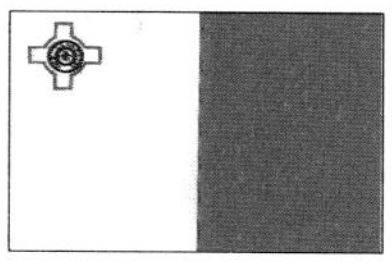

## MALTA

THE island state of Malta has an involvement with the sea almost without parallel, having been colonized from the sea by Phoenicians. Greeks, Carthaginians, Romans, Arabs, the Knights of St John, the French and, finally, the British. During WWII it was the key to British survival in the Mediterranean and was the base from which Axis resupply convoys were subjected to endless attack.

Post-war it continued to be the main base of the British Mediterranean Fleet until it became independent in 1974 and the British forces departed in 1979. Thereafter Malta adopted a policy of independent "positive neutrality", expelling NATO and becoming fairly close to the Ghadaffy régime in Libya.

Malta has a tiny naval force which constitutes the "maritime squadron" of the Malta Armed Forces. The vessels in service have been obtained from various sources and are generally in a poor condition. There are seven patrol boats, an ex-US LCVP and several patrol launches and cabin cruisers. There are two ex-Yugoslav Type 131 boats, *President Tito* and *Ganni Bonnici*, which are armed with six 1.12in (30mm) Hispano Suiza guns. Two boats have been acquired from Libya: C26, built in Yugoslavia and armed with one 0.5in (12.7mm) Browning, and C28, built at Thornycroft in the UK and armed with one 0.8in (20mm) Oerlikon. There are two ex-US Swift class boats, C23 and C24, and an ex-RAF launch, PC20.

**Below:** Units of the Malta Maritime Squadron. From left to right they are: C-26 and C-25 (now struck), *Ganni Bonnici* (C-39) and *President Tito* (C-38) transferred in 1982.

## NETHERLANDS

THE Royal Netherlands Navy (RNethN) has a history stretching back many enturies and at one time it was one of the most powerful navies in the world. It achieved its peak at the time of the three Anglo-Dutch wars in the seventeenth century under admirals such as Maarten Tromp, his son Cornelis van Tromp and Michael de Ruyter. Today it is a small navy, but highly-efficient and with a demonstrable record for producing outstanding warship designs.

As one of the major European colonial powers the Dutch needed to protect their overseas possessions, a task in which the navy played a predominant role. Until the 1950s by far the most important colonial territory was the enormous sprawl of islands which constituted the Dutch East Indies (present-day Indonesia). For many years this commitment to the East Indies meant, in effect, the existence of two fleets and, in many cases, even two types of ship. Thus, during WWII the RNethN found itself fighting in two quite separate theatres — in the North Atlantic and North Sea, and in the South China Sea. This Far Eastern commitment ended with Indonesian independence in the 1950s and the RNethN's overseas role has now reduced to a naval "presence" in the Caribbean, based on Willemstad in Curacao and Oranjestad in Aruba, to protect the Netherlands Antilles.

Today, the primary commitment is in European waters in support of NATO. Fleet headquarters are at Den Helder and a second base is at Vlissingen (Flushing). The navy consists of some 17,000 men and women in uniform, supported by 6,500 civilians and 2,800 marines. The Dutch fleet's war plans are to provide three escort groups, each comprising about seven frigates and a combat support ship, which would operate under NATO command in the North Atlantic. One of these groups, known as The Task Group, is permanently operational in peacetime. The RNethN also routinely provides a frigate for NATO's Standing Naval Force Atlantic (STANAVFORLANT). There is also a commitment to keep Dutch territorial and coastal waters and ports free of mines, for which purpose a number of minesweepers and hunters are operated, of which one is usually committed to NATO's Standing Naval Force Channel (STANVFORCHAN).

The RNethN has an especially close relationship with the British Royal Navy. This covers such areas as submarine operations, marine commandos and sea training. One specific example is that all submarine patrols start from and finish at the RN's base at Faslane in Scotland, where the clip-on towed arrays are maintained. There is also close liaison with the smaller navy of neighbouring Belgium.

**Above:** *Jan Van Brakel*, the ninth out of 10 of the Kortenaer class frigates to be built for the Dutch Navy. The weapons on the foredeck are a 3in (76mm) OTO Melara dual-purpose gun and a twin, four-cell Mk 29 Sea Sparrow SAM launcher.

**Left:** *De Ruyter*, one of the Dutch Navy's two Tromp class destroyers. This view shows a Westland Lynx helicopter on the flight-deck and (just forward of the hangar) the Mk 13 launcher for Standard SM-1 MR SAMs, 40 of which are carried.

**Above:** *Jacob Van Heemskerk* is one of the two air-defence versions of the Kortenaer design in which the flight-deck and hangar have been replaced by a magazine and launcher for Standard SM-1 MR missiles. There is an eight-cell Harpoon launcher on the fore-deck, but no 3in (76mm) gun. The Dutch produce four balanced ASW task groups in the Atlantic, with Tromp and Van Heemskerk class flagships.

**Right:** There are four battalions of the elite Royal Dutch Marines. These troops work closely with the British Royal Marines, with whom they form a joint force for the NATO seaborne reinforcement role.

The largest ships in the fleet are the two frigates of the Tromp class. Displacing 4,310 tons, they have a mixed armament of missiles (Harpoon and Standard), two 4.7in (120mm) guns, six torpedo tubes and a Lynx helicopter. They are instantly recognizable by their huge radome above the bridge housing a three-dimensional radar. Commissioned in the mid-1970s, they are due to be phased out of service during the 1990s. The main part of the fleet consists of 10 Kortenaer class frigates (3,786 tons), very powerful units with a primary anti-submarine role. The two most recent ships of this design (known as the Jacob van Heemskerk class) were modified to accept a Standard missile system in place of the helicopter facilities, and also to accomodate an admiral and his staff. This design has been a great success and has been sold abroad (Greece and Portugal have taken two each) and also built in Germany (eight ships of the Bremen Type 122 class).

The latest frigates are the Karel Doorman class. These are officially intended to patrol the 200-mile economic zone and for fisheries protection, but they are, in fact, very powerful and, with a displacement of 3,320 tons, only marginally smaller than the Kortenaer class. The first four will join the fleet in 1992 and the remaining four between 1993 and 1995.

The RNethN also operates a large number of minesweepers. There are 15 of the Tripartite design, which was developed in conjunction with France and Belgium. It is also planned to purchase 10 of a new class of deep-sea minesweeper to replace the elderly wooden Dokkum class, of which 11 remain in service.

There are only a few Dutch-built submarines, but these are commonly acknowledged to be of exceptional quality. Oldest are two Potvis class submarines, which were constructed in the 1960s and which, by use of an unique triple-hull design, achieved a diving depth unequalled by their contemporaries. These were complemented in 1972 by two boats of the Zwaardvis class (2,640 tons submerged displacement), whose overall design, and especially that of the teardrop hull, was based upon the US Navy's Barbel class. Two boats of an Improved-Zwaardvis design have been constructed for the Republic of China (Taiwan) Navy.

Latest submarines are the Zeeleuw class, of which four will be in service by 1993. Displacing 2,800 tons, they are among the finest diesel-electric submarines in service anywhere in the world.

There are some small landing craft but there are no large amphibious warfare ships, the Dutch marines being transported by other nations' shipping, principally that of the British. The Dutch fleet is rounded out by two large replenishment ships and the normal infrastructure of training ships and auxiliaries.

The Royal Netherlands Marine Corps has recently been reorganized into the Groep Operationele Eenheden Mariniers (GOEM) consisting of four marine battalions, two regular and two reserve, together with the Dutch national anti-terrorist unit (the BBE), a combat support battalion and a logistics battalion. The bulk of GOEM is located at Doorn. Under existing war plans approximately half the GOEM would be allocated to the ACE Mobile Force, the balance to the UK/Netherlands Commando Group. This organization and that of the rest of the navy is undergoing revision due to the end of the Cold War.

The naval air arm consists of two main elements. There are three squadrons of Lockheed P-3C Orions for maritime reconnaissance and ASW. There are also 22 Westland Lynx helicopters allocated to the frigates for afloat ASW support.

### EQUIPMENT

**Submarines:**
Zeeleuw class
Zwaardvis class
Potvis class
**Frigates:**
Tromp class
Kortenaer class
Jacob van Heemskerk class
Karel Doorman class
**Mine Warfare:**
Tripartite class
Dokkum class
**Naval Aircraft:**
Lockheed P-3C Orion
Westland Lynx Mks 25, 27 & 81
**Marines:**
Four battalions (two reserve)

## NORWAY

NORWAY is a sparsely populated country with 13,000 miles (20,921km) of coastline indented with many deep-water fjords and 150,000 islands.

The Royal Norwegian Navy (RNorN) is 5,300 strong, 3,500 of them in the naval-manned coastal artillery. There is also a large naval Home Guard and a coastguard force (kystvak) which would operate 13 craft in support of the navy, including the three well-armed Nordkapp class.

Naval headquarters is in Oslo and there are bases at Bergen, Horten, Ramsund and Tromsø. The principal mission is the defence of Norwegian waters in support of NATO plans, and the protection of national oil platforms and fishing.

Virtually the entire surface fleet has been constructed in Norwegian yards. The largest vessels are five Oslo class frigates (1,850tons) whose hull design was based on that of the US Navy's Dealey class. Norwegian refinements offer greater freeboard, to cope with the sea conditions in northern waters, and mainly European weapons and electronic systems. All have recently undergone a major modernization and are now armed with four launchers for the very successful Norwegian Penguin SSM, a single launcher for NATO Sea Sparrow SAMs, two 3in (76mm) DP guns, and one 1.6in (40mm) and two 0.8in (20mm) AA guns. For ASW there is one Terne-III rocket-launcher, six 12.7in (324mm) torpedo tubes and a depth-charge rack.

Two 790ton Sleipner class corvettes remain in service, KMN *Skipper* and KMN *Aeger*, but are now used for training. The largest single element of the navy is the guided-missile patrol boat fleet with 38 in three classes. The oldest are 18 Storm class (125tons) which entered service in the mid-1960s. They are armed with six Penguin SSM launchers, a 3in (76mm) Bofors gun and a 1.6in (40mm) Bofors AA gun (a depth-charge rack can be fitted at the expense of two Penguin launchers). In the 1970s came six Snögg class (140tons) with four Penguin SSM launchers, one 1.6in (40mm) Bofors and four 21in (533mm) torpedo tubes with, again, the possibility of depth-charge racks in place of two SSM launch-bins. These boats are being modernized for service into the next century. The latest class is the 14 strong Hauk class (155tons) which has an identical hull to the Snögg and Storm and is armed with up to six of the latest Mk II version of the Penguin SSM, a 1.6in (40mm) Bofors and 0.8in (20mm) Rheinmetall AA guns, and two 21in (533mm) torpedo tubes. The bulk of the Hauk entered service in the 1980s and a new class, as yet unnamed, is scheduled to enter construction soon with a proposed build of 24 to replace both the Snögg and Storm classes in the late 1990s.

There is a small mine warfare element with three minelayers and eight minesweepers. The largest are two Vidar class minelayers (1,722tons), KMN *Vidar* and KMN *Vale*, which are capable of carrying 320 mines. They have been designed to be flexible in peace, however, and are also able to serve as torpedo-recovery ships, transports for men or materiel and fishery-protection. In wartime they can be used as ASW escorts; their armament comprises two 1.6in (40mm) AA guns and six 12.7in (324mm) ASW torpedo tubes. The other is KMN *Borgen* (282tons), an unusual vessel — a mine-planter — which is designed to place remotely-controlled mines with great precision using a crane.

The minesweepers are all ex-USN vessels from the 1950s which now form the Sira class (372tons). A replacement minehunter/minesweeper class is now under construction which will displace some 375tons. These Oksøy class will be of a rigid sidewall air-cushion design with a catamaran hull, a very bold choice indeed.

The surface fleet is completed by seven amphibious LCTs, all Norwegian designed and built: two Kvalsund class and five Reinøysund class, both capable of carrying seven tanks and 200 troops.

After WWII Norway operated a number of ex-British submarines, but with the start of the Cold War the RNorN sought their own modern submarines. They eventually selected the German IKL Type 205 modified to meet Norwegian requirements, most particularly increased diving depth. Designated Type 207, or Kobben class, 14 were purchased in the 1960s and paid for jointly by Norway and US mutual assistance funds. This was a very successful programme and nine have been modernized between 1988 and 1992: six for continued service with the RNorN and three for possible sale to Denmark.

The latest submarine in RNorN service is the Ula class (1,150tons) built in Germany. Five of six of these very sophisticated submarines have been delivered and the order will complete in 1992. They are fitted with eight torpedo tubes and have X-configured after control surfaces.

There are neither marines nor an aviation branch of the RNorN. The air force operates F-16s in the maritime strike role and P-3 Orions for over-water reconnaissance. The coastguard operates Westland Lynx helicopters on its Nordkapp class, while the air force uses Westland Sea Kings and Bell UH-1D helicopters for SAR.

### EQUIPMENT

**Submarines:**
Kobben class
Ula class
**Frigates:**
Oslo class
**Patrol Boats:**
Storm class
Snögg class
Hauk class
**Corvettes:**
Sleipner class
**Amphibious Warfare:**
Reinøysund class
Kvalsund class
**Mine Warfare:**
Vidar class
Borgen class
Sira class

**Below:** The Royal Norwegian Navy's Hauk class guided-missile patrol boat *Terne* launches a Penguin anti-ship missile. Six Penguin launchers are mounted aft.

**Below:** The Norwegian frigate *Bergen*, one of a class of five built in Norway in the 1960s. All were completely rebuilt in the late 1970s, a task repeated in the late 1980s.

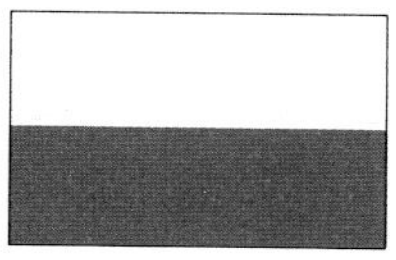

## POLAND

THE Polish Navy was created on 28 November 1918 with the shadow of impending war with the newly-created USSR hanging over the country. Poland won that short war (1919-20), but two decades later was overrun in the opening weeks of WWII. The Red Army later installed a Communist government and Poland remained a key member of the Warsaw Pact until its disbandment in 1991. The navy, as a result, is equipped with predominantly Soviet equipment, although Poland does have a ship-building industry of its own and has constructed warships of both Soviet and Polish designs.

The Polish Navy is intended only for missions within the Baltic and during the Warsaw Pact-era it had a major amphibious warfare role in support of potential Soviet operations against targets in West Germany and Denmark. Today its missions are solely concerned with protection of the Polish coastline and territorial waters. In 1990 the navy was some 20,000 strong, including substantial coastal defence artillery forces, although with the disbandment of the Warsaw Pact this figure may well reduce. There is also a 2,000 strong coastguard and a small maritime border guard. Naval bases are at Gdynia, Hel, Swinoujscie and Gdansk.

ORP *Warszawa* (4,950tons) is the flagship of the fleet, it is an ex-Soviet Modified Kashin class destroyer. She is armed with four SS-N-2C Styx SSMs, two SA-N-1 SAM launchers, four 3in (76mm) DP guns, four 1.12in (30mm) CIWS, five torpedo tubes and two RBU-6000 ASW rocket launchers. A helicopter-deck is fitted at the stern but, as far as is known, no suitable aircraft are in use with the Polish Navy. ORP *Warszawa* was commissioned into the Polish Navy in 1988 after having served in the Soviet Navy as *Smely* since 1974.

There is one frigate, ORP *Kaszub* (1,200tons), and she was the first major warship to have been built in Poland since 1939. She was built in Gdansk, completed in1987 and entered service in 1990. It is a modification of the Soviet Grisha class and lacks a main gun. Her armament consists of one SA-N-4 Gecko twin launcher and two SA-N-5 Grail twin launcher SAMs, six 0.9in (23mm) guns, four 21in (533mm) torpedoes, two RBU-6000 ASW mortars, and two rails of depth-charges.

There are four corvettes of the Soviet Tarantul-I class which came into service during the 1980s. They carry SS-N-2C Styx SSMs and SA-N-5 Grail SAMs, plus one 3in (76mm) gun. Now named Gornik class, it is thought four more may be acquired. Poland is also finishing three former-East German Sassnitz class, renamed Orkan class, and may well get more.

The patrol boat fleet is 18 strong. There are 10 ex-Soviet Osa-I class, most of them Polish-built, which carry guided-missiles and four 1.12in (30mm) guns; and eight Modified Obluze class with four 1.12in (30mm) guns, developed from a design used by the Polish Border Guard.

The mine wafare force is equipped with eight Krogulec class (484tons) ocean minesweepers and 13 Notek class coastal minesweepers. These Polish designs are aided by three Soviet T-43 class ocean minesweepers and two Leriwka class coastal vessels, making an overall total of 26 ships.

No less than 16 Polnocny class landing ships remain in use for the Baltic coast landing role with the 5,000 strong naval infantry force. There are also five Lublin class LCTs which entered service in 1991. One Eichstaden class LCP remains from the 1960s but will be replaced by the Deba class LCUs shortly.

In the 1950s Poland was supplied with three Whiskey class submarines. These served for many years and were due to be replaced by four Kilo class. However, following delivery of the first Kilo, ORP *Orzel*, in 1986 some difficulties with the USSR over the nature of the deal led to a delay and two Foxtrot class, ORP *Wilk* and ORP *Dzik*, have been supplied instead.

There is an aviation arm which has 2,500 men and is organized into one reconnaissance squadron, three fighter-bomber squadrons plus helicopter units. Most are land-based Ilyushin Il-28 Beagles and Mikoyan MiG-19 Farmers, plus a host of Mil Mi-2 Hoplite, Mi-8 Hip and Mi-14 Haze helicopters.

### EQUIPMENT

**Submarines:**
Orzel (Soviet Kilo) class
Wilk (Soviet Foxtrot) class
**Destroyers:**
Warszawa (Soviet Modified Kashin) class
**Frigates:**
Kaszub class
**Patrol Boats:**
Soviet Osa-I class
Grozny (Modified Obluze) class
**Corvettes:**
Gornik (Soviet Tarantul-I) class
Orkan (East German Sassnitz) class
**Amphibious Warfare:**
Lublin class
Lenino (Soviet Polnocny-A/B) class
Grunwald (Soviet Polnocny-C) class
**Mine Warfare:**
Krogulec class
Tur (Soviet T-43) class
Notek class

**Left:** A finely turned-out honour guard of officers and ratings of the Polish Navy.

**Above:** During the Cold War the Warsaw Pact planned amphibious operations in the Baltic Sea and as a result Poland operates a large force of Polnocny class landing ships.

## PORTUGAL

PORTUGAL has one of the greatest seafaring traditions in the world and her navy not only conducted many great voyages of discovery but also helped to establish one of the major European colonial empires. Portugal remained neutral in both world wars, although it granted both Britain and the USA certain basing rights in the Azores during WWII. Despite this long period of neutrality Portugal became a founder member of NATO and remains a staunch supporter.

The navy is responsible for the defence of home waters, for fulfilling national obligations to NATO, and for protecting the remaining overseas territories. There are three naval commands: Continental (HQ Portimao), Azores (HQ Punta Delgado) and Madeira (HQ Funchal). There is also a major naval base at Lisbon, the capital. The navy has a peacetime strength of some 13,000 officers and ratings, about 35 per cent of them conscripts.

There is a large number of frigates. The four Comandante Joao Belo class (2,250tons) were built in France in the late 1960s and are virtually identical to the French Navy's Commandant Riviere class. Some new sonar and EW gear has been installed recently and they will remain in service for a few years more. Six Joao Coutinho class (1,410tons) were also built in the late 1960s, three each by Bazan in Spain and Blohm und Voss in Germany. They have a relatively light armament of two 3in (76mm) DP guns, two 1.6in (40mm) AA guns and a Hedgehog ASW mortar. The Joao Coutinho class has been very successful and four more were constructed to an improved design in the mid-1970s: the Baptiste de Andrade class (1,348tons). These vessels have a single 3.9in (100mm) gun, two 1.6in (40mm) AA guns and six 12.7in (324mm) ASW torpedo tubes. They also have a helicopter flight-deck, but no hangar. There are plans to modernize all three classes which would include fitting more powerful weapons, particularly SSMs and SAMs, and more sophisticated electronics. These have been shelved due to lack of funds.

Meanwhile, three new German-designed and built MEKO 200 frigates — the Vasco da Gama class (3,200tons) — have recently joined the fleet. They were financed jointly by Canada, Germany, the Netherlands, Norway and the USA. They are thoroughly up-to-date and are armed with eight Harpoon SSMs, a Mk 29 launcher for NATO Sea Sparrow SAMs, a 3.9in (100mm) Creusot-Loire Compact DP gun, a 0.8in (20mm) Vulcan Phalanx CIWS and six 12.7in (324mm) ASW torpedo tubes. A large flight-deck and hangar accommodate a single Westland Lynx ASW helicopter. These three splendid ships represent a major increase in the Portuguese Navy's capabilities.

**Above:** *Comandante Roberto Ivens* is one of four of the handy and capable Comandante Joao Belo class frigates built in France for the Portuguese Navy in the late 1960s.

**Below:** Six Joao Coutinho class frigates are in service, such as *Augusto Castilho* seen here. Each has a platform (but carries no helicopter) and a marine detachment.

**Above:** The pride of the Portuguese fleet is *Vasco da Gama*, the first of three new German-designed and -built MEKO 200 frigates to enter service. They are well-armed, have gas-turbine engines and carry one Westland Super Navy Lynx Mk 99 ASW helicopter.

**Below:** *Dom Alexio* dates from the late-1960s and has a top speed of 16kts.

The navy operates several dozen patrol boats: 10 of the Portuguese Cacine class (310tons); four Sao Roque class minesweepers (452tons) which have had their sweeping gear removed; six Albatroz class; two Dom Aleixo class; and one new Rio Minho class. In 1990 plans for the new Argos class were announced and five Portuguese-built vessels should enter service in 1991.

The submarine force consists of three French Daphne class boats (1,043tons), which are known as the Albacora class in Portuguese service. Four boats were originally purchased in 1967-69 but one was sold to Pakistan in 1975. It is planned to modernize these three submarines, but in view of the navy's financial problems it is unlikely that they will be replaced soon.

There are some 2,600 men in the marines who are formed into two infantry battalions and a police unit. They require amphibious transport and the navy meets this need with three Bombarda class LCTs which can take a load of 350 tons, plus six LCMs of the LDM 400 and LDM 100 classes.

There is no naval air arm and all aviation support comes from the air force. This includes six Lockheed P-3P Orion and eight Casa 212 Aviocar aircraft for maritime surveillance; plus five Lockheed C-130H Hercules and 12 Aerospatiale SA.330 Puma for SAR. It appears that the air force will also operate the five Westland Mk99 Super Lynx purchased for service aboard the Vasco da Gama class frigates and expected in 1992.

**Above:** Westland Super Navy Lynx Mk 99, one of five bought for service aboard the Vasco da Gama class frigates in the anti-ship and ASW roles. It has a top speed of 125kts.

### EQUIPMENT

**Submarines:**
Albacora (French Daphne) class
**Frigates:**
Comandante Joao Belo (French Commandant Riviere) class
Joao Coutinho class
Baptiste de Andrade class
Vasco da Gama (German MEKO 200) class
**Patrol Boats:**
Cacine class
Sao Roque class
**Naval Aircraft:**
Westland Super Navy Lynx Mk99

## ROMANIA

THE Romanian Navy was formed from a river flotilla which existed as long ago as 1881. It is made up of three elements: one a riverine force on the Danube, the second a sea-going force on the Black Sea and the third a coastal defence force. The navy is some 9,000 strong, as many as one-third of them conscripts. Black Sea bases are at Constanza and Mangalia, while Braila, Giurgiu, Sulina and Tulcea are the main Danube bases.

Romania's largest warship is something of a mystery. The destroyer *Muntenia* (6,000tons), launched in 1983, was designed and built in Romania and published photographs suggest that she is a very modern and handsome-looking ship. Her armament includes eight Soviet SS-N-2C SSMs, four guns, eight AA cannon and six ASW torpedo tubes. A very large flight-deck and hangar are sufficiently roomy to operate three Alouette III helicopters. But, the ship has been laid-up since the mid-1980s. The first mystery about this ship is why she was built, because the Romanian Navy can have had no operational use for such a large and expensive ship. Secondly, it is not clear what has happened to her, although it appears that she never completed fitting-out.

The navy operates four frigates of the Tetal class (1,800tons) which have two twin 3in (76mm) DP guns, four 1.12in (30mm) AA cannon and four 0.6in (14.5mm) AAMGs, two RBU-2500 ASW rocket launchers and four 21in (533mm) torpedo tubes. They are also fitted with a helicopter flight-deck but there is no hangar. These ships were designed and built in Romania, probably to a modified Koni blueprint; the weapons and electronics are of Soviet origin.

There are three Soviet-supplied Poti class corvettes (400tons) and four Democratia clas (775tons). The latter were originally laid down during WWII, to the German M-40 minesweeper design, but were not completed until 1951. Since completion they have had their steam plant replaced by diesels, their minesweeping gear removed, their armament updated and their superstructure completely remodelled. The latest acquisition is a Soviet Tarantul-I class vessel transferred in late-1990.

There are over 60 patrol boats, all of foreign design but most built in Romania. The oldest are five Osa-Is supplied by the Soviets in the early 1960s. They are now of limited value and some have already been stricken. The Romanians then built their own version of the Osa, the Epitrop class, with four torpedo tubes in place of the SS-N-2 missiles. They have 12 of these in service. The Romanian government then became friendly with China and one result was that Romanian shipyards began to produce Chinese designs, including 27 Shanghai class gunboats and 29 Huchuan class torpedo-armed hydrofoils. There are also 18 river monitors, three minelayers and 31 minesweepers, nearly all designed and built in Romania. The Danube flotilla actually comprises a number of these gunboats, patrol craft and minesweepers.

Romania operated its own submarines during WWII, but only recently did they take delivery of their first one since the war — a Soviet Kilo class named *Delfin*.

There is a sizeable coastal defence force which consists of some 2,000 officers and men. The HQ is at Constanza and there are about 10 artillery batteries and eight AA batteries. This force may also include a unit of naval infantry. All aircraft are operated by the air force and their support for the navy includes six Soviet Mil Mi-14 Haze and six Aerospatiale SA.316 Alouette III helicopters.

### EQUIPMENT

**Submarines:**
Soviet Kilo class
**Destroyer:**
Muntenia class
**Frigates:**
Tetal class
**Corvettes:**
V 31 (Soviet Poti) class
Democratia (German M-40) class
Tarantul-I class
**Patrol Boats:**
Soviet Osa-I class
Chinese Shanghai class
Epitrop (modified Soviet Osa-I) class
Chinese Huchuan class
**Mine Warfare:**
Cosar class
Soviet T301 class

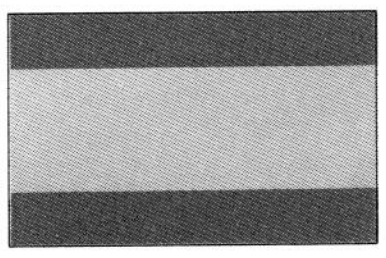

## SPAIN

**T**HE Spanish Navy has a long and very distinguished history and for several centuries was one of the mightiest naval forces in the world, a power that was necessary to maintain a global empire. This empire gradually broke up and the fleet stagnated. Spain was neutral during WWI and then plunged into civil war and nearly 50 years of dictatorship. Not until the 1970s did the navy re-equip itself and then in 1975 Franco's death restored Spain to democracy. In 1982 she joined NATO and today possesses a well-balanced and efficient force.

The Spanish Navy consists of some 32,000 officers and ratings, of whom about 55 per cent are conscripts. There is one major functional command or Flota with its HQ at Rota. It has five constituent parts: the Grupo Aeronaval Alfa based on *Principe de Asturias*; the Escuadrillas de Escoltas with four squadrons; the Grupo Anfibio Delta; the Fuerza de Medidas contra Minas; and the Flotilla de Submarinos. There are four regional commands: Cantabria Zone (HQ El Ferrol), Mediterranean Zone (HQ Cartagena), Straits Zone (HQ Cadiz) and Canarias Zone (HQ Las Palmas). The main submarine base is also at Cartagena, and there are other bases at Palma de Mallorca and Port Mahon.

The primary task of the navy is its contribution to NATO. This is achieved principally by the provision of a battle group for deployment in the North Atlantic, centred upon the aircraft carrier *Principe de Asturias*. Spain also provides naval forces for the defence of the Straits of Gibraltar; this is a crucial choke-point in NATO's naval strategy for the Mediterranean and a vital area adjoining volatile North Africa and the Middle East. Nationally, the Spanish Navy is responsible for the protection of the 200nm economic zone and for the routes to the remaining Spanish overseas possessions, including the Canary Islands off the African coast.

The fleet is being enhanced and modernized to take it into the next century; the blueprint for this being the Plan del Alta Mar outlined in 1989. This entails a large construction programme which, by 2002, will have added a number of vessels to the navy: two Santa Maria class, four F-100 and five F-110 frigates, eight minehunters and four minesweepers, four Modified Halcon class, four submarines, two fleet replenishment ships and one LPD. The air arm will also receive a significant boost with new acquisitions and developments.

Pride of the existing fleet is the carrier *Principe de Asturias* (16,200tons) which entered service in 1988. Based on the US Navy's Sea Control Ship (SCS) design, she operates an air wing comprising up to eight EAV-8B Harrier IIs and up to 14 helicopters in various combinations of Sikorksy SH-60B and SH-3D/G, and Agusta-Bell AB.212. Deliberately designed to be "austere" she has only one propeller and her sole defensive armament consists of four Spanish-designed Meroka 0.8in (20mm) CIWS. She represents a significant capability.

Four WWII-vintage US Gearing class destroyers were transferred in the 1970s and designated Gravina class. They are now very outdated and are being stricken some time in 1992.

There are 15 frigates in service. The oldest are five Baleares class (4,177tons) ships which were built in Spain to a design similar to that of the US Navy's Knox class, the main differences being in the weapons systems (although, the Spanish ships do not have any helicopter facilities). They are well-armed and after recent modernizations will have eight Harpoon SSM launchers, a Mk 22 launcher for Standard SM-1 MR SAMs, a single 5in (127mm) DP gun, two Meroka CIWS, an ASROC launcher and six ASW torpedo tubes. The design of the second frigate class was based on the "Improved Joao Coutinho" (Portugal) and, like them, the vessels were built by Bazan at Cartagena and El Ferrol. These neat little Descubierta class ships have a displacement of 1,575tons and a useful armament of four Harpoons, a Sea Sparrow SAM launcher, a 3in (76mm) OTO Melara Compact DP gun, two 1.6in (40mm) AA guns, a Bofors ASW rocket-launcher and six ASW torpedo tubes. Not surprisingly, they do not have room for a helicopter but they do have accommodation for 30 troops if needed.

The newest frigates in the fleet are the four ships of the Santa Maria class (4,100tons) which are essentially copies of the long-hulled version of the US Navy's Oliver Hazard Perry class. Like the US ships they are armed with a single launcher on the foredeck, which fires both Harpoon SSMs and Standard SAMs; a single 3in (76mm) OTO Melara Compact DP gun, which sits atop the superstructure between the mast and funnel; and an ASW armament which comprises six 12.7in (324mm) torpedo tubes and close-in air-defence provided by the Spanish Meroka system. A large hangar has room to accommodate two Sikorsky SH-60B Seahawk ASW helicopters, although only one is presently carried by the ships in service. Two more will be complete and in service by late-1994.

The four Atrevida class (1,136tons) corvettes were built over 30 years ago and are now employed on offshore patrol duties. Their replacements, the Serviola class (1,100tons), are now entering service and the four vessels ordered should all be serving by early 1992. The Modified Halcon design enables a number of armament modifications to be made, but at present these AB.212 carrying ships have one 3in (76mm) gun and two 0.5in (12.7mm) machine guns.

Bazan has proposed a fast, guided-missile ship known as the BES-50. It is trialling and may well go ahead. Either way, the navy maintains a significant patrol/fast attack craft ability with four 1980's designs in service: 10 Anaga class, four Conejera class, two Toralla class, and one Cormoran

**Below:** *Blas de Lezo* is one of four ex-US Navy Gearing class destroyers remaining in service with the Spanish Navy. It is used on economic zone patrols and carries a Hughes 369 helicopter. It will strike by 1993.

**Below:** *Cataluna*, a Baleares class frigate, is seen here taking part in a naval review. Note her bow-mounted 5in (127mm) gun and ASROC launcher. Now updated, the class has many more years of service life left.

**Above:** The Descubierta class frigate *Infanta Christina* is named after King Juan Carlos's daughter. Several of this class have been sold abroad.

**Below:** Latest frigates in the Spanish fleet are five ships of the Santa Maria class. They have a broader beam than the US Navy's Oliver Hazard Perry class.

**Right:** An EAV-8B Harrier II of the Spanish Navy. Eleven are in service and operate from the 16,000ton carrier *Principe de Asturias*.

design. There are other older vessels too, including 22 P101 class, three ex-US Adjutant class, six Lazaga class and six Barceló class.

There are 12 former US Navy minesweepers which have been in service for well over 30 years. These are to be replaced by 12 new minehunters of the British Sandown class which will be constructed by Bazan at Cartagena, with the first entering service in 1993.

The navy operates a sizeable amphibious warfare fleet for its 9,000 man marine force. Principal ships are two 16,838ton troop transports purchased second-hand from the US Navy in 1980. They have a helicopter flight-deck and carry seven LCM(6) and 16 LCVPs. There are also two large ex-US Navy LSTs, three Spanish-built LCTs, two ex-US Navy LCUs, eight LCMs and numerous smaller craft.

Spain was one of the pioneers of submarines and has had them since the beginning of this century. In the 1970s she built four French Daphne class submarines as the Delfin (S-60) class. These were followed in the 1980s by four more submarines of the Galerna (S-70) class — Spanish-built versions of the French Agosta class. These eight submarines will all continue in service for some years, with a plan to replace the Delfin (S-60) class with a new S-80 class in the late 1990s.

The Arma Aerea de la Armada (fleet air arm) was one of the first to see the potential of the Harrier V/STOL aircraft for naval operations, although for political reasons it preferred to purchase the aircraft (seven AV-8As and two TAV-8As) from the USA rather than direct from the UK. The AV-8A aircraft were operated from the old carrier *Dedalo* which is now a museum in the USA; the 12 EAV-8B Harrier IIs have been purchased for the *Principe de Asturias'* air wing (one has since crashed), although the AV-8As will continue to be used for some years. The fleet air arm uses a large number of helicopters. For the ASW mission there are six Sikorsky SH-60B Seahawks, 11 Agusta-Bell AB.212, 10 Sikorksy SH-3D Sea Kings and 11 Hughes 500MD (ASW). A further three SH-3Ds are fitted with special radar for AEW.

## EQUIPMENT

**Submarines:**
Galerna (French Agosta) class
Delfin (French Daphne) class
**Aircraft Carriers:**
Principe de Asturias class
**Destroyers:**
Gravina (US Gearing FRAM I) class
**Frigates:**
Santa Maria (US Oliver Hazard Perry) class
Descubierta class
Baleares class
**Patrol Boats:**
Serviola class
Atrevida class
Lazaga class
Barceló class
Anaga class
Conejera class
Nalón (US Adjutant) class
**Amphibious Warfare:**
Castilla (US Paul Revere) class
Velasco (US Terrebonne Parish) class
**Mine Warfare:**
Guadalete (US Aggressive) class
Jucar (US Adjutant) class
**Naval Aircraft:**
BAe/McDonnell Douglas Matador (AV-8A/TAV-8A Harrier I)
BAe/McDonnell Douglas EAV-8B Harrier II
Agusta-Bell AB.212
Hughes 369M (500M) Cayuse
Sikorsky SH-3 D/G Sea King
Sikorsky SH-60B Seahawk
**Marines:**
Four Tercios and two groups

## SWEDEN

SWEDEN remained resolutely neutral in both world wars and the Cold War. The Swedes have long made a point of being as independent in defence equipment as is both possible and sensible.

Today's Royal Swedish Navy (RSwedN) consists of some 3,100 regular officers and ratings, plus some 6,000 conscripts. The main bases are at Karlskrona and Musko (Stockholm), with minor bases at Harnosand and Göteborg The Swedes, however, also have lots of other smaller bases, many of them hewn out of rock for maximum survivability against both conventional and nuclear attack.

The armed forces' mission is to defend Sweden's neutrality against threats from any direction. This entails naval operations in the Baltic right up the Gulf of Bothnia, and including the many islands, the Belts and the Skaggerak. The reality of the threat was demonstrated only too clearly in 1982 when a Soviet Whiskey class submarine ran aground off the main naval base in clear contravention of Sweden's sovereignty. There have been numerous other incursions into the country's territorial waters, but none so blatant.

The navy's surface force is composed solely of corvettes, patrol boats and mine warfare vessels; there are no frigates or destroyers. The two Stockholm class (320tons) corvettes, *Stockholm* and *Malmö*, were completed in 1985 and are intended to be leaders for groups of fast-attack craft (FACs). Their armament comprises eight Saab RBS-15 SSMs, a single Bofors 2.25in (57mm) gun, one 1.6in (40mm) AA gun, two 21in (533mm) torpedo tubes and four ASW rocket launchers. Extra command facilities are included for the flotilla leader role.

The next class, the Göteborg class (400tons), are rather larger. Their weapons fit is similar, except that they mount a Bofors Trinity AA gun in place of the single 1.6in (40mm) gun and four 15.75in (400mm) torpedo tubes — all on the starboard side — in place of the two 21in (533mm) tubes. *Göteborg* and *Gälve* are in service with two more to follow by mid-1992. These ships will form the core of four surface attack flotillas which the navy wants to have operational by the turn of the century.

The oldest missile boats still in service are the 12 Nörrkopping (Spica-II) class (230tons); these are long, mean-looking vessels with the superstructure well aft and a very long foredeck whose lines are broken only by a large turret for the Bofors 2.25in (57mm) gun. The armament also includes two Saab RBS-15 SSMs, two 21in (533mm) torpedo tubes and two ASW rocket launchers. Three Rolls-Royce Proteus gas-turbines give a maximum speed of 40kts.

The next class to be built was the Hugin class (150tons). Built in Norway, there are 16 in Swedish service and they are similar to the Norwegian Navy's Hauk class. Like the Nörrkopping class they have a single (57mm) gun on the foredeck, but they mount up to six Norwegian Penguin SSMs on the quarterdeck which can be replaced by either two sets of mine-rails (24 mines) or depth-charge racks.

Mine warfare is an obvious threat in Baltic waters. All the corvettes and FACs can lay

**Above:** The launch of this Västergötland boat shows the unique hull shape, X-shaped aft hydroplanes and heavy torpedo battery. To the rear is the minelayer *Älvsborg*.

**Below:** Västergötland at sea. This design is also being built in Australia as the Collins class, having won the contract in competition against some good designs, including Germany's.

**Above:** The Spica II class guided-missile patrol boat *Pitea*. There is a single 2.25in (57mm) gun forward, while the launch bins for Saab RBS-15 missiles are on the afterdeck.

**Above:** Boeing-Vertol 107 (HKP-4) helicopters are used by the Swedish Navy for ASW patrols, a very necessary task in view of the many illegal submarine incursions into Swedish waters.

mines, but there are three large minelayers too. *Carlskrona* (3,300tons) is capable of carrying a load of 105 mines in war, but in peacetime she is employed as a cadet training ship, MCMV support ship or torpedo target. The other two belong to the Älvsborg class (2,660tons) and can each carry 300 mines in war: in peacetime *Älvsborg* is employed as a submarine tender and *Visborg* as the fleet flagship. There are also 12 coastal minesweepers and 18 inshore minesweepers from a variety of classes.

The navy has put great effort into submarine development and today Sweden has one of the most modern and effective fleets in the world. Oldest in service are the five boats of the Sjöormen class (1,400tons) which entered service between 1967 and 1969. They are fitted with four 21in (533mm) tubes for Swedish-made Type 61 torpedoes or mines and two 15.75in (400mm) tubes for Type 427 ASW torpedoes. The next to join the fleet (in 1980/81) were three Näcken class (1,125tons) with a considerably revised hull and fin shape, an armament of six 21in (533mm) and two 15.75in (400mm) torpedo tubes. The first-of-class, *Näcken*, has a 26.25ft (8m) plug inserted to fit two Sterling V4-275R engines to give the boat an air-independent, non-nuclear propulsion capability.

The latest in service are four Västergötland class (1,140tons) boats. They have a very heavy bow battery of nine torpedo tubes — six 21in (533mm) and three 15.75in (400mm) — and can also carry 22 mines in an external belt designed by the Swedish submarine company, Kockums. (It is a version of this class that has been put into production in Australia). A particular feature of Swedish submarine design is the extensive use of automation, thus cutting down the number of crew and saving on manpower and training costs. The Sjöormen class is due for replacement in the mid-1990s and the chosen design to do this is the Götland class which Malaysia has expressed a strong interest in too.

The naval aviation branch is entirely shore-based, as only a few Swedish ships have a flight-deck and none have a hangar. The navy has just one fixed-wing aircraft — a Casa 212 Aviocar for maritime patrol — although the air force operates a number of other types of maritime reconnaissance aircraft. All the remaining aircraft are helicopters and they comprise nine Agusta-Bell AB.206 JetRangers and 17 Boeing 107s and Kawasaki KV-107s.

There are no marines, but there is a strong coastal defence organization with a strength of some 4-5,000 men and women. This service operates anti-ship missiles, air-defence guns, anti-ship artillery, barriers and minelayers. It is organized into six amphibions battalions equipped with craft for inshore patrols and amphibious landings.

## EQUIPMENT

**Submarines:**
Sjöormen class
Näcken class
Västergötland class
**Patrol Boats:**
Dalaro class
Hano class
Hugin class
Jägaren class
Nörrkoping (Spica-II) class
Skanör class
SVK class
**Corvettes:**
Göteborg class
Stockholm class
**Amphibious Warfare:**
Combat boat 90H
Ane class
**Mine Warfare:**
Älvsborg class
Arkö class
Arkosund class
Carlskrona class
Furusund class
Gässten class
Gillöga class
Hisingen class
Landsort class
M15 class

## SWITZERLAND

THE neutral Swiss employ 11 glass-reinforced plastic Patrouillenboot 80 of the Aquarius class as part of their integrated force. These vessels are armed with machine-guns and patrol Lakes Constance, Geneva and Maggiore.

**Right:** Switzerland may not have a coastline, but its defence force uses these fast and efficient armed boats to deter any intruders on its vast system of lakes which cover over 500sq miles.

## TURKEY

**Above:** This former US Carpenter class destroyer is now the Turkish Navy's *Anitepe*. Her flight-deck can accept the hovering AB.212 helicopter, but the hangar is too small.

TURKEY, once the centre of the Ottoman Empire, lies at the junction of Europe and Asia, with shores on the Mediterranean, the Black Sea and the Aegean. She shares borders with the USSR, Syria and Iraq to the east; while to the west lies her old enemy Greece, with whom there exists a very uneasy relationship despite a common membership of NATO; and to the north is Bulgaria, which during the Cold War was a significant threat as it would have been the staging point for a Soviet land attack to capture the Dardanelles, an important area which has hosted many historic naval battles. Loss of the straits to a hostile power would not only be a disaster for Turkey, but would also make a very significant change to the balance of power in the region. Thus, naval power is vital to Turkey and she maintains a large navy, the primary element of which is one of the strongest and most up-to-date submarine forces in the Mediterranean region.

The Turkish Navy has some 52,000 men, of whom about 80 per cent are conscripts. Naval headquarters, and the NATO headquarters for the Commander North-East Mediterranean (COMEDNOREAST), are at Ankara; the Fleet Headquarters is at Gölcük. There are four area commands: Northern Area and Bosphorus (HQ Istanbul), Southern Area and Aegean (HQ Izmir), Black Sea Area (HQ Eregli) and Mediterranean Area (HQ Mersin).

Turkey has its own shipbuilding capability, with a very successful naval shipyard at Gölcük which is currently building 3,000ton frigates and sophisticated submarines. The majority of the fleet, however, still consists of somewhat ageing ex-US Navy ships and submarines.

The core of the fleet consists of 12 destroyers and a growing number of large frigates. The destroyers are all ex-US Navy types of WWII-vintage and in need of replacement, despite having undergone various modernization programmes. All have 5in (127mm) main guns and an assortment of AA weapons from 3in (76mm) downwards; most also have ASROC and ASW torpedo tubes.

Of increasing significance, however, is the MEKO 200 frigate. The original order, placed in 1983, was for four, (of which two have been built in Germany and two at Gölcük in Turkey). Designated the Yavuz class (3,000tons) in Turkey, these are excellent vessels and an increasing number are entering service around the world. One of their major attractions is that they incorporate a modular system which enables weapons, $C^3$ and sensor fits to be changed easily. The first four Turkish ships have a main armament of eight Harpoon SSM launchers, one Mk 29 launcher for Sea Sparrow SAMs, a 5in (127mm) gun turret on the foredeck and three Contraves 1in (25mm) Sea Guard CIWS systems — one before the bridge and two aft, either side of the hangar. The principal ASW system is a bank of six 12.75in (324mm) torpedo tubes. They carry one AB.212 helicopter in an anti-ship role, its main weapon being the British Sea Skua missile. Four more vessels have been ordered to a more advanced design, with a different propulsion system and armed with vertical-launch SAMs.

There are four smaller frigates in service: two 30-year-old former German ships of the Gelibolu class (2,970tons) and two Berk class (1,950tons) built in Turkey in the early 1970s and based on a US Navy design (USS *Claud Jones*).

The requirement for offshore patrols, particularly in the Black Sea and around the Aegean islands, is met by 50 patrol boats. The most modern are those of the Dogan class (398tons), a German design of which the first was built in Germany and the remainder in Turkey. They are armed with eight Harpoon launchers, a 3in (76mm) OTO Melara turret, two (35mm) Oerlikons in a second turret at the stern and two light machine-guns. The remainder are a mixture of German, US and French designs,

There are no less than 10 ships with a major minelaying capacity, of which five have been designed for use as landing craft once their minelaying tasks have been completed. Additionally, there are 26 small minesweepers; all are now somewhat old and plans are being considered to produce the Tripartite Minehunter as a replacement. The amphibious warfare element is similarly large, with two ex-US Navy LSTs, 37 LCTs and 14 smaller craft.

The Turkish Navy was the first in Europe to commission a submarine — the *Nordenfelt* in 1887 — and today 15 boats are in service. The oldest are seven former US Navy Guppy types, post-war conversions of WWII hulls which are now at the end of their useful lives. There are also two ex-US Navy Tang class (2,600tons) which were built in the early 1950s.

When the Turkish Navy started to look for new submarines in the late 1960s there were no United States' designs on the market, so they turned to a previous source, Germany, and 12 of the new Class 209/Type 1200

**Below:** A splendid sight as three of Turkey's four Yavuz (MEKO 200) class frigates steam in company. More may be bought now that the USN Garcia class deal has fallen through.

**Below:** Eight Lürssen FPB-57 patrol boats for the Turkish Navy, like *Tayfun* seen here, and there are plans for at least two more. The first was built in Germany, the rest will be Turkish.

**Below:** The Kocatepe class destroyer *Fevzi Cakmak* firing a Harpoon anti-ship missile and (inset) the effect of the impact, on a surplus destroyer, which would have put the ship completely out of action. The Harpoon is in wide-scale service around the world.

(1,185tons) were ordered. The first three were built in Germany by Howaldtswerke, but all the subsequent boats have been constructed by the Turks themselves at the Gölcük Naval Shipyard. Six of the Type 1200 are now in service, but the remainder were cancelled to be replaced on the ways at Gölcük by six of the larger Type 1400 (1,586tons). The first two of these, *Preveze* and *Sakaraya*, are laid down and will most likely complete in 1994.

The Turkish submarine force's Type 1200 boats are equipped with modern torpedoes and sensors, while the new Type 1400s will be even more effective with Sub-Harpoon SSMs. The two Tang class will serve on for some years, but the seven very elderly Guppy conversions will doubtless be stricken in the near future.

There is one 4,000-man regiment of marines which consists of three infantry battalions, an artillery battalion and a support group. The naval air arm has nearly 1,000 men and operates 26 Grumman S-2E Tracker maritime patrol/ASW aircraft, and three Agusta-Bell AB.204 and nine AB.212 helicopters. Maritime strike is an air force responsibility.

## EQUIPMENT

**Submarines:**
Atilay (German Type 209) class
Burak Reis (ex-US Guppy-IIA) class
Hizir Reis (ex-US Tang) class
Ikinci Inönü (ex-US Guppy-III) class
**Destroyers:**
Alcitepe (ex-US Carpenter) class
Kocatepe (ex-US Gearing FRAM I) class
Muavenet (ex-US Robert H Smith) class
Yücetepe (ex-US Gearing FRAM II) class
Zafer (ex-US Allen M Sumner FRAM II) class
**Frigates:**
Berk class
Gelibolu (ex-German Köln) class
Yavuz (MEKO 200) class
**Patrol Boats:**
AB 25 class
Bora (ex-US Asheville) class
Dogan (German FPB 57) class
Girne (German PB 57) class
Kartal (German Jaguar) class
Tufan (ex-German Jaguar) class
**Amphibious Warfare:**
Ertugrul (ex-US Terrebonne Parish) class
**Mine Warfare:**
Bayraktar (ex-US LST 542) class
Cakabey class
Nusret (Danish Falster) class
Osman Gasi class
Sarucbey class
**Naval Aircraft:**
Agusta-Bell AB.204
Agusta-Bell AB.212
Grumman S-2E Tracker
**Marines:**
One brigade and four battalions

**Above:** In the 1960s the Turkish Navy received a Danish Falster class minelayer, paid for out of US "offshore funds". Carrying no less than 400 mines, she remains in service as *Nusret*.

**Below:** The navy's varied capabilities extend to amphibious warfare. These LCTs are three of a Turkish-built class of 24 in service and used here in an exercise.

## USSR

SINCE 1945 the Soviet Navy has achieved one of the most remarkable expansions in naval history, transforming itself over a period of 40 years from a small, inefficient and essentially coastal force into a fully-fledged bluewater navy. It is a force whose ships and capabilities are admired throughout the naval world and one which is second only to that of the United States in size and sophistication.

Despite its advances, however, the modern Soviet Navy cannot overcome a unique and insoluble geographical strategic problem: it must plan to fight campaigns in four totally separated areas; the Arctic Ocean/North Atlantic, the Baltic Sea, the Black Sea and the Pacific Ocean. The fleets in each area are quite incapable of providing mutual support to one another. Furthermore, the exits from the Baltic and Black Seas are dominated by hostile powers, and even in the Far East the majority of bases lie on the mainland coast with their exits from the Sea of Japan and the Sea of Okhotsk also dominated by foreign powers, the sole exception to this being the base at Petropavlovsk on the Kamchatka Peninsula. Both the Imperial Russian and Soviet Navies have had to wrestle with this problem and if their fleets have at times been very large in total, they have seldom been a dominant feature in any one theatre of operations.

In the early years of the Cold War the Soviet Navy developed a strong force of fast, well-armed cruisers and long-range diesel-electric submarines. Both threatened NATO's lines of communication across the Atlantic, causing considerable concern to Western naval commanders.

It soon became apparent that the Soviet Navy had global ambitions and under the remarkable Admiral of the Fleet of the Soviet Union, Sergei Gorshkov, a successful expansion plan was carried out. Under this plan the Soviet Navy has developed a fleet with capabilities in all areas; its last remaining gap — in fixed-wing aircraft carriers — is currently being filled.

The Soviet Navy is divided into four major operational fleets. The Northern Fleet has its headquarters (HQ) at Severomorsk, with other bases at Motovsky Gulf, Polyarny and Severodvinsk. This is the strongest of all Soviet naval forces and its task in war would be to break out into the Atlantic and dominate northern waters. Its SSBNs would operate from under the ice-pack and SSGNs would attack any approaching enemy carrier battle groups.

The second major fleet is the Pacific Fleet, with its HQ at Vladivostok and bases at Sovietskaya Gavan, Magadan, Petropavlovsk and Komsomolsk. This fleet controls the second great SSBN bastion in the Sea of Okhotsk and, apart from operating aggressively in the northern Pacific, would defend the area against attack.

The Baltic Fleet operates in confined waters, its only exit to the open oceans being through the Great and Little Belts between Denmark and Sweden, an operation which would just not be possible without Soviet command of the landward defences. The Baltic is large, although somewhat shallow, and any part of the sea can be reached by land-based aircraft within a matter of minutes, giving naval operation there a unique character. The fleet's HQ is at Kaliningrad, with other ports in the rebellious Baltic states of Tallin, Paldiski, Riga, Liepaja, Klaiepada and Baltiysk, as well as at Kronstadt in the Russian Republic.

The Black Sea Fleet operates in another closed environment, with the sole and very narrow exit totally controlled by Turkey. The fleet maintains a large squadron in the Mediterranean, whose ships come from all three western fleets. There is also a small squadron in the Caspian Sea. The fleet's HQ is at Sevastapol and there are ports at Balaklava, Odessa, Poti and Tvapse.

The might of the Soviet Navy is very apparent and their global capability has been demonstrated repeatedly. With half-a-million men serving and the same in reserve, plus some 1,300 vessels, they appear formidable. However, they have had no experience of naval combat since 1945

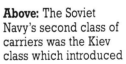

**Above:** The Soviet Navy's second class of carriers was the Kiev class which introduced a unique layout, with the flight-deck offset to port and a foredeck bristling with weapons.

**Left:** The helicopter cruiser *Moskva* (seen here) and her sister *Leningrad* were built in the 1960s as the first Soviet carriers. Each operates an air wing of 14 Kamov Ka-25 Hormone ASW helicopters but are thought to have poor sea-keeping qualities.

**Left:** An efficient young Soviet Navy officer makes a last minute check on the honour guard before a foreign dignitary comes aboard during a rare Soviet visit abroad.

**Above:** *Admiral Gorshkov*, the fourth of the Kiev class. A new system is the Sky Watch radar, with four fixed planar arrays mounted on the island, for control of the air battle.

**Below:** *Admiral Gorshkov* with good views of Sky Watch and Cake Stand (the large cylinder above the superstructure for aircraft control) radars. It carries torpedoes.

and, as the RN learned to its cost in the Falklands in 1982, there is a considerable difference between peacetime exercises under carefully controlled conditions and war, where the enemy behaves with great unpredictability. In particular, the Soviet Navy could find that command-and-control of four large fleets is a much more complex undertaking than they have estimated.

The two Moskva class ASW helicopter cruisers were the first Soviet warships to carry an air wing and were designed to hunt and destroy US SSBNs operating in the eastern Mediterranean. They can accommodate 18 Kamov Ka-25 Hormone helicopters in the large hangar. Unlike most other carrier designs they also have a large forward superstructure which houses a comprehensive outfit of ASW and air defence sensors and weapons, including SA-N-3 Goblet SAM launchers and SUW-N-1 torpedo system. Only two units were built, *Moskva* and *Leningrad*, and they continue to serve the Soviet Navy well.

Next came the Kiev class ASW carriers with added surface warfare capability. They carry 19 Ka-25 Hormone helicopters and 13 Yak-38 Forger strike aircraft. The flight-deck is angled at 4.5deg to port, but does not have a ski-jump because the Forger is not capable of rolling take-offs. The Kiev class have a heavy weapons fit with eight SS-N-12 Sandbox SSMs, two SA-N-3 Goblet and two SA-N-4 Gecko, two twin 3in (76mm) DP gun mounts, eight 1.12in (30mm) Gatling CIWS turrets giving good all-round protection, an SUW-N-1 ASW missile launcher forward, two RBU-6000 ASW rocket-launchers, and 10 fearsome 21in (533mm) torpedo tubes.

The first two ships, *Kiev* and *Minsk*, are essentially identical, but the third, *Novorossiysk*, has minor differences — one of the most notable being that the new SA-N-9 vertical launch SAM has replaced the SA-N-4. There are also small variations in the electronics fit and in the flight-deck layout.

The fourth ship of the Kiev class is equipped with 3D planar radar and is often classified as a Modified Kiev. *Admiral Gorshkov* (ex-*Baku*) has the same hull and propulsion systems, but has many different weapons and electronic systems. These also appear on the later Kuznetsov class (ex-Tbilisi), and it is now clear that she was acting as a test-bed for these complex systems. *Admiral Gorshkov* carries the same air wing as her sisters, but the weapons fit is somewhat different with 12 SS-N-12 Sandbox missile launchers, four more than in the earlier ships but without any reloads. The long-range SA-N-3 SAM launchers have been replaced by SA-N-9 vertical launch silos. The two twin 3in (76mm) DP gun mounts on the earlier ships are replaced by two single 3.9in (100mm) mounts. The SUW-N-1 and RBU-6000 ASW launchers, as well as the torpedo tubes, have been deleted; ASW armament now consists of just two of the new RBU-12000 ASW rocket launchers.

The design of the new carrier *Admiral Kuznetsov* (67,000tons) is much more akin to Western design practice. She is the first-of-class and was commissioned in early 1991, a second, *Varyag*, will follow in 1992. She has a large, full-length flight-deck with an angled portion offset at some 10deg to port; and, continuing their innovative approach to carrier practice, the Soviet designers have employed a large 12deg ski-jump to enable CTOL aircraft to be launched without the use of a catapult. According to Soviet sources, *Admiral Kuznetsov* is intended to carry an air wing of some 60 aircraft, a logical design progression from the earlier helicopter carriers.

The armament of the Kuznetsov class includes 16 SS-N-19 Shipwreck SSMs, 24 SA-N-9 vertical launchers and the SA-N-11 close-in air-defence system (eight launchers). No DP guns have been seen, but there are the usual 1.12in (30mm) gatling CIWS mounts.

A new carrier, *Ulyanovsk* (75,000tons), is currently under construction. Of an entirely new design, she will have a conventional flat flight-deck with steam catapults rather than a ski-jump for take-off. She will be nuclear-powered and should enter service in about 1995. According to Soviet sources she will be the last aircraft carrier to be built for the Soviet Navy, although this seems somewhat improbable.

The three Kirov class (24,000tons) battle-cruisers are among the most powerful warships afloat. The first, *Kirov*, joined the fleet in 1980 followed by *Frunze* and *Kalinin* at four-year intervals. The final ship, *Yuri Andropov*, will enter service in 1992. Each has incorporated new weapons and electronics systems, so that none of them are identical. Taking *Kalinin* as an example, her main surface warfare battery consists of 20 SS-N-19 shipwreck SSMs, supported by two 5.1in (130mm) DP guns in single turrets. Her air-defence systems are very extensive, consisting of 12 long-range SA-N-6 Grumble vertical launchers (96 missiles), two SA-N-4 Gecko medium-range SAM systems (40 missiles), 16 short-range SA-N-9 vertical launch SAMs (128 missiles) and six of the new CADS-1 close-in systems, each of which comprises two 1.12in (30mm) gatling turrets and an SA-N-11 missile launcher. ASW systems comprise one RBU-12000 ASW mortar and two RBU-1000 torpedoes, together with two Ka-27 Helix-A helicopters. A Ka-25 Hormone-B helicopter is also carried to provide over-the-horizon (OTH) targeting information for the SS-N-19 missiles. *Kirov* lacks some of these weapons systems but has others too, as does *Franze*. *Kalinin* and *Kirov* serve in the Northern Fleet and *Frunze* in the Pacific.

Propulsion is by a unique combined nuclear and steam system. Top speed is 32kts and the nuclear reactors give almost limitless range. These ships will make ideal escorts for the new carriers, but could also be deployed as the central vessel in a surface-warfare battle group. In this role their exceptionally sophisticated air-defence systems should give them a reasonable chance of survival against all but the heaviest threats.

**Left:** In May 1990 the latest Soviet carrier design, *Admiral Kuznetsov* (then named *Tbilisi*), is moved to Sevastopol for final fitting-out. Note the wide flight-deck and the sharply angled (12deg) ski-jump.

**Below:** The nuclear battlecruiser *Kirov*. Only the hatches on the foredeck hint at the hidden missile power.

**Above:** *Slava* showing her ungainly battery of 16 SS-N-12 Sandbox anti-ship missiles. Note the large number of big, old-fashioned radar antennas.

**Left:** A Kamov Ka-25 Hormone departs from a Kresta-II guided-missile cruiser. The huge antenna is for the widely-used Top Sail 3-D air-search radar with a range of 300nm (555km).

The last of the Sverdlov class cruisers has been stricken and all 26 cruisers now in service have guided-missile main armaments. The oldest are three missile cruisers of the Kynda class (5,500tons), *Grozny, Admiral Fokin* and *Admiral Golovko*, designed for the surface warfare mission. These ships have an inadequate armament by today's standards and will be stricken.

The Kresta-I class (7,500tons) was based on the Kynda but with a much improved armament. Three ships have been in service since the 1960s, *Admiral Zozulya, Vladivostok* and *Vitse-Admiral Drozd*. A fourth, *Sevastapol*, was paid off in 1990 and it is possible the rest of the class may follow.

There are 10 Kresta-II class (7,700tons) which were built, like the Kresta-Is, at Leningrad using the same hull. These, however, are intended for the ASW mission, although they also managed to mount improved missile systems for other roles. The centrepiece of the ASW system is the SS-N-14 Silex which is mounted in two quadruple launch bins under the bridge wings and fixed in both azimuth and elevation. The remaining ASW armament is the same as for the Kresta I, but with the very important addition of a Ka-25 Hormone-A ASW helicopter. For air-defence the SA-N-3 Goblet replaced the SA-N-1 Goa, while the two twin 2.25in (57mm) turrets were retained and boosted by four 1.12in (30mm) gatling guns installed abreast of the tower mast.

The seven Kara class (9,700tons) cruisers were built at the same time as the Kresta-II class (mid-1960s — mid 1970s), but in the yards at Nikolayev on the Black Sea. Optimized for the ASW mission their armament was very similar to that of the Kresta-II, but with the addition of two SA-N-4 Gecko SAM twin launchers and the mounting of two twin 3in (76mm) gun turrets in the waist rather than 2.25in (57mm) ones.

**Above:** An automatic 5.1in (130mm) gun aboard the Sovremenny class destroyer *Otlichnyi*. The fully stabilized mount is capable of 65 rounds per minute.

**Below:** *Bezuprechnny* of the Sovremenny class enters the main British naval base at Portsmouth, England, on a 1990 official visit to the Royal Navy, one of very few since WWII.

**Above:** The Slava class cruiser *Marshal Ustinov* coming alongside during a July 1989 visit to the USA. The large bins for the SS-N-12 SSMs can be seen below the bridge.

The largest of the current cruisers are the three ships of the Slava class (12,500tons), *Slava, Marshal Ustinov* and *Chervona Ukraina*, which were completed between 1982 and 1990, and thought to have been built as an insurance policy against the failure of the Kirov class. A fourth, *Admiral Lobov*, should commission in 1993. They use only well-tried equipment in straightforward installations; for example, the main armament is 16 SS-N-12 Sandbox SSMs mounted in two fixed rows of eight angled launch tubes either side of the bridge superstructure. They are also fitted with SA-N-6 Grumble (eight launchers), SA-N-4 Gecko (two launchers), six 1.12in (30mm) gatling guns, 10 21in (533mm) torpedo tubes, two RBU-6000 ASW rockets and two 5.1in (130mm) guns. They also carry one Ka-25 Hormone-B OTH targeting helicopter.

There are nearly 40 destroyers in the fleet. The oldest ones are the 14 Kashin class (4,750tons), three of them modified, which were once the most advanced of their type in any navy and the first major warships to be powered solely by gas-turbines. With rakish lines and high power their maximum speed when built was some 38kts, although it is doubtful whether they could reach it now given wear and tear.

The main strength of the fleet at the moment lies in two types, both built in Baltic yards: a surface combat destroyer, the Sovremennyy class, and an ASW type, the Udaloy class. The Sovremennyy class (7,850tons) first appeared in 1981 and a total of 13 are believed to be in service. They are equipped with eight SS-N-22 Sunburn SSMs in two quadruple launch bins either side of the bridge, while air-defence armament is provided by two SA-N-7 Gadfly SAM systems and four 1.12in (30mm) gatling turrets. The gun armament of two twin 5.1in (130mm), fully automatic, water-cooled gun turrets, one on the forecastle and one on the stern, is very heavy by modern standards and is intended for shore bombardment, air-defence and anti-ship fire missions. ASW weapons are four 21in (533mm) torpedo tubes and two RBU-1000 rocket launchers. The helicopter landing-deck is mounted much further forward than in other Soviet ships (just abaft the funnel) and the hangar is telescopic — another unusual feature. The helicopter is a Ka-25 Hormone-B for OTH targeting. Those of the class currently in service are split between the Northern and Pacific Fleets, with about half in each. Surprisingly, these ships are powered by steam rather than gas turbines.

**Above:** Udaloy class ASW destroyer *Vitse-Admiral Kulakov*, showing the complex array of antennas and multiple weapons systems common to many Soviet warships.

**Above:** A Krivak-II class ASW frigate. Like the contemporary US Navy Oliver Hazard Perry class frigates these ships are now used as general-purpose destroyers.

The Udaloy class (8,100tons) joined the fleet concurrently with the Sovremennyys. The main ASW armament is the SS-N-14 Silex fitted, as in other classes, in quadruple bins beneath the bridge wings. This is complemented by two Ka-27 Helix-A ASW helicopters and two of the RBU-6000 rocket launchers which are fitted to almost every Soviet warship. There are two 3.9in (100m) DP guns in single turrets before the bridge and there are eight launchers for the SA-N-9 short-range, vertical launch SAM system. These are capable ships and like the Sovremennyy class are split between the Pacific and Northern Fleets with approximately 50 per cent in each. There are 12 of them and no more will be built because an uprated design is now undergoing construction: the BALCOM-12 class will mix features from the Udaloy and Sovremennyy classes, and the first may appear in 1991.

At least 38 examples have been built of the excellent and widely admired Krivak class. They would be designated frigates by NATO but the Soviet Navy prefers to see them as patrol ships. There are 21 of the well-armed Krivak-I class, displacing 3,575tons. The only major shortcomings are poor range at constant high speeds and the lack of any helicopter facilities.

In 1975 the first of a revised design appeared, the 11 strong Krivak-II class (3,670tons). The four SS-N-14 Silex ASW missiles remain but the guns are mounted slightly higher and they have two single 3.9in (100mm) gun turrets instead of the twin 3in (76mm), plus a larger variable-depth sonar (VDS) housing at the stern. This apart they appear the same as the Krivak-I.

The third type was the Krivak-III (3,900tons) built for use by the KGB Maritime Border Guard in the Far East. In these the ASW equipment, apart from two RBU-6000s and eight torpedo tubes, has been removed together with one of the two SA-N-4 Gecko SAM systems. This has created the room necessary to accommodate a large flight-deck and hangar aft, as well as space for one 3.9in (100mm) gun turret to be mounted on the foredeck and two 1.12in (30mm) gatlings, one either side of the hangar. These six vessels seem to be very large and well-armed warships, perhaps too much so to be operated by a "border patrol service".

A totally new frigate design appeared in 1991. The Neustrashimy class (4,000tons) will replace Krivak-I frigates and Kashin class destroyers; it has extensive sonar equipment to enable it to perform its ASW tasks and also has full helicopter facilities. There is a new SSM system with six SS-N-X fixed in three horizontal tubes each side of the ship. Its other armament consists of four SA-N-9 and eight SA-N-11 SAMs, one 3.9in (100mm) gun, one RBU-12000 ASW rocket and two CADS-N-1 gun systems.

A large number of warships with displacements between 1,000 and 2,000tons are in service. These "light" frigates are used by the Soviet Navy as patrol vessels with a primary ASW function. The oldest of those in service are 10 Mirka-I and Mirka-II class

**Below:** *Bditel'nyi* of the Krivak-I class which completed in 1981. An attractive design, it has two twin 3in (76mm) guns, the SA-N-4 Gecko SAMs and a Silex launcher.

**Below:** Another view of *Bditel'nyi* during a visit to Antwerp in 1991. This shows her large transom door for the variable-depth sonar (VDS) and the twin 3in (76mm) gun mounts.

ships (1,150tons). Also of 1960s vintage is the Petya class (1,180tons) which exists in four classes: Petya-I (two), Modified Petya-I (five), Petya-II (11) and Modified Petya-II (one). The Petya-II class has sold well abroad.

The Grisha class frigate has been a considerable success with more than 70 produced for the Soviet Navy and many others for export over a period of 25 years. Again, it exists today in several modified forms: Grisha-I (15), Grisha-II (12), Grisha-III (31) and Grisha-V (22). All are designed for the ASW mission, although many of them serve with the KGB Maritime Border Guards.

Some 10 Riga class (1,393tons) frigates remain in service. Built in the 1950s, large numbers of this handsome design have been exported and those remaining with the Soviet Navy have been reduced greatly in recent years. The Soviet Navy ordered 12 East German-built Parchim-II class (1,200tons) during the late-1980s to replace the Poti class in the Baltic Sea.

The navy has large numbers of corvettes, many of them equipped with guided missiles. Displacing between 400 and 800tons, this is a type in which the Soviet Navy has developed great expertise and reaped the rewards with large numbers being exported. The old Poti class (400tons) is now phasing out, (35 remained in 1991) and the main ASW corvette is the 36 strong Pauk class (440tons). These vessels mount a 3in (76mm) turret on the foredeck, with SA-N-5/8 missiles and a 1.12in (30mm) gatling turret for air-defence; ASW weapons are an RBU-1200 rocket launcher, four 21in (533mm) torpedo tubes and two depth-charge racks. There is the usual plethora of sensors, including a large dipping sonar mounted in a prominent housing on the transom.

The Tarantul class (450tons) missile corvettes use the same hull as the Pauk class. They exist in three versions, all with SSMs; the first type was all for export except for two trials/training boats retained in the USSR. The first Soviet Navy type was the Tarantul-II armed with four SS-N-2C Styx SSMs, an SA-N-5 Grail SAM system, a 3in (76mm) gun and two 1.12in (30mm) gatling turrets. There are 18 Tarantal-II but production has now switched to the Tarantul-III in which the SS-N-2C missiles are replaced by SS-N-22, a new missile with a 60nm range and a speed of Mach 2.5. Production here has also reached 18 boats.

Also in service are 34 Nanuchka class missile corvettes (850tons), armed with six SS-N-9 Siren SSMs in triple bins either side of the bridge and a single SA-N-4 Gecko SAM launcher. The Nanuchka-I, of which there are 16, has twin 2.25in (57mm) guns in a single turret at the stern, which has been replaced by a single 3in (76mm) and one 1.12in (30mm) turret gatling in the later Nanuchka-III and IV versions.

The corvette element is completed by the 17 T-58 vessels which have had several classifications during their 30-year service. Of more interest is the 750ton Dergach class air-cushion vessel which first appeared in 1989. It is based at Sevastapol and carries eight SS-N-22 Sunburn SSMs and an SA-N-4 Gecko SAM launcher.

The patrol boat/fast attack craft is a further area of Soviet expertise. There are several hundred examples in service, ranging widely in capability from slow, long-endurance, lightly armed vessels to very fast, missile-armed hydrofoils. A significant number of these vessels are operated by the KGB Maritime Border Patrol Service. There are also a number of patrol flotillas on the USSR's many rivers, including the Amur, Danube, Ussurio and Yenesei. Among the more significant types are the long-serving Osa-I and Osa-II class which serve around the world, the Matka and Turya classes of hydrofoil, and the Stenka and Shmel classes which still have 200-plus boats in service between them.

Virtually all Soviet surface warships and submarines are capable of laying small numbers of mines and there are only three known specialist minelayers belonging to the Alesha class (3,500tons). They were built in the late 1960s and can carry an estimated 300 mines. Like Western navies the Soviet Navy uses minesweepers and minehunters, although they do not seem to have produced any large GRP vessels to date. The ocean-going types in service include 42 Yurka class (460tons), 34 Natya-I (750tons) and one Natya-II (780tons), 20 T-43 class and one of the most recent Gorya class (1,100tons). There are also some 130 coastal and at least 50 inshore minesweepers, among the latter some 13 different classes — the most numerous being the Sonya and Yevgenya. In addition to all these, at least four Polnocny class landing craft have been fitted with special equipment to enable them to act as assault minesweepers.

**Above:** Tarantul-III corvettes are well-armed and capable of a speed of 36kts. Many of this class have been sold abroad to India, Yemen and eastern Europe.

**Below:** An Osa-II class patrol boat, a type which led the way in FAC design. Less than 30 remain in Soviet service. Over 200 have been sold to various foreign navies.

One of the areas in which the Soviet Navy has made rapid developments over the past 20 years is amphibious warfare. From a position where they were capable of only the most limited coastal operations they are now able to conduct a long-range opposed landing, if necessary. The largest units to date are three Ivan Rogov class (13,000tons) landing ships, *Ivan Rogov, Aleksandr Nikolaev* and *Mitrofan Moskalenko*, the first appearing in 1978, the second in 1982 and the third in 1989. These ships are each capable of carrying a naval infantry battalion group with all its men, stores, equipment and vehicles, as well as 10 tanks or self-propelled guns. There are two large flight-decks for helicopters and a stern-well for air-cushioned vehicles (ACVs). Bow doors and ramps enable these ships to land troops and vehicles across a beach. The large superstructure also accommodates the extensive command-and-control facilities essential for an amphibious operation. It also carries impressive defensive weaponry, including SA-N-4 Gecko and SA-N-5 Grail SAMs.

The 26 Ropucha class (3,600tons) landing ships are among the most sophisticated of their type in any navy and can carry some 250 troops and 24 armoured vehicles. Surprisingly, there are no facilities for helicopters. They have both bow and stern doors and facilitate a "roll-on-roll-off" approach with a tank deck that runs the length of the ship. In addition, there are 14 slightly older Alligator class (4,700tons) LSTs which were produced between 1964 and 1977 and can carry about 20 tanks and 300 troops. Finally, there are 36 of the smaller Polnocny class medium landing ships, many of which have been exported. There are over 100 smaller landing craft.

The Soviet Navy was one of the first to see the potential of the British-invented air-cushion vehicles (ACVs) and several different types have been produced for amphibious warfare duties. The most impressive to date is the Pomornik class (350tons) which can carry five PT-76 tracked vehicles or up to 220 troops and has SA-N-5 Grail SAM defences. It is powered by five gas-turbines which give it a top speed of 55kts. Other types in service include the Lebed, Aist and Gus classes.

**Above:** The three *Ivan Rogov* class landing ships were the first long-range assault ships to go into Soviet service. A fourth is being built.

**Left:** A Pomornik class ACV discharges its armoured vehicles onto a sharply shelving beach. It can take a 100ton load.

Once the Soviet Navy had recovered from the aftermath of WWII its submarine force followed four major lines of development: diesel-electric patrol submarines (SS), nuclear-powered attack submarines (SSN), ballistic missile submarines (SSB/SSBN) and guided-missile submarines (SSG/SSGN). In those 45 years they have constructed some 758 new-build submarines (excluding conversions) and today there are well over 300 submarines in service: nearly 60 armed with strategic ballistic missiles, over 60 with cruise missiles and approximately 200 attack boats with torpedoes. In this area, as in so many others, the Soviet Navy has expanded steadily and produced some excellent and innovative designs (although they have also built some poor and unreliable types as well).

The first SSN, a November class boat (5,300tons), was commissioned on 8 April 1958. It had a long narrow hull which would almost certainly have prevented her obtaining maximum advantage from the 22,000shp nuclear reactor. Like USS *Nautilus* she had two propellers which enabled four 16in (406mm) stern torpedo tubes to be fitted. The last of the class was stricken in 1991 and the oldest SSNs now in service are the 15 boats of the Victor-I class built between 1965 and 1974. These were followed by seven of the longer Victor-II (5,900tons) which carry SS-N-16 missiles, in addition to the original SS-N-15 and torpedoes. Latest in this line are 26 of the even longer Victor-IIIs (6,000tons). These have a large streamlined pod atop the vertical rudder; its purpose still causes intense speculation in Western intelligence circles and it is thought to be a towed array dispenser.

In the early 1980s two new SSNs appeared: the Sierra class (8,000tons) and the Akula class (9,000tons). (The development of two apparently competing designs is a not infrequent occurrence in areas the Soviet military consider very important.) There are two Sierra-I and a slightly longer version designated Sierra-II. Powered by two nuclear reactors with two turbo alternators, the Sierra class's heaviest armament is her SS-N-21 Sampson SLCMs with a range of 1,620nm (3,000km). There are seven of the long-finned Akula class in service, a class which is the follow-on to the Victor-III. She is slightly slower when dived than the Sierra but carries the same weaponry.

There has been a third, complementary strand of development. The Alfa class (3,680tons) appeared in 1967 with a totally new hydrodynamic hull design and powered by a liquid-metal cooled nuclear reactor which gave it underwater speeds in excess of 40 knots. The first Alfa was scrapped, but five others are in service today. Its apparent successor, the single Mike class (9,700tons), was commissioned in 1983 but sank in 1989 and is unlikely to be replaced.

The Soviet Navyhas produced many hundreds of diesel-electric patrol submarines since WWII. The majority of these were of the Whiskey (1,350tons) and Foxtrot classes (2,400tons), but they are now obsolete and are being stricken in increasing numbers. Highly successful export designs, the navy retains 40 front-line Foxtrot and 18 Whiskey.

**Above:** A Victor-III nuclear-powered attack submarine with the pod housing a towed, linear, passive hydrophone array, which was once thought to be a new propulsion system.

**Above:** An Oscar-II class. The 24 cruise missiles are housed in 12 bins on each side of the sail and angled at about 40deg. The hump abaft the sail houses a communications buoy.

The first Tango class (3,900tons) was commissioned in 1972 and a total of 18 have been produced. The largest diesel-electric submarine built since WWII, nearly all serve in the Northern Fleet. None were offered for export and it is assumed that they fulfil some special purpose in the navy's war plans.

Production has since switched to the Kilo class (3,000tons), of which at least 17 serve with the Soviet Navy and numerous others have been exported. The first Soviet conventional submarine with a "teardrop" hull, the Kilo is armed with six 21in (533mm) tubes for 12 SS-N-15 ASW missiles.

The Soviet Navy concluded in the mid-1950s that one of the most serious threats came from US Navy carrier task forces operating in the Pacific and North Atlantic Oceans. One of their main responses was to develop a force of submarines armed with cruise-missiles tasked to attack the carriers before they could get within aircraft range of the USSR. The first class intended for this role was the Echo-II (6,000tons), a group of 29 nuclear-powered submarines armed with eight SS-N-3A (later replaced by SS-N-12) surface-launched, anti-ship missiles mounted in four pairs in elevating bins. Some 17 of these submarines remain in service, as do 15 of the diesel-electric-powered Juliett class SSGs (3,750tons) which were built in parallel with the Echo-II and were armed with four SS-N-3A missiles.

The much more sophisticated Charlie class SSGNs (5,000tons) have a better designed hull and are armed with eight SS-N-7 anti-ship missiles, mounted in fixed-angle launch bins in the bows, launched while the submarine is submerged. There are 10 Charlie-I class SSGNs in service together with six improved Charlie-II class equipped with eight SS-N-9 Siren missiles and fitted with extra fire-control equipment.

After a long gap the new Oscar class (16,700tons) appeared in 1980. They are armed with 24 SS-N-19 Shipwreck SLCMs. This huge submarine has a central pressure-hull some 30ft (9.1m) in diameter with a row of 12 missile bins along either side. There are two Oscar-I class; subsequent boats are 32ft 10in (10m) longer and are designated Oscar-II (18,000tons) class. There are six Oscar-II class in service.

The Soviet Navy was just as quick to see the potential of ballistic missiles launched from submarines; something which offered a means of directly threatening the continental USA. A design finally appeared in 1967 which would match the SSBNs then appearing in Western navies: the Yankee class (9,600tons) armed with 16 SS-N-6 Serb SLBMs mounted under a small "turtleback" abaft the fin. The first of these boats took station off the United States' eastern seaboard in 1968, followed by a similar west coast deployment in 1971. The 33rd and last Yankee was launched in 1974 and in 1991 there were 11 still in service together with one uprated Yankee-II class armed with 12 SS-N-17 missiles. The first of an enlarged version, designated the Delta-I (11,300tons), launched in 1972. This design, which has progressed through to the current Delta-IV class, is still in production in 1991. Each successive design has become bigger and better armed: there are 18 Delta-I, four Delta-II, 14 Delta-III and seven Delta-IV.

The latest Soviet SSBN is the Typhoon class (25,000tons). This is a true milestone in submarine development, being by far the largest underwater vessel ever built. It is armed with 20 solid-fuelled SS-N-20 SLBMs and production appears to have ended at six submarines. All the Typhoons so far built operate from two bases on the Kola Peninsula: Zapadnaya Litsa and Gremikha. The latter appears to have been constructed specifically for the Typhoons and includes huge submarine pens blasted out of the granite rocks to provide what is, perhaps, the ultimate in survivable facilities. No Typhoons are known to have deployed outside Arctic waters.

The Soviet Navy has been involved in submarine development from the very earliest days and has frequently possessed the largest submarine fleet in the world, although its effectiveness has been limited by its enforced split into four elements. At the end of the Cold War in 1989 the Soviet submarine fleet was at least the equal of that of the United States, although how long that will remain so is open to question.

Accompanying the large underwater fleet is an enormous range of tenders plus surface auxiliary vessels, repair ships, fleet replenishment ships, tankers, rescue ships and intelligence collectors (AGIs), with over 60 of the latter identified.

**Below:** The mighty Typhoon SSBNs, largest submarines ever built, carry 20 SS-N-20 missiles, each with nine 100KT MIRV warheads. Only six boats have been built so far.

**Above:** The Morskaya Pekhota or naval infantry are one of the few areas of expansion in the Soviet military. They specialize in raids and coastal assaults with tough exercises.

**Above:** The largest marine detachment is 7,000 strong and based at Vladivostok on the Sea of Japan. An elite unit, their training puts much stress on a form of combat wrestling.

**Right:** The Yakovlev Yak-38 Forger V/STOL fighter is not a great success as an aircraft, but has given the Soviet fleet its first taste of complex fixed-wing operations at sea.

The Soviet Naval Infantry (marines) were re-established in 1961-62 and since then they have expanded into a major force which currently numbers some 18,000. This well-trained and highly-disciplined force is probably second only to the paratroops in morale and effectiveness. They are formed into one division and three brigades. The division is composed of three infantry regiments, supported by an amphibious tank regiment and a self-propelled artillery regiment. The three independent brigades each include four infantry battalions and also have tank and artillery support. There are also a number of Spetznaz (special forces) brigades.

In addition there are some 7-10,000 officers and men in the coastal defence organization. Their primary mission is to protect the approaches to naval bases and major ports. They are bolstered by the existence of the KGB Maritime Border Guard which is responsible for the security of the coastline frontiers of the USSR. It is manned by some 25,000 naval personnel under KGB command and operates a number of frigates, patrol ships and other minor craft.

There are some 65,000 men in Soviet Naval Aviation, operating approximately 750 combat aircraft, 320 combat helicopters and 400 support types. This force is responsible for both shore-based aviation and the growing number of aircraft afloat.

For many years the principal helicopter type has been the Kamov Ka-25 Hormone which exists in three versions: Hormone-A for ASW; Hormone-B for OTH targeting for ship-launched missiles; and Hormone-C for SAR and troop carrying. This successful type has 120 examples in service but is now being replaced by the larger and more modern Kamov Ka-27/32 Helix. This also exists in three versions: Helix-A (Kamov Ka-27) for ASW; Helix-B (Kamov Ka-29) as an assault troop carrier; and Helix-D (Kamov Ka-32) for SAR.

The first shipboard fixed-wing aircraft was the Yakovlev Yak-38 Forger VTOL, which exists in single-seat strike and two-seat trainer/strike versions. Although this aircraft has given the fleet invaluable experience of carrier operations it would be ineffective in combat and a new type, the Yakovlev Yak-41, is entering service. The new carriers, with their ski-jumps, enable conventional aircraft to be used and the Sukhoi Su-25 Frogfoot, Sukhoi Su-27 Flanker and Mikoyan MiG-29 Fulcrum are all being developed for such a role.

Ashore Soviet Naval Aviation is responsible for air operations in support of the fleet. For maritime reconnaissance the Tupolev Tu-95 Bear-D continues to be used, supported by the shorter-ranged Tupolev Tu-16 Badger, Sukhoi Su-24 Fencer-E and Tupolev Tu-22M Backfire. There is a very large EW fleet, mirroring the intelligence-collectors in the fleet, flying specially fitted-out aircraft, such as Tupolev Tu-16 Badger-H, Ilyushin Il-20 Coot-A and -B. There are over 300 long-range bombers, including the Tupolev Tu-22M Backfire-B and -C, and the ageing Tu-22 Blinder and Tu-16 Badger. Fifty Badger-As have also been converted to the in-flight refuelling role.

Shore-based attack fighters include a number of Sukhoi Su-17 Fitters, most of which are based on the Baltic coast and specially configured for the ship-attack mission. The MiG-23 Flogger is also used by the navy and has been seen operating from the former Soviet base at Cam Ranh Bay in Vietnam. There are also specialized ASW aircraft, including the Tu-142 Bear-F, Ilyushin Il-38 May and Beriev Be-12 Mail flying boat.

In addition to the sea-based helicopters there are many more which operate from shore bases. These include the Mil Mi-14 Haze, which is used for both mine countermeasures and ASW, and a variety of other types such as Mil Mi-8 Hip-C and Mil Mi-6 Hook. There are also some 400 further aircraft for training, transport and general support missions.

## EQUIPMENT

**Aircraft Carriers:**
Moskva class
Kiev class
Admiral Gorshkov (modified Kiev) class
Kuznetsov class
**Cruisers:**
Kirov class
Kynda class
Kresta-I & II classes
Kara class
Azov (Modified Kara) class
Slava class
**Submarines:**
Whiskey class
Foxtrot class
Tango class
Kilo class
Victor-I, II & III classes
Alfa class
Sierra class
Akula class
Juliett class
Echo-II class
Charlie-I, II & III classes
Papa class
Oscar-I & II classes
Yankee-I & II classes
Delta-I, II, III & IV classes
Typhoon class
**Destroyers:**
Kashin class
Modified Kashin class
Sovremennyy class
Udaloy class
**Frigates:**
Krivak-I, II, III & IV classes
Neustrashimmy class
Mirka-I & II classes
Petya-I, II & III classes
Grisha-I, II, III, IV & V classes
Riga class
Parchim-II class
**Corvettes:**
Pauk class
Poti class
Dergach class
Nanuchka-I & IV classes
Tarantul-I, II & III classes
T-58 class
**Patrol Boats:**
Babochka class
Matka class
Mukha class
Muravey class
Osa-I & II class
SO1 class
Shershen class
Stenka class
Svetlyak class
Shmel class
Turya class
Zhuk class
Yaz class
**Amphibious Warfare:**
Ivan Rogov class
Ropucha-I & II classes
Polnocny class
Pomornik class
**Mine Warfare:**
Alescha class
Gorya class
Ilyusha class
Natya-I & II classes
T-43 class
Yurka class
Sonya class
Yevgenya class
Zhenya class
Vanya class
**Naval Aircraft:**
Beriev Be-12 Mail
Beriev A-40 Albatross
Ilyushin Il-20 Coot-A
Ilyushin Il-38 May
Kamov Ka-25 Hormone-A, -B & -C
Kamov Ka-27 Helix-A
Kamov Ka-29 Helix-B
Kamov Ka-32 Helix-D
Mikoyan MiG-23 Flogger-K
Mikoyan MiG-29 Fulcrum-A
Mil Mi-8 Hip-C
Mil Mi-14 Haze -A & -B
Sukhoi Su-17 Fitter-C & -D
Sukhoi Su-24 Fencer-E
Sukhoi Su-25UT Frogfoot
Sukhoi Su-27 Flanker-B
Tupolev Tu-16 Badger-C, -D, -E, -F, -G & -J
Tupolev Tu-22 Blinder-A & -C
Tupolev Tu-22M Backfire-B & -C
Tupolev T-95 Bear-D & -J
Tupolev Tu-142 Bear-F
Yakovlev Yak-38 Forger-A & -B
**Marines:**
One division
Three independent brigades
Four Spetsnatz brigades

## UNITED KINGDOM

THE Royal Navy (RN) was the strongest navy in the world for a long period of time, but by the end of WWII th RN was clearly not as strong as the US Navy. The RN remained large and versatile through the 1950s and 1960s but its strength was reducing inexorably.

The Royal Navy has one major command — Commander-in-Chief Fleet (CINCFLEET) — based at Northwood just outside London. This officer commands all RN ships afloat anywhere in the world, a role he combines with two NATO appointments as CinC Channel and CinC Eastern Atlantic. The bases and naval shore establishments are commanded by CinC Naval Home Command (CINCNAVHOME) based at Portsmouth. The major bases are at Devonport, Portsmouth and Portland in England, and Rosyth and Faslane in Scotland. The last two of the navy's once numerous overseas bases are at Gibraltar and Hong Kong.

There are 56,000 men and women in the Royal Navy and nearly 8,000 in the Royal Marines. The reserves are nearly half the strength of the regular force. Organiza-

**Above:** Westland Sea King HAS.5 anti-submarine helicopters warm up aboard an Illustrious class carrier, while a BAe Sea Harrier FRS.1 awaits its turn to leave the deck.

**Below:** HMS *Invincible* with part of her air wing on deck, the crew "manning ship" and the Royal Marines band playing. "Showing the Flag" is an important activity for all navies.

**Below:** HMS *Invincible* of the Illustrious class. She was the second of the three carriers to be refitted and has a range of 5,000 miles at 18kts, offering considerable power. Note the Mk 15 CIWS and the Sea Dart launches on the foredeck.

tionally, there is the Submarine Flotilla, with four squadrons; the First Flotilla, with seven frigate squadrons and two destroyer squadrons; the Second Flotilla; the Third Flotilla; the MCM Flotilla with five squadrons; the Surveying Flotilla; and the Dartmouth Training Squadron.

The RN's primary role is in support of NATO naval forces in the Atlantic. To achieve this it has the largest European navy, which consists of three ASW aircraft carriers, some 48 destroyers and frigates, 26 submarines, 33 mine warfare vessels and some 70 amphibious or patrol ships, with large support organizations in the Royal Fleet Auxiliary (RFA) and the Royal Maritime Auxiliary Service (RMAS). RN ships provide about 70 per cent of NATO's ready maritime forces in the eastern Atlantic and the English Channel, and contribute to the two NATO forces in these areas.

The RN also contributes to the UK's commitments around the world. These include a small force in Falkland waters in the South Atlantic, in Hong Kong, and a long-standing patrol force in the Persian Gulf. The RN probably has more post-1945 "hot war" experience than any other navy, having taken part in the Korean War, the Suez Operation (1956), the Falklands War (1982), the Armilla Patrol, the Gulf deployments of 1987-89 and the Gulf War of 1990-91.

Following the end of the Cold War it is clear that the RN will suffer some reductions. The government appears to be planning very severe cuts and these, if effected, could well lead to a situation in western Europe where the RN loses its dominant position to the French Navy, which is increasing rather than contracting. The French are also self-sufficient in strategic nuclear weapons, which the British are not, as they depend upon the United States for missiles.

The core of the fleet is the three Invincible class (20,600tons) aircraft carriers, HMS *Invincible*, HMS *Illustrious* and HMS *Ark Royal*, which entered service between 1980 and 1985. Today, two ships are active at any one time, with the third either in refit or in an inactive status for use as a training platform.

Initially described as "through-deck cruisers", these ships were intended to operate ASW helicopters but, rather late in the design process, provision had to be made to operate Sea Harriers to intercept hostile reconnaissance and ASW patrol aircraft. HMS *Invincible* and HMS *Illustrious* were constructed with a 7 deg ski-jump and HMS *Ark Royal* was the first to have the full 12deg device, (which is also some 39ft/12m longer), thus enabling the full load-carrying capability of the Sea Harrier to be exploited. In 1986 HMS *Invincible* began a refit which completed in 1989; it extended the ski jump to 12deg, improved the storage facilities to accommodate 21 aircraft, fitted larger magazines for the new Sea Eagle missiles and Stingray ASW torpedoes, and replaced the Mk 15 Vulcan Phalanx CIWS — which had been fitted in haste during the Falklands War — with three Dutch Goalkeeper systems. HMS *Illustrious* began its refit in 1991 and it includes fitting of Sea Wolf. All three ships are fitted with extensive flag-ship facilities enabling them to take command of task groups, and all three can carry a Royal Marine commando group (of 960 men) for short periods.

There are 13 destroyers, all but one of which are Type 42s. The original series of nine, known as the Sheffield class (4,250tons), were built in two batches in the 1970s as air-defence and radar picket ships. Their principal weapon system is the Sea Dart SAM, for which 20 missiles are carried. There is also a 4.5in (114mm) DP gun and four 0.8in (20mm) AA guns, while the sole onboard ASW weapon system is the ASW torpedo with six tubes fitted. There is a large flight-deck aft and one Westland Lynx HAS.3 helicopter is carried. During the Falklands War the name-ship of the class, HMS *Sheffield*, was lost after she was hit by an air-launched Exocet missile. This showed up a number of deficiencies, including inadequate close-in air-defences and limitations in sensor capability and damage-control arrangements. This led to many improvements in subsequent refits, including fitting two 0.8in (20mm) Mk 15 Vulcan Phalanx CIWS.

The original Type 42s proved to be very cramped, relatively poor seaboats and so it was decided to produce four Type 42Cs (4,775tons), which are some 52ft (16m) longer. The weapons fit is improved with the Sea Dart magazine carrying 40 missiles and two Sea Wolf launchers are being installed in place of the two Phalanx systems, with one of the latter being retained but moved to the forecastle. The increase in length has led to problems of its own and hull strakes and strengthening plates have had to be fitted.

The remaining destroyer is HMS *Bristol* (7,100tons), a Type 82, which was originally intended as the prototype of a class of large escorts for the proposed aircraft carrier CVA-01. She has proved troublesome and is generally considered to have been an expensive failure. She is now used as a training ship for cadets.

**Left:** HMS *Gloucester*, a Type 42C destroyer. The large white radomes cover the Type 909 fire-control radar antennas, which control both Sea Dart SAMs and the 4.5in (114mm) gun.

**Below:** HMS *Liverpool*, a Type 42 destroyer. On her foredeck are a single 4.5in (114mm) Mk 8 DP gun and a twin-arm Sea Dart launcher.

**Above:** HMS *Minerva,* one of the Leander class frigates converted to take Exocet missiles; the four launchers can be seen positioned immediately forward of the ship's bridge.

**Below:** HMS *Andromeda*, one of the final version of the Leander class, with Exocet launchers, Sea Wolf SAM and a hangar capable of accepting a Lynx ASW helicopter.

**Above:** The Type 21 frigate HMS *Ambuscade*. Two of this class were lost to enemy action during the 1982 Falklands War and the six remaining all have problems.

**Below:** The squat lines of the original British Type 22 frigates were transformed by the lengthened hull of the Batch 2 version, as shown by the elegant HMS *Brave*.

The main concern of the RN has, for many years, been with ASW and there are dozens of frigates in service to meet this requirement. The very successful Leander class was built in the 1960s (23 for the RN and numerous others for foreign navies) and those that remain have undergone a process of modification and improvement. Today's 12 exist in two groups of six each: the "Exocets" and the "Broad Beamed". The "Exocets" displace 3,200tons and divide into two groups of three. All have four Exocet SSMs, but HMS *Cleopatra*, HMS *Sirius* and HMS *Argonaut* all have towed sonar array and only two 0.8in (20mm) Oerlikon Mk7A; whereas HMS *Minerva*, HMS *Danae* and HMS *Juno* lack towed sonar but have two Bofors 1.6in (40mm) Mk 9, two Oerlikon 0.8in (20mm) GAM-B01 and two 0.8in (20mm) Oerlikon Mk7A. The "Broad Beamed" also come in two groups. All displace 2,962tons but five of them are armed with four Exocets, a Sea Wolf SAM system, two 0.8in (20mm) Oerlikon GAM-B01, two 0.8in (20mm) Oerlikon Mk7A and six 12.7in (324mm) torpedo tubes for Marconi Stingrays. HMS *Ariadne* by contrast has a Sea Cat SAM, two 4.5in (114mm) guns, two Oerlikon 0.8mm (20mm), one 0.8in (20mm) Oerlikon GAM-B01 and a Mk10 A/S mortar.

Eight Type 21 Amazon class (3,600tons) were built and two have subsequently been lost in action to aircraft-delivered bombs during the Falklands War. Armament consists of four Exocet SSMs, a 4.5in (114mm) DP gun, a Sea Cat SAM launcher, four 0.8in (20mm) Oerlikon Mk7A AA and a Westland Lynx HAS.3 ASW helicopter. Two of the class also have six ASW torpedo tubes. These ships have long been subjected to criticism for being insufficiently robust, for incorporating too much aluminium and for being top heavy.

There are 14 Type 22 frigates which have been built in three batches. The first four of these ships displaced 4,400tons and formed the Broadsword class which joined the fleet in 1979-82, just in time for some of them to take part in the Falklands War. They are well-armed with missiles — four Exocets, two Sea Wolf SAM launchers and six 12.75in (324mm) torpedo tubes — and guns: two 0.8in (20mm) Oerlikon GAM-B01 and four 1.12in (30mm) Oerlikon GCM-A03. They also operate one or two Westland Lynx HAS.3 or HAS.5 Sea King ASW helicopters. As with the Type 42 destroyers it was found that too much equipment and too many men had been squeezed into too little space; the same remedy of a longer hull was adopted. The Batch Two and Three ships all have the same 55ft (17m) longer hull, but differ in detail from each other.

This deficiency has been rectified in the four Cornwall class (4,900tons) Type 22 (Batch Three) ships, which are the largest frigates currently in service in any navy. Acknowledging one of the major lessons of the Falklands War they have a 4.5in (114mm) gun on the forecastle which has displaced the eight Exocet launchers to an amidships location. There are two Sea Wolf launchers, two 1.12in (30mm) Oerlikon cannon and a Goalkeeper CIWS for air-defence, plus six ASW torpedo tubes. The hangar and the deck can handle either two Westland Lynx HAS.3s or one and a Sea King HAS.5.

Production of the Type 22 was completed in 1990 and the new 4,200tons Duke class Type 23 frigates are now joining the fleet. Ten of an originally planned 16 have been ordered to replace the Leander class. By 1991, three had been commissioned, HMS *Norfolk*, HMS *Argyll* and HMS *Marlborough*. These are highly-capable ships with, unusually for the RN, a flush-deck hull. Their armament consists of eight Harpoon SSMs, one vertical-launch Sea Wolf SAM, one 4.5in (114mm) gun, two 1.12in (30mm) Oerlikon cannon and four fixed 12.75in (324mm) ASW torpedo tubes. Rather surprisingly, there is no CIWS — presumably on the grounds that the Seawolf system can handle all incoming targets. Structurally, the Duke class is interesting because it incorporates design features based on stealth technology in order to reduce acoustic, infra-red, magnetic and radar signatures. This has been achieved by rounding out edges and sloping the vertical surfaces, as well as adopting methods to suppress noise and emissions.

The RN does not possess any fast attack craft, but has a number of patrol boats for various missions. There are three of the original five Peacock class remaining (712tons) which are armed with the OTO Melara 3in (76mm) Compact and used for patrolling Hong Kong waters. There is HMS *Endurance* and two vessels of the Castle class which patrol South Atlantic waters; fishery protection duties undertaken by seven Island class; and a variety of others which train recruits or patrol coastal or base waters, these include HMS *Sentinel*, two Bird class, five Attacker class and 14 Archer class.

There is a very strong mine countermeasures force. Seven of the old 1950's Ton class (440tons) remain in service, as does HMS *Wilton* (450tons) which is of a similar design but with a hull constructed totally of glass-reinforced plastic (GRP). The GRP hull was a success and as a result 13 of the larger and very sophisticated Hunt class (725tons) minesweepers were produced in the 1980s. These have been very successful and were deployed to the Gulf on several occasions. The latest Sandown class (465tons) are designated single-role minehunters (SRMH) (they have no sweeping capability). The first of five entered service in 1989; two more should follow in 1991. The navy has plans to buy more, Saudi Arabia has ordered six and Bazan at Cartagena will build 12 for the Spanish Navy. Finally, there are 12 River class (890tons) "Extra-deep Armed Team Sweeps". Another 1980's design, they have been built to operate a Vickers-designed system which requires two ships with a wire catenary stretched between them. The Royal Naval Reserve (RNR) operates 11, but one is regular-manned and operates in peacetime with the Fisheries Protection Squadron.

The navy's amphibious warfare capability consists of seven major units and about 30 LCVs and LCVPs. There are two Intrepid class assault ships (12,120tons), HMS *Fearless* and HMS *Intrepid*, which are equivalent to the US Navy's Landing Platform, Dock (LPD). They can carry a complete commando unit (equivalent to a battalion) and land them by helicopter or by smaller landing craft. These ships are now very old (built in the 1960s) and in urgent need of replacement. A decision on whether to proceed with a new 24,400ton ship is still awaited.

Six Landing Ships Logistics (LSLs) were procured by the army in 1963, but were later transferred to the navy where they are operated by the Royal Fleet Auxiliary (RFA). They are in constant use and played an invaluable role in the Falklands and Gulf wars. One was so severely damaged in the Falklands War, RFA *Sir Galahad*, that she had to be scuttled and replaced by a new ship of the same name to a modified design. The five Sir Bedivere class (5,766tons) can carry 340 troops, 16 tanks and 34 vehicles. The newest ship, although larger (8,541tons), has a similar capacity. Despite the two assault ships and five LSLs there is a perpetual shortage of amphibious lift, and commercial vessels are frequently on charter to meet the shortfall.

The first post-war British submarines were the Porpoise and Oberon classes which entered service in the 1960s. (Six of the latter still remain in service.) It was thought that these would be the final diesel-electric submarines in the Royal Navy, but in the 1970s it was decided to build a new class. This appeared in the late 1980s as the Upholder class (2,400tons). They are designed to operate for 15,000 hours (equivalent to seven years in commission) between major refits and are armed with six bow-mounted 21in (533mm) torpedo tubes firing a mix of Mk 24 Tigerfish and Spearfish torpedoes, Sub-Harpoon ASMs and Stonefish mines. The Royal Navy intended to buy 10 of the Upholder class, with the fifth onwards being of a stretched design capable of greater endurance. That plan may now be shelved because of the defence cuts and the number in the class remains at four with HMS *Upholder* and HMS *Unseen* commissioned, with HMS *Ursula* and HMS *Unicorn* to follow by 1993.

The RN's first SSN was completed in 1963, since when three further classes have been produced. A British SSN, HMS *Conqueror*, sank an Argentine warship in 1982 making her the only SSN ever to have sunk an enemy warship in combat. A seven strong fourth class was also planned to (SSN-20 or W class) take the RN into the next century with a radical new design. The future, however, seems to lie with a less expensive design instead.

The latest SSN in service is the Trafalgar class (5,208tons) consisting of six boats which joined the fleet between 1983 and 1990, with one more to follow. These are a development of the Swiftsure class and all are coated with a layer of rubber-compound anechoic tiles to reduce radiated and reflected noise. All except the first of class, HMS *Trafalgar*, are fitted with a shrouded pump-jet propulsion system. The Trafalgar class has a similar weapons fit to the Swiftsure with its five tubes. There are six Swiftsure class which have been refitted to extend their service lives by a dozen or so years. Two further operational classes of SSN, the Valiant and Churchill, represented by HMS *Valiant* and HMS *Courageous*, are being laid off.

**Below:** HMS *Hurworth* is one of many British Hunt class minehunters to have operated in the Gulf since 1987 with the Armilla Patrol. These are very effective and capable warhips.

**Below:** HMS *Torbay*, fourth of seven submarines in the Trafalgar class. She has a dived speed of 32kts and a diving depth of 1,000ft (300m). She has a complement of 97.

Even more important than the SSNs are the SSBNs, the first of which, HMS *Resolution* (8,500tons), became operational in 1967. Since then at least one of the four Polaris submarines have been on constant deterrent patrol. The Vanguard class (15,850tons) of Trident-armed SSBNs is now being constructed and the first-of-class is due to enter service in 1992. Following the end of the Cold War the British government's defence review proposed a future British submarine fleet of four SSBNs, 12 SSNs and four SSKs. These will form a very capable force, but their numbers, especially of SSNs and SSKs, are worryingly meagre.

The global commitments of the RN necessitate a large afloat support organization, and this is provided by the Royal Fleet Auxiliary (RFA). Comprising some 2,500 officers and ratings, the RFA, who are civilians under RN control, operate 10 large replenishment vessels and 10 smaller types. One of these, RFA *Argus* (26,421tons) is a former merchant-ship which has been rebuilt as an "aviation support ship" and can provide a base for up to 12 Sea Harriers and six Sea King helicopters. Although designated an auxiliary, and manned primarily by RFA personnel, she has a combat role and during the Gulf War deployed well within the combat zone — although serving then as a forward medical ship.

Despite the demise of the large carriers the Fleet Air Arm is still a significant force which operates some 125 fixed-wing aircraft and 219 helicopters. Land-based ASW and MR aircraft (BAe Nimrods) are operated by RAF crews as part of Strike Command, but they are under the operational control of the naval CINCFLEET.

The RN's strike aircraft are the BAe Sea Harrier FRS.1 and FRS.2, special navalized versions of the very successful Harrier V/STOL aircraft which are only operated by the RN and the Indian Navy. There are 42 single-seat strike fighter FRS.1s in service, together with seven two-seat trainers, and orders have been placed for the FRS.2 version (which is equivalent to the AV-8B Harrier II).

The large ASW force consists of 76 Sea King HAS.5 and HAS.6 helicopters, 80 Lynx HAS.3s, and one EH.101 Merlin. These operate from the Invincible class carriers and the destroyers and frigates. There are 10 Sea King AEW.2 specially equipped for the airborne early warning role which was shown by the Falklands War to be a significant deficiency.

**Right:** HMS *Minerva* pounding through a North Atlantic swell, while a Westland Lynx HAS.3 ASW helicopter flies overhead, armed with two Stingray anti-submarine torpedoes.

The RN is also responsible for operating troop-carrying helicopters for the Royal Marines and for this purpose they have 35 Sea King HC.4s, 12 Gazelle AH.Mk1s and six Lynx AH.Mk1. Other front-line, land-based aircraft are the RAF's BAe Buccaneer S2 and Nimrod MR.2, both of which are now rather elderly types.

The 700 officers and 7,200 men of the Royal Marines (RM) are under naval command, even though they will often undertake tasks under the operational control of the army. Equipped as navalized light-infantry, the RM provide a brigade consisting of three commandos (a unit equivalent in size and organization to an army infantry battalion). The RM provide the Special Boat Section (SBS) which, with the Army's Special Air service (SAS), forms the British Special Forces which have a reputation second to none.

**Left:** HMS *Resolution*, name-ship of the class of four SSBNs which provide the British nuclear deterrent. She carries 16 Polaris A3TK missiles, each with three 200KT MRV Chevaline warheads.

**Below:** The BAe Sea Harrier FRS.2 is the Royal Navy's equivalent of the AV-8B Harrier II and will serve well into the next century.

### EQUIPMENT

**Aircraft Carriers:**
Invincible class
**Submarines:**
Oberon class
Valiant class
Swiftsure class
Trafalgar class
Resolution class
**Destroyers:**
Bristol (Type 82) class
Manchester (Type 42C) class
Sheffield (Type 42) class
**Frigates:**
Amazon (Type 21) class
Boxer (Type 22, Batch Two) class
Broadsword (Type 22, Batch One) class
Cornwall (Type 22, Batch Three) class
Duke (Type 23) class
Leander class
**Patrol Boats:**
Castle class
Island class
Peacock class
**Amphibious Warfare:**
Intrepid class
Sir Bedivere class
Sir Galahad class
**Mine Warfare:**
Hunt class
River class
Sandown class
Ton class
**Naval Aircraft:**
Agusta-Westland EH.101 Merlin
BAe Sea Harrier FRS.1/2
Westland Gazelle AH.Mk1
Westland Lynx AH.Mk1 & HAS.3
Westland Sea King AEW.2, HAS.2, HC.4, HAS.5 & HAS.6
**Marines:**
One brigade of three battalions
Special Boat Section of three squadrons
Two assault squadrons

## YUGOSLAVIA

AFTER WWII the navy was gradually built up in parallel with the army and air force, with considerable use being made of the small, but efficient and imaginative, Yugoslavian defence manufacturing industry. Today, the navy has a strength of some 11,000 officers and ratings, of whom about 40 per cent are conscripts. The main headquarters is at Split, and there are also naval sectors at Pula, Sibenik and Boka. A riverine squadron is under the operational command of the army.

The main units are four frigates, two of the Split class (Soviet Koni class) and two of the Yugoslavian-designed and constructed Kotor class. The main armaments of the Split class (1,900tons) are four SS-N-2C Styx missile launchers abaft the funnel, an SA-N-4 SAM system and four 2.25in (57mm) guns in two twin turrets, one on the foredeck, the other right aft. There are also four 1.12in (30mm) gatlings and two RBU-6000 ASW RLS. The Kotor class (1,850tons) are of similar size and appearance but are not copies of the Koni. They have different armament and propulsion systems.

The navy has two 1950's-era corvettes of the home-built Mornar class. These were modernized in the 1970s but are now dated. A replacement, Type 400 or Kobra class, has begun building.

The main strength of the fleet lies in some 60-odd patrol boats. Some of them, such as 10 Osa-Is and 14 Shershen class, were designed in the USSR, but most of the latest are designed and built in Yugoslavia. Many of those built in the 1970s have Soviet weapons and sensors, but in the 1980s more Western equipment has been used, including Swedish guns and missiles (Koncar and Mirna classes). There are about 30 minesweepers and 40 or so smaller amphibious warfare craft; a larger Silba class LCT with ro-ro features is on order.

All the submarines are diesel-electric and have been designed and built in Yugoslavia. Three Heroj class (960tons) were built in the late 1960s and two Sava class (964tons) some 10 years later. Both types are armed with six 21in (533mm) torpedo tubes. Yugoslavia is one of the few countries constructing midget submarines and small numbers have been exported. The R-2 Mala class (1.4tons) is a two-man swimmer delivery vehicle; but of greater significance is the six strong M100-D Una class (88tons), which has a crew of four and can transport six swimmers and four swimmer delivery vehicles.

Naval aviation operates mainly helicopters, all of which are Soviet supplied. There are also some Canadian Beaver utility aircraft and CL-215 amphibians. The air force has a "naval cooperation regiment" which is responsible for maritime surveillance and strike. Finally, there is a coastal defence organization which comprises some 2,300 men and women manning anti-ship missiles and guns.

### EQUIPMENT

**Submarines:**
Heroj class
Sava class
**Frigates:**
Split (Soviet Koni) class
Kotor class
**Corvettes:**
Mornar class
**Patrol Boats:**
Mitar Acev (Soviet Osa-I) class
Koncar class
Pionir (Soviet Shershen) class
Mirna class
**Naval Aircraft:**
Kamov Ka-25 Hormone A
Kamov Ka-28 Helix A
Mil Mi-8 Hip

# NORTH AFRICA AND MIDDLE EAST

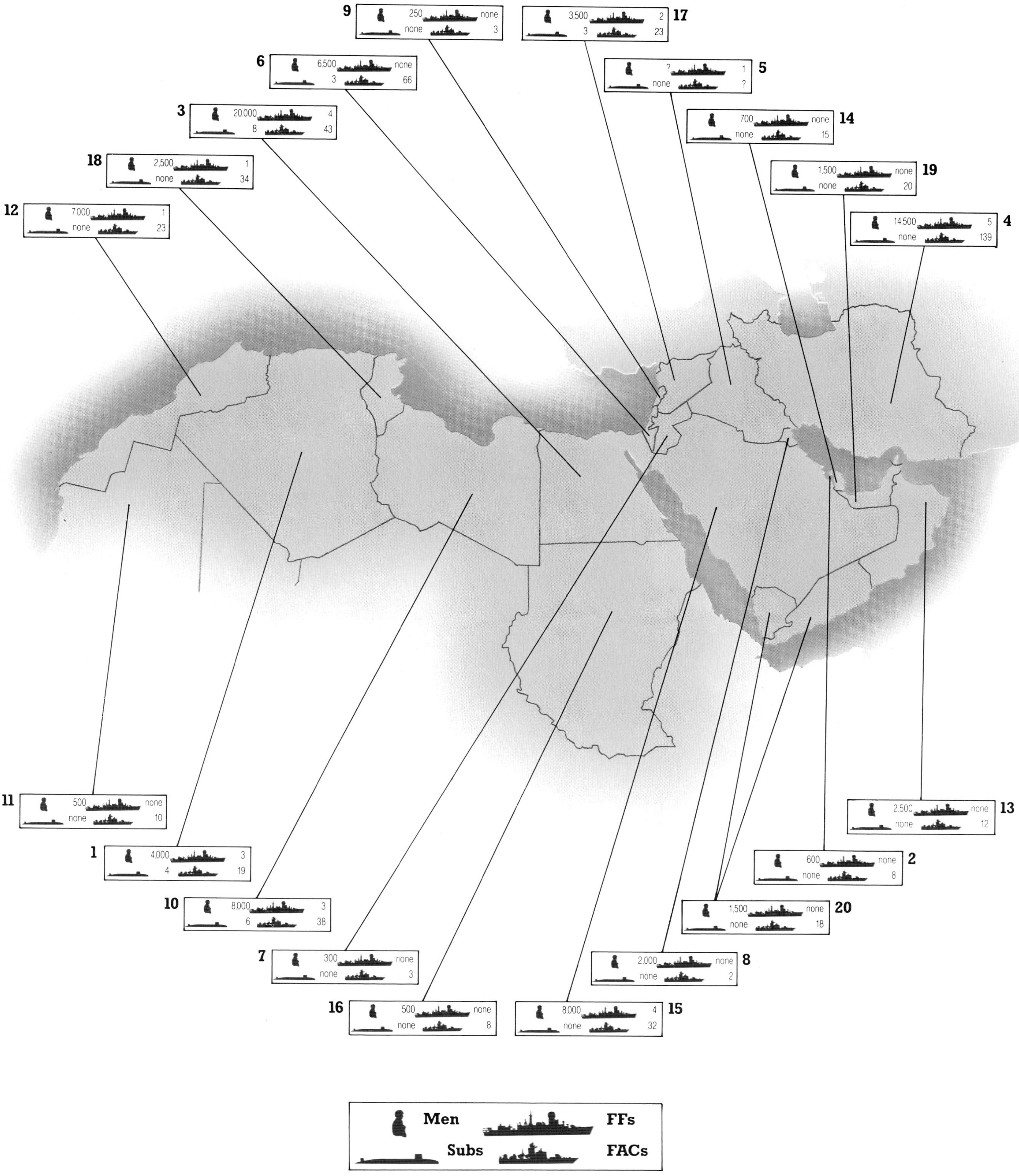
9 250 none none 3
17 3,500 2 3 23
6 6,500 none 3 66
5 ? 1 none ?
3 20,000 4 8 43
14 700 none none 15
18 2,500 1 none 34
19 1,500 none none 20
12 7,000 1 none 23
4 14,500 5 none 139
11 500 none none 10
13 2,500 none none 12
1 4,000 3 4 19
2 600 none none 8
10 8,000 3 6 38
20 1,500 none none 18
7 300 none none 3
8 2,000 none none 2
16 500 none none 8
15 8,000 4 none 32
Men
FFs
Subs
FACs

## ALGERIA

SINCE gaining her independence from France in 1962, the Mediterranean Sea state of Algeria has pursued a policy of strict non-alignment and has earned considerable respect for its role in resolving various international problems.

The liberation movement had a strong army but no navy or air force, and with the departure of the French these had to be created from scratch. The 4,000 strong navy is equipped almost entirely with Soviet vessels, although some ships have been purchased recently from the United Kingdom. The main bases are at Mers-el-Kebir, Algiers and Annaba.

The principal element in the fleet is a force of four Soviet submarines. There are two elderly Romeo class built in the USSR in the 1950s and transferred to Algeria in the early 1980s on a long-term loan. Two of the later Soviet Kilo class diesel-electric submarines were then sold to Algeria (one in 1987 and the second in 1988).

The major surface units are three Soviet Koni class frigates (1,900tons full-load displacement) supplemented by three Nanuchka class corvettes armed with four SS-N-2C cruise missiles. There are also nine Osa-II and two Osa-I guided-missile patrol boats which have proved less thansatisfactory in service. In addition, there are four Kebir class fast attack craft and three Chinese boats of the SAR type. Attempts to establish a local shipbuilding capability producing a version of the Bulgarian C-58 patrol boat design (the Kebir class) do not appear to have been successful and only one of the three ordered in 1983 has so far been commissioned.

**Above:** *Kalaat Beni Rached* is one of two British-built landing ships in service with the Algerian Navy. A similar ship serves with the Omani Navy as the *Nasr el Bahr*.

The largest ships are two British-designed and built amphibious warfare ships of the Kalaat beni Hammed class. These vessels displace 2,130tons and can carry up to 240 troops or 650tons of stores. There is also one Soviet Polnocny class landing ship.

The coastguard operates some 40 patrol boats, all of them armed with light weapons. In contrast to the navy's policy of buying mainly Soviet equipment, the coastguard operates British and Italian designs; earlier purchases were built abroad but there is a noticeable trend towards building the foreign designs in the Algerian yards at Mers-el-Kebir. The main types are made by Baglietto: the Mangusta A and Type 20 craft.

There are no marines and aerial maritime surveillance is carried out by the air force using the Fokker F-27 and Beech Super King Air 2000.

### EQUIPMENT

**Submarines:**
Soviet Kilo class
Soviet Romeo class
**Frigates:**
Mourad Rais (Soviet Koni) class
**Patrol Boats:**
Soviet Osa-I & and II classes
Kebir class
**Corvettes:**
Rais Hamidou (Soviet Nanuchka-II) class
**Amphibious Warfare:**
Kalaat beni Hammed (British Brooke Marine) class
Soviet Polnocny class

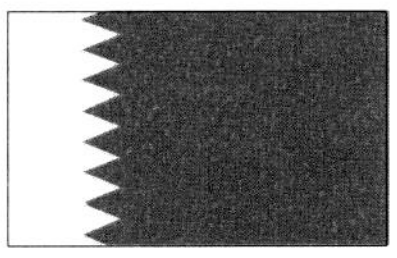

## BAHRAIN

FORMERLY a British protectorate, the Emirate of Bahrain consists of a group of islands in the Persian Gulf and since Britain's withdrawal in the 1960s it has gradually built up its defence forces. Today, the navy is 600 strong and Bahrain has a bilateral defence treaty with Saudi Arabia and was a founding member of the Gulf Cooperation Council in 1981.

Bahrain was a bystander in the Iran-Iraq War, but then became an active participant in the 1990/91 Gulf War. With the successful resistance to Iraqi aggression all the Gulf states have started to review their defence arrangements.

The majority of the small navy's vessels have been built by the German firm of Lürssen; the largest are two FPB 62-001 corvettes known as the Al Manama class. These are similar to the *Victory* class boats supplied by Lürssen to Singapore, except that the Bahraini boats are fitted with a flight-deck for a Dauphin helicopter. The raised helicopter platform incorporates a lift to lower the aircraft into the hangar below, an arrangement reminiscent of the British Tribal class frigates of the 1960s (now serving in the Indonesian Navy as the Martha Khristina Tiyahahu class). These corvettes manage to accommodate four Exocet launchers, a 3in (76mm) DP gun, two 1.6in (40mm) AA guns, two 0.8in (20mm) cannon and the helicopter facilities onto a 632ton displacement hull — no mean achievement for the designers.

There are six other Lürssen fast patrol boats: four El Fateh class (TNC-45) displacing 259tons and two Al Riffa class (FPB-38) displacing 205tons; plus two US Commercial Cruiser class 33ton patrol boats.

There is an even smaller coastguard which, in common with many other Gulf states, reports to the Ministry of the Interior rather than to the Ministry of Defence. It is equipped with 12 motor boats. There are two landing craft, the larger of which displaces 428tons, also operated by the coastguard rather than the navy.

At the end of the Iran-Iraq War, when the danger of mining in the Gulf had become clear, the Bahrain Ministry of Defence announced an intention to purchase three minehunters. No orders had been placed by the time the Gulf War broke out, but it seems likely that the order will be pursued now that the effectiveness of mines has been demonstrated once again.

**Below:** *Al Manama*, one of two Lürssen FPBs with the Bahraini Navy, is very similar to the P6201s serving with the UAE. Note the Exocet tubes just forward of the hangar.

## EGYPT

THE Arab Republic of Egypt has been involved in several wars with Israel in which there has been limited naval action, and despite the Camp David accords the principal threat to Egyptian security remains Israel.

Today the Egyptian Navy is large in manpower terms — some 20,000 men, including 12,000 conscripts — but the number of ships seems rather small in comparison. The navy's task is complicated by the fact that it must cover two areas, the Mediterranean and the Red Sea; although the Suez Canal, provided it is not cut by Israeli action, allows rapid transit between the two. The main naval base and Mediterranean HQ is at Alexandria, with the Red Sea HQ at Hurghada. Other bases are at Port Said, Mersa Matruh, Bur Safaqa, Port Tewfiq and Ras al Tum.

The primary combat element is the eight strong submarine force. There are four Chinese-built Romeo class diesel-electric patrol submarines which were delivered in 1983-84. They are currently being refitted in a joint US/PRC programme which will enable them to launch US Mk 37 torpedoes and Sub-Harpoon missiles. These boats are joined by four ex-Soviet Romeo class which are undergoing refits. Plans to acquire ex-British classes came to nought and these eight make Egypt's force the second strongest submarine force in the eastern Mediterranean (after Turkey).

There are two Chinese-built Jianghu class frigates. These 1,586tons displacement vessels are visually impressive but less so on a more detailed examination. The main weapon system is the Chinese HY-2 anti-ship cruise missile, a land-launched Silkworm version of which was used by Iraq against the Coalition naval forces in the Gulf War and shot down with ease by British Sea Dart missiles.

The Egyptian Navy also operates two Spanish Descubierta class frigates which were originally built for the Spanish Navy but were sold prior to completion. Displacing 1,363tons they have a comparatively heavy armament for their size which, when coupled with a much more comprehensive electronic fit, makes these vessels greatly superior to the Chinese frigates.

The navy operates some 43 patrol boats. Seven of the Soviet Osa class remain in service, each armed with four SS-N-2A Styx missiles; there are also six Chinese Hoko class each armed with two HY-2 SSMs. The 6 October class patrol boats were built in Egypt, using the Soviet *Komar* class hull design, and fitted out in Britain.

The best of the missile patrol boats are six Ramadan class vessels of 312tons displacement which were built by Vosper-Thornycroft in Britain between 1978 and 1982. They are armed with four Otomat anti-ship missiles, a single 3in (76mm) OTO Melara Compact DP on the foredeck and a single twin 1.6in (40mm) Breda mount on the stern.

Finally, there are 12 Chinese boats: eight Hainan class and four Shanghai-II class, all transferred to Egypt in the early 1980s; and six Soviet *Shershen* class torpedo boats.

An attempt to buy two Tripartite minesweepers from The Netherlands in 1986 failed through lack of funds, which means that nine elderly Soviet-designed minesweepers must continue in service. The most up-to-date of these are four Yurka class vessels, displacing 450tons, which were delivered new in 1969, and there has been some talk of modernizing them. The others consist of three T-43 class and two T-301 class, the latter now being confined to harbour tasks.

The remainder of the navy consists of three of the ubiquitous Soviet Polnocny class landing ships and a number of smaller utility landing craft. The only support ships are eight small Soviet-built coastal tankers.

Naval aviation operates 18 Westland Sea King Mk 47 helicopters which are armed with Otomat missiles and used for both ASW and anti-shipping tasks. There are 12 Gazelle helicopters mounting AS-12 wire-guided anti-ship missiles. Other types of air support come from the air force whose inventory includes ELINT, ECM and AEW aircraft, as well as two Beech maritime surveillance aircraft.

To counter the threat of raids from Israeli warships there is a large coastal defence organization which is manned by army troops but is under naval operational control. They are armed with 5.1in (130mm) SM-4-1 guns, and Otomat missiles.

There is a coastguard of some 2,000 men which operates as a branch of the navy. It uses 24 patrol boats and about 60 small craft. There are no naval marines although the army has seven commando groups, one of whose roles would be amphibious.

### EQUIPMENT

**Submarines:**
Soviet Romeo class
**Frigates:**
Najim Al Zafir (Chinese Jianghu) class
El Suez (Spanish Descubierta) class
**Patrol Boats:**
Ramadan class
Chinese Hoku class
6 October class
Soviet Osa class
Chinese Hainan class
Chinese Shanghai-II class
Soviet Shershen class
**Amphibious Warfare:**
Soviet Polnocny class
**Mine Warfare:**
Aswan (Soviet Yurka) class
Assiout (Soviet T-43) class
**Naval Aircraft:**
Westland Sea King Mk 47
Aerospatiale SA.341/342 Gazelle

**Below:** The 6 October class FPBs carry two twin 1.12in (30mm) guns and are fitted with racks for an Otomat SSM system. The design is based on the Soviet Komar class.

**Below:** The Egyptian navy has two Spanish Descubierta class frigates. This is *El Suez*; she is armed with guns, rockets, Harpoon SSMs and NATO Sea Sparrow SAMs.

**Below:** The seven elderly Osa class patrol boats are armed with four SS-N-2A Styx SSMs, but their capability in a modern ECM environment is limited quite considerably.

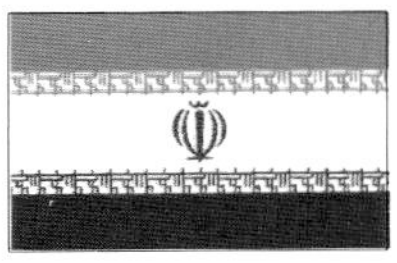

## IRAN

THE Islamic Republic of Iran lies on the Persian Gulf and the Caspian and Arabian Seas. In the 1970s under the last Shah the Iranian armed forces were among the most powerful in the region and were receiving some very sophisticated and modern equipment from the West. It was quite clear that he intended to make Iran the predominant power in the Gulf (if not in the Middle East as a whole) and his naval ambitions were on the grand scale. After 1979 the new revolutionary regime headed by the Ayatollah Khomeini quickly antagonized its former allies, particularly the United States, and the supplies of new equipment and spares dried-up virtually overnight.

Then followed the eight-year Iran-Iraq War. Although the naval theatre was less important than the land to both sides there was still considerable activity in the Gulf, especially when attacks on unarmed merchant ships started and the Western powers began to send warships to protect their oil supplies. The Iranian Navy lost a number of ships, some to Iraqi forces and others to the United States, which sank at least one frigate and one patrol boat as well as a number of smaller craft.

In the 1990/91 Gulf War Iran remained outside the anti-Saddam coalition. However, it was careful not to antagonize the West and this may well lead to a restoration of the supply of new equipment and spare parts which it craves for.

The navy is some 14,500 men strong and includes both a naval air wing and marines. The main base and fleet HQ is at Bandar Abbas, with subsidiary bases at Bushehr, Banda-e-Anzelli, Banda-e-Khomeini, Khorranshar and Kharg Island, with facilities also at Chah Behar, a strategically important port which lies on the Arabian Sea outside the Straits of Hormuz.

The largest units in the navy are three WWII destroyers. The *Damavand* is an ex-British Battle class ship which was modernized, once before her transfer in 1967 and then again during a refit in South Africa in 1975-76. She is armed with four Standard SM-1 SAM launchers, four 4.5in (114mm) guns, four 1.6in (40mm) and two 0.9in (23mm) Soviet AA guns (which replaced a Sea Cat SAM launcher), plus one Squid mortar for ASW. The other two destroyers are the *Babr* and *Palang*, ex-USN Allen M. Sumner class vessels which are also fitted with four Standard SAM launchers. They have retained four of their original 5in (127mm) guns in two twin turrets fore and aft but, like *Damavand*, have had a Soviet twin 0.9in (23mm) cannon mount installed on the quarterdeck.

The most modern surface warships are three Saam class frigates which were built in the UK in 1967-1972. A neat and modern design, these Vosper Mk 5 frigates are armed with a single 4.5in (114mm) DP gun, Sea Killer SSM launchers and two 1.4in (35mm) and two 0.9in (23mm) AA cannon. Four of this class were originally in service but *Sahand* was lost on 19 April 1988 when she was hit by three Harpoon missiles and cluster bombs from American ships and aircraft. A second ship, *Sabalan*, was damaged in the same engagement but has since been repaired. There are also two US PF 103 class frigates which were supplied in the early 1960s and operate today as the Bayandor class.

The 10 French-built Kaman (Combattante II) class patrol boats have had an adventurous career. They were under construction at the time of the Shah's overthrow and delivery of the final three was delayed by the French Government in 1979. They were later released in 1980 but one was then captured at sea by an anti-Khomeini group, although it was later abandoned and eventually reached Iran. Another of the class was later sunk by US forces in the same engagement as *Damavand*, and a further one was captured by Iraqi forces in November 1980. They carry Harpoon

**Below:** Iranian Vosper Mk 5 frigate at sea in the Gulf in April 1988. That same month one Mk 5 was sunk and another damaged by US naval forces using Harpoon SSMs.

**Above:** The Iranian frigate *Alborz* visiting Portsmouth, England, in 1977. The Limbo three-barrelled ASW mortar (which can just be glimpsed near the stern) is still fitted.

**Below:** Twelve of these Combattante-III patrol boats were built for Iran in France between 1977 and 1981. One was sunk by Iraqi forces in 1980 and a second by US forces in April 1988.

missiles and an OTO Melara 3in (76mm) bow gun. There is one ex-USN patrol boat.

There is a small amphibious warfare fleet of 11 vessels. There are four Hengam class (2,940ton displacement) and three Iran Hormuz 24 class (2,014ton) LSTs, two Iran Hormuz 21 class (1,400ton) landing ships and two Iran Asr class (2,274ton) LCTs.

At the time of the revolution two refurbished US Tang class diesel-electric submarines were on order from the USA and six new Type 209s were on order from West Germany. Both governments cancelled the orders, although the Iranians later tried to renew the German contract. The Iranians have since obtained one midget submarine from North Korea and are reported subsequently to have built another to their own design. In late 1990 the commander of the Iranian Navy announced that Iran would soon have a "fleet of submarines". There are only two countries likely to undertake such a deal — the PRC and North Korea — but which of the two has yet to be revealed.

A complicating factor in the Iranian armed forces is the Pasdaran or Revolutionary Guard whose naval element operates a significant number of small attack craft (over 100 various types) as well as controlling the coastal defence artillery and a force of marines. These fanatical forces proved a great nuisance in the Gulf in the mid-1980s, using recoilless rifles and rocket launchers to attack unarmed merchant ships.

Reflecting the Shah's grandiose plans for a bluewater navy are the six large auxilaries. The *Kharg* (33,014tons) is a replenishment oiler built to a modified British Olwen class design, while two smaller oilers of the Bandar Abbas class (5,000tons) were built in Germany. There are also two large water tankers of the Kangan class (12,000tons) which are operated by the navy to supply fresh water to Iranian-owned offshore islands in the Gulf. Finally, the *Chah Bahar* (14,450tons) is a former USN Amphion class repair ship.

The Shah placed orders for a number of hovercraft, including six large BH-7 and eight smaller SR-N6, for fast offshore patrols in Gulf waters. Four of the larger type, which were overhauled in the UK in 1984-85, remain in service but the remainder are inoperable.

The naval air arm inventory includes three Sikorsky SH-3Ds, six Agusta-Bell AB.212 ASWs, and two RH-53D mine counter-measure helicopters. It also has a small transport component with a mixture of fixed-wing and helicopter types. It is not clear how many of these aircraft remain operational.

With the destruction of the Iraqi Navy in the recent war the Iranian Navy is the most powerful single indigenous maritime force in the Gulf. It has the potential to become a significant force in the area, second only in size to the Indian Navy, but first it needs to resolve its maintenance problems.

### EQUIPMENT

**Destroyers:**
Damavand (British Battle) class
Babr (US Allen M Sumner) class
**Frigates:**
Saam (British Vosper Mark 5) class
Bayandor (US PF 103) class
**Patrol Boats:**
Kaman (French Combattante-II) class
Keyvan (US Coastguard Cape) class
**Amphibious Warfare:**
Hengam class
Iran Hormus 24 class
Iran Hormuz 21 class
Iran Asr class
**Mine Warfare:**
Shahrokh (US Falcon) class
**Naval Aircraft:**
Sikorsky SH-3D Sea King
Agusta-Bell AB.212
Sikorsky RH-53D Sea Stallion
Lockheed P-3F Orion

## IRAQ

THE sole Iraqi access to the sea is a narrow strip of coastline at the head of the Persian Gulf with two highly vulnerable bases at Basra and Umm Qasr. Indeed, the frustration caused by this strategic disadvantage is one of the main reasons for Iraq's disputes with Iran, and that with Kuwait over the islands of Bubuyan and Warba.

At the time of the outbreak of the Iran-Iraq War a number of vessels were on order for the Iraqi Navy in what can now be seen to have been the first stage of an ambitious naval expansion plan whose aim was to displace Iran as the major power in the Gulf. Many of the orders were embargoed throughout the war, but when this was lifted the Iraqi Government was so heavily in debt that it found itself unable to finance the deals and so the ships concerned were still not delivered; indeed, some have now been offered for sale to other countries.

During the Gulf War the Iraqi Navy was subjected to devastating attacks by Coalition naval and air forces. It will be some time before the full extent of the damage can be reliably assessed, although it seems highly likely that it has virtually ceased to exist as a viable force. The whereabouts of some of the vessels at the start of the war was unclear and they may have managed to ride-out the conflict in some foreign port.

The largest warship in service at the outbreak of the war in August 1990 was the training frigate *Ibn Marjid* (1,850tons) which was completed in Yugoslavia in 1980. Although armed, she had been considered too vulnerable to operate in the Gulf in the Iran-Iraq War and had been employed as a transport to deliver goods from Europe to the Jordanian port of Al Aqaba from where they were sent overland to their destination.

The main combat strength of the Iraqi Navy lay in a number of elderly Soviet-supplied patrol boats: six Osa-II class (240tons), four Osa-Is (215tons), three SO-1s (215tons) and five Zhuks (60tons). There were also two T-43 class ocean-going minesweepers and three Yevgenya class inshore minesweepers. The fleet was rounded out by six amphibious warfare vessels: three Danish-built modified ro-ro ships (Al Zahraa class of 5,800tons) and three Soviet Polnocny-C class (Atika class of 1,150tons).

Awaiting delivery to Iraq in mid-1990 were a number of vessels which had been embargoed during the conflict with Iran. The most important of these were four Italian Lupo class frigates (2,525tons), one of which had actually been commissioned into the Iraqi Navy in 1985. All of them lay in Italian ports awaiting payment. There were also six modified Wadi M'ragh class patrol boats (685tons) with which the Iraqis intended to form two flotillas, each of one command boat (equipped with a helicopter) and two attack boats. Built by Fincantieri in Italy none had been delivered by mid-1990. Also from Italy was a Stromboli class replenishment oiler commissioned into the Iraqi Navy in 1984, but which has lain in Alexandria in Italy since 1986. The whereabouts of a troop transport and a luxurious presidential yacht are unknown. It will take years to redevelop the Iraqi Navy which is now a spent force.

### EQUIPMENT

**Frigates:**
Hittin (modified Italian Lupo) class
**Corvettes:**
Assad (modified Wadi M'ragh) class

**Right:** Two of the four Italian Lupo class frigates built for the Iraqi Navy which have languished in Italian ports since 1985, due to non-payment of the purchase price.

## ISRAEL

THE Israeli Navy was created during the first Arab-Israeli War of 1948-49, but has always been the junior and smallest of the three services. Its first major success was in the 1956 war when Israeli patrol boats attacked the Egyptian destroyer *Ibrahim el-Awal* so ferociously in a running battle at sea that they were able to board and capture her, then tow her into Haifa harbour in triumph.

In the Six Day War the Israeli Navy sent four LCTs on huge lorries overland to Eilat by day and then returned them northwards at night before repeating the move next day. This so convinced the Egyptians that a major amphibious operation was planned that they sent a number of naval units from the Mediterranean into the Red Sea to counter the apparent threat. This enabled the Israelis to undertake a number of naval actions in the Mediterranean during which they lost a destroyer to a Styx missile. Three Israeli motor torpedo boats (MTB) captured Sharm-el-Sheikh and other MTBs took part in the controversial attack on USS *Liberty*, an electronic surveillance ship which was operating some 14 miles off the Israeli coast.

After 1967 the Israelis decided to purchase patrol boats and submarines. They selected West German designs in both cases, but for political reasons both types had to be constructed abroad — the submarines in the UK and the patrol boats in France. The last five of the 12 patrol boats were embargoed on President de Gaulle's instructions. This led to a daring operation by the Israeli Navy whose crews hijacked their boats from the French port of Cherbourg on 24 December 1969 and sailed them direct to Haifa in a remarkable and skilled operation.

The Egyptians started the naval part of the Yom Kippur War in 1973 by declaring a blockade of Israel in both the Mediterranean and Red Seas. The Israeli Navy fought back with their Sa'ar class patrol boats, armed with Gabriel missiles, dominating the coastal waters off Syria and Egypt to such an extent that not one naval shell or missile was fired at the Israeli coast during the short conflict. Despite this, the Egyptian blockade did have an effect and caused a substantial reduction in commercial traffic to and from Israeli ports.

Since that time the Israeli Navy has been in regular action, both defending its country's coastline from guerrilla attack and carrying out offensive operations, particularly against targets in Lebanon. The Israeli Navy is some 6,000 strong in peacetime, of whom about half are conscripts. Naval headquarters and the main base are at Haifa, with subsidiary bases at Ashdod and Eilat. The navy also has an elite, 500 strong force of commandos and frogmen.

The principal combat strength of the navy lies in its force of 22 missile patrol boats and three missile hydrofoils. Six of the French-built Sa'ar-IIs and four of the Sa'ar-IIIs remain in service. Displacing 250tons and with a top speed of 40kts they are excellent seaboats and, as their voyage from Cherbourg so clearly demonstrated, have an excellent range! The Sa'ar-IIs are armed with five Gabriel SSM launchers, two 1.6in (40mm) Breda cannon and two 0.5in (12.7mm) machine guns (MGs); the Sa'ar-IIIs are armed with two Harpoon launchers, three Gabriels, an OTO Melara 3in (76mm) DP gun and four 0.5in (12.7mm) MGs.

The next class is the Reshev (Sa'ar-IV), built in Israel and somewhat larger with a displacement of 450tons. Thirteen were built, of which three were sold to South Africa and two to Chile with the remaining eight being kept for the Israeli Navy. They have a very heavy armament for boats of this size, consisting of four Harpoon SSMs, eight Gabriels, a 3in (76mm) OTO Melara Compact, a 0.8in (20mm) Mk 15 Vulcan Phalanx CIWS on the foredeck, two 0.8in (20mm) AA cannon and two 0.5in (12.7mm) MGs. The 3in (76mm) gun is specially modified for shore bombardment and is mounted on the quarterdeck. These boats are fully air-conditioned and carry two speedboats on fitted davits.

In the late 1970s a number of navies showed an interest in patrol hydrofoils and various designs were produced. The Israeli Navy ordered three from Grumman, of which one was built in the USA and the other two in Israel between 1982 and 1985.They are armed with four Harpoon and two Gabriel launchers, together with two 1.12in (30mm) cannon and two 0.5in (12.7mm) MGs. Fifteen were to have been bought but delays in the programme, cost overruns and a failure to meet the design top speed of 52kts led to the order being reduced to three. These Flagstaff-IItype are known as Shimrit in IDF service.

At one stage a flight-deck for a light helicopter was fitted to one of the Reshev class in place of its 3in (76mm) gun, but the deck was later removed and the gun re-mounted. A new design of patrol boat, the Aliyah (Sa'ar-4.5) class, is slightly larger, displacing 500tons and is fitted with a hangar and a permanent flight-deck. These

**Above:** *Nirit* of the Romat class fitted out to test systems for the proposed Saar 5 class. Note the Barak VLS and the mast which houses all the sensors and fire-control radar.

**Below:** *Aliya* was the first of the Saar 4.5 class and is capable of 31kts with her four engines. The OTH targeting helicopter gives extra range and sensor abilities.

**Right:** *Shimrit* of the US Flagstaff II design of hydrofoil from the Grumman Lantana Yard. In IDF service it is known as the Zivanit class and an improved type may yet appear.

vessels are armed with four launchers each for Harpoon and Gabriel SSMs, a 0.8in (20mm) Mk 15 Vulcan Phalanx CIWS on the foredeck, two 0.8in (20mm) cannon and four 0.5in (12.7mm) MGs. The helicopter is an SA.366 Dauphin 2 whose primary mission is to provide over-the-horizon targeting for the Harpoon missiles. The same hull was used for two other patrol boats of the Romat class which do not have the helicopter hangar and flight-deck; the extra deck-space is used instead to mount an additional four Harpoon SSM launchers and a 3in (76mm) OTO Melara Compact DP gun. Two Aliyah were built, both being launched in 1989, and two Romats, one being commissioned in 1981 the second in 1982. It is planned to upgrade the Reshev class even further with the addition of the Barak anti-missile missile system.

The Israeli Navy appreciated from an early stage the importance of submarines. As a result they purchased three British T class boats in 1967-68, of which one, *Dakar* (the former HMS *Totem*), disappeared with all hands somewhere in the eastern Mediterranean on 26 January 1968. The two surviving boats were replaced by three Type 206 submarines which were designed in West Germany but constructed by Vickers at Barrow in the UK. These 600ton displacement boats are to be replaced by two new submarines which will be built by Howaldtswerke in Germany, the estimated completion date being 1994.

Also under construction are three 1,168tons displacement corvettes of the Lahav (Sa'ar-V) class. These are being built by Ingalls in the USA and will be the largest ships in the Israeli Navy when they are completed. They are designed to offer minimum infra-red, radar and noise signatures and will mount eight Harpoon and eight Gabriel launchers together with the new Barak SAM system. This consists of 32 vertical launch cells mounted before the bridge, with two missiles for each cell. The Lahav class ships will also be fitted with two 1in (25mm) Sea Vulcan Gatling AA guns, a single 0.8in (20mm) Mk 15 Vulcan Phalanx CIWS and ASW torpedoes. A large flight-deck on the stern will enable two SA.366 Dauphin 2 helicopters to be operated.

The balance of the fleet consists of tens of patrol craft (Dabur and Dvora classes) and seven landing craft. Naval aviation operates three IAI Westwind Sea Scan maritime reconnaissance aircraft and a number of Dauphin helicopters.

## EQUIPMENT

**Submarines:**
Gal (British Vickers Type 500) class
**Patrol Boats:**
Mivtach (Sa'ar-II) class
Sa'ar (Sa'ar-III) class
Reshev (Sa'ar-IV) class
Aliyah (Sa'ar-4.5) class
Romat class

**Above:** *Gal*, name-ship of the three strong submarine class. It carries a totalof 10 Sub Harpoon SSMs and NT 37E torpedoes. The fire-control system is due to update soon.

**Below:** A Super Dvora FAC capable of 36kts and armed with MGs, an Oerlikon gun and rocket launcher. It can also fit SSMs, depth charges and torpedoes if they are needed.

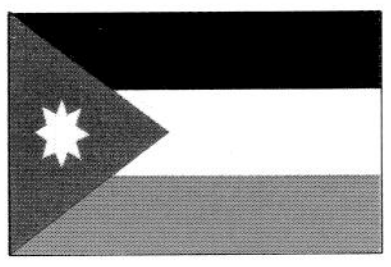

## JORDAN

THE Hashemite Kingdom of Jordan has only one outlet to the sea at the port of Aqaba. The navy consists of some 300 men who operate three Al Hussein class patrol boats (British-built Hawk) and four small GRP craft.

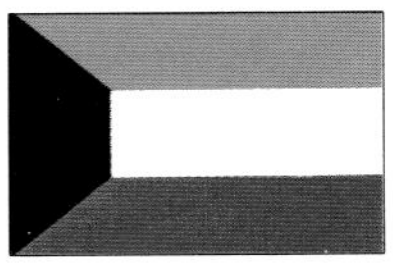

## KUWAIT

THE Sheikhdom of Kuwait was created by the post-WWI settlements and has been repeatedly threatened by Iraq ever since. Situated at the head of the Gulf, Kuwait remained slightly aloof from the military cooperation agreements among the emirates and her defences were shown to be of little value when the Iraqis overwhelmed them by sheer weight of numbers in August 1990.

At the time of the invasion Kuwait had a very small navy consisting of only eight fast patrol boats, a landing-craft and a tug. All the patrol boats were built by Lürssen in West Germany and entered service in 1983/84. Six were of the fast TNC-45 class (259tons and 41.5 kts) armed with four Exocet launchers, a single OTO Melara 3in (76mm) DP, two 1.6in (40mm) cannon and two 0.30in (7.62mm) MGs. There were also two FPB-57 FPBs which acted as flotilla leaders for the TNC-45s. They were slightly larger (398tons displacement) and had identical armaments, with the extra space being devoted to additional sensors and command-and-control facilities. The other naval vessels were four British-built Loadmaster landing craft capable of carrying two 60ton tanks or 150tons of cargo. The navy also operated six Aerospataile AS.332F Super Puma helicopters armed with Exocet missiles. There were two battalions of commandos under naval command.

Quite how many of these vessels and aircraft survived the Iraqi invasion and the Allied bombing is not clear, but it is thought only three did. It is almost certain that the Kuwaiti Navy will have to start again.

## LEBANON

THE troubled country of Lebanon, once an oasis of relative calm in the Middle East, is now a shattered hulk but there is hope of reconstruction. Situated on the Mediterranean its ports are ancient trading posts now being taken back into government control after years under various militias. The small 250-man navy has six small Crestitalia craft, three Biblos and two Edic patrol craft.

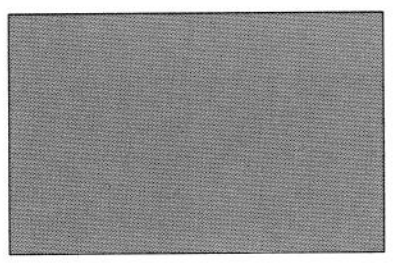

## LIBYA

LIBYA, once home to the Barbary Pirates, lies on the Mediterranean and achieved independence from Italy in December 1951. King Idris was overthrown in September 1969 in a coup d'etat led by Captain Mu'ammar Ghadaffy who remains in charge to this day. Libya's political course has been somewhat erratic and at one stage there were armed clashes with US forces over Libyan claims to territorial waters in the Gulf of Sidra.

The Libyan Navy has an overall strength of 8,000 men (including the coastguard) and the bases are at Benghazi, Dernah, Al Khums, Tarablus, Tobruk and Sidi Bilal.

Its latest surface warships are two Soviet Koni class missile frigates, *Al Hani* and *Al Ghardabia*, which were acquired in 1986/87. These 1,600ton vessels have a useful armament, their major system being four SS-N-2C SSM launchers. Air-defence is provided by one SA-N-4 Gecko SAM launcher, two twin 3in (76mm) turrets and two twin 1.12in (30mm) AA guns, while ASW systems comprise one RBU-6000 rocket launcher and four 15.75in (400mm) torpedo tubes. There are also mine rails. The third frigate in service is the *Dat Assawari* (1,650tons), a British-built Vosper Mark 7 design with four Otomat SSMs, a 4.5in (114mm) Mark 8 DP gun, an Albatros SAM system, two 1.6in (40mm) and two 1.4in (35mm) AA guns, and six ASW torpedo tubes.

There are eight corvettes from three

**Left, above:** Vosper Mk 7 frigate *Dat Assawari* of the Libyan Navy. Since this picture was taken she has refitted and now has an Albatros SAM launcher forward of the bridge and four Otomat SSM launchers.

**Left:** *Assad El Tougour*, an Assad class corvette of the Libyan Navy. This class of four was built in Italy in the late 1970s and the main armament is four Otomat SSMs, although the ships have often been seen without them.

different sources. Oldest is *Tobruk* (500tons), a British Vosper Mk 1B design with a rather poor weapon fit of one 4in (102mm) low-pressure gun and four single 1.6in (40mm) AA guns, with an electronic suite of precisely one navigation radar. The accommodation includes a luxury suite, and it seems more likely that this ship is used as a yacht rather than as a warship. Of greater military value are the Soviet Nanuchka-IIs, four of which were acquired between 1983 and 1985 (one was sunk by US aircraft in March 1986). The third source of corvettes is Italy which provided four Wadi M'ragh class between 1977 and 1981. Armed with four Otomat SSM launchers, these are identical to those built for Iraq.

Ten French Combattante-II missile patrol boats were delivered between 1982 and 1983, of which one was sunk by US Navy aircraft on 24 March 1986. With a displacement of 311tons they are armed with four Otomat SSM launchers, one 3in (76mm) OTO Melara DP gun and two 1.6in (40mm) Bofors AA guns. They are complemented by 12 Soviet Osa-IIs and three light missile boats of the British-built Susa class which are armed with eight French SS-12 launchers, a very outdated missile with a small warhead and poor accuracy. A new type of patrol boat is believed to have been ordered from Yugoslavia in 1985, but as far as is known no deliveries have yet taken place.

It is rather surprising that the small Libyan Navy operates no less than six Soviet-supplied Foxtrot class diesel-electric submarines. These are solid and reliable boats which have served many Third World navies well over the past 20 years. It is probable that Libya will receive some of the new Kilo class Soviet submarines sometime in the future.

The Libyan Navy is completed by six Soviet Natya class ocean-going minesweepers and five landing ships: three Polish Polnocny-C (1,150tons) and two Ibn Ouf class (2,800tons); the latter were built in France in the late 1970s. A fourth Polnocny-C was lost at sea in 1978 in a fire. There are also approximately 25 Turkish-built 600ton C-107 landing craft.

Naval aviation operates only helicopters. There are some 18 Mil Mi-14 Haze and six French Super Frelons, both of which are used for ASW. There are 12 Alouette IIIs for liaison and reconnaissance. There are no dedicated marines.

### EQUIPMENT

**Submarines:**
Al Badr (Soviet Foxtrot) class
**Frigates:**
Al Hani (Soviet Koni) class
Dat Assawari (British Vickers Mk 7) class
**Patrol Boats:**
Sharara (French Combattante-II) class
Al Katum (Soviet Osa-II) class
**Corvettes:**
Ain al Ghazala (Soviet Nanuchka-II) class
Assad (Italian Wadi M'ragh) class
Tobruk (Vosper Mk 1B) class
**Naval Aircraft:**
Aerospatiale SA.316/319 Alouette III
Mil Mi-14 Haze

## MAURITANIA

THIS Islamic Republic has a 500 strong navy with 10 vessels and two Piper Cheyenne II coastal surveillance aircraft. Most boats are from Europe: *El Nasr* is a 148ton PATRA class patrol boat acquired from the French Navy; it is armed with two AA guns, one 1.6in (40mm) Bofors and one 0.8in (20mm) Oerlikon, and two 0.30in (7.62mm) machine-guns. There are three Barcelo class from Bazan (Lürssen FPB 36 class) which are powerful, well-armed vessels. There is also the *Z'bar*, a moderately-armed ex-German Neustadt class vessel. Finaly there is the *N'madi*, a British-build, and four light craft from India.

## MOROCCO

WITH access to the Atlantic Ocean and the Mediterranean Sea, the Kingdom of Morocco's important geographic position was the reason for it being split between France and Spain from 1912 until 1956, when it was reunited and regained full autonomy. Since than a small navy has been maintained, which today numbers some 5,500 officers and ratings. It has bases at Agadir, Casablanca, Dakhla and Al Hoceima; with one exception warships have been obtained from Spain and France.

The largest warship is the *Lieutenant Colonel Errhamani*, a Spanish Descubierta class frigate (1,479tons) which was commissioned in 1983. Unlike the Spanish Navy's ships, she is armed with an Albatros SAM system with 24 Aspide missiles, one 3in (76mm) OTO Melara DP, 14.75in (375mm) Bofors ASW rocket launcher, two 1.6in (40mm) AA guns and six 12.7in (324mm) ASW torpedo tubes. Plans to install four Exocet launchers have never been implemented and orders for two more ships to the same design have yet to be finalized.

Morocco is one of four countries to operate the Osprey 55 class design of patrol boat, although in their case there are no facilities for helicopters. The two ships of the El Lahiq class (500tons) were delivered by Danyard of Fredrikshavn, Denmark, between 1987 and 1990. These ships have a large beam: length ratio which makes them very stable; slowly but surely they are increasing in popularity as their merits become more widely appreciated. They are used by the Moroccans for fishery protection and search-and-rescue duties.

The remainder of the combat fleet consists of similar, light patrol boats. Spain has supplied many types: six Vigilance class, (425tons) armed with one 1.6in (40mm) and two 0.8in (20mm) guns, and four Lazaga class, (420tons) with four Exocets, a single DP gun and three machine guns. All are from Bazan. The French too have been big suppliers: there are two vessels of the Okba class (440tons PR-72 type) and one each of the now elderly *Lieutenant Riffi* (Fouguex class) and *El Sabiq* (Sirius class). In addition there are six El Wacil (French P-92) type wooden-hulled boats.

The fleet is completed by three Daoud Ben Aicha class landing ships (French Champlain class) and one utility landing craft of the French EDIC class (*Lieutenant Malghagh*). There are several auxiliaries and some 1,500 marines in a naval infantry regiment.

### EQUIPMENT

**Frigates:**
Lieutenant Colonel Errhamani (Spanish Descubierta) class
**Patrol Boats:**
El Lahiq (Danish Osprey 55) class
Lieutenant de Vaisseau Rabhi (Spanish Vigilance) class
Commandant al Khattabi (Spanish Lazaga) class
Okba (French PR-72) class
**Amphibious Warfare:**
Daoud Ben Aicha (French Champlain) class

**Below:** *Lieutenant Colonel Errhamani*, seen alongside in Casablanca, is a Spanish Descubierta class frigate. Her 16,000bhp diesel engines give a speed of 25kts and a range of 4,000 miles at 18kts. It is thought two more may be acquired.

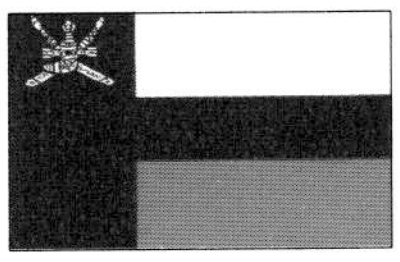

## OMAN

THE Sultanate of Oman lies in a strategically critical position at the south-eastern end of the Arabian Peninsula. It faces Iran across the Gulf of Oman. The powerful sultan has overcome a rebellion in the south and was an enthusiastic member of the Coalition against Iraq in the 1990/91 Gulf War.

The navy is some 2,500 strong and has its headquarters at Seeb, with the main base at Wudham and subsidiary bases at Alwi, Ghanam Island and Raysut. The main combat element is three classes of patrol boats constructed in the UK. The four Vosper Thornycroft 363ton guided-missile boats are in the Dhofar class (named after Omani provinces) and are armed with six Exocets, a 3in (76mm) OTO Melara DP, two 1.6in (40mm) cannon and two 0.5in (12.7mm) machine guns. These are supported by four Brooke Marine 123ft (37.5m) gunboats of the Al Wafi class, with one 3in (76mm) OTO Melara gun which dwarfs everything else on the foredeck, two 0.8in (20mm) and two 0.3in (7.62mm) machine guns. There are also four 82ft (25m) class boats from Vosper designated the Al Seeb class.

Oman has a long coastline with very poor landward communications and a detached territory called Muscat; there is, therefore, a requirement for coastal movement and this is met by a relatively large amphibious warfare component. By far the largest ship in the navy is the 10,900tons *Fulk al Salamah*, a purpose-built troop and vehicle transport from Germany. She is not capable of delivering men and equipment directly over a beach, but carries two Sea Truck landing craft on davits and also has full facilities to operate two Super Puma transport helicopters. At least 240 troops can be carried and vehicles can be offloaded through a large door in the starboard side below the helicopter hangar.

The logistic support ship *Al Munassir* (2,169tons) has a large flight-deck aft, a squat superstructure, stubby foredeck and a perpendicular stem. She can carry eight heavy tanks or a battalion of infantry, but despite being only 12 years old she has been relegated to reserve. Brooke Marine then developed the design into a much more capable (and visually pleasing) ship, one of which serves in the Omani Navy as the *Nasr al Bahr* (2,200tons). This has bow and stern ramps and can land a battalion of infantry or seven heavy tanks over a 1-in-40 beach gradient.

The navy operates two Dornier 228-100 for coastal surveillance plus the Westland Sea King. There are no marines. Importantly, the Royal Oman Police also have a substantial naval element of 13 patrol craft.

### EQUIPMENT

**Patrol Boats:**
Dhofar class
Al Seeb class
Al Wafi class
**Amphibious Warfare:**
Fulk al Salamah class
Nasr al Bahr class
Al Munassir class

**Below:** The heavily armed Omani patrol boat *Dhofar*. The class is similar to Kenya's Nyayo class and is sometimes called the Province class. It has a speed of 38kts.

**Below:** *Al Waafi* was built for Oman by the British firm of Brooke Marine in 1976-77. Although well-armed they are likely to be replaced in the 1990s by 1,200ton vessels.

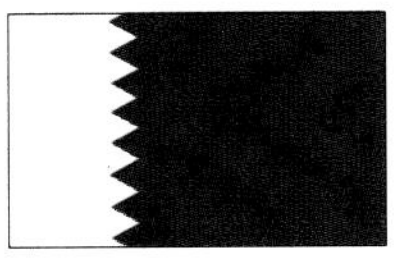

## QATAR

A LARGE peninsula in the southern Persian Gulf, Qatar has a small 700-man navy. Its main element is its three boat Combattante-III compliment known as the Damsah class. These French guided-missile boats are armed with Exocet SSMs, a 3in (76mm) OTO Melara DP and AA gun systems. There are six Barzan class boats, a 103ft (31m) design of Vosper Thornycroft, and six Polycat 1450, a glass reinforced plastic design from The Netherlands. The fleet is completed by 25 Spear class craft from Fairey Marine. There are six Agusta-Sikorsky SH-3D Sea King helicopters engaged in search-and-rescue.

**Above:** The Gulf state of Qatar operates patrol boats, such as *Fateh Al Khair*. Built by Vosper Thornycroft in England in 1975-76 she is armed with four 1.12in (30mm) Oerlikon guns.

## SAUDI ARABIA

THE Saudi Navy has trailed behind its service rivals during the country's military expansion over recent decades. In the late 1970s, however, a naval expansion programme was formulated under the designation "Sawari" and the orders were won by France.

Saudi Arabia has some interesting maritime strategic problems. It has a long western coastline on the Red Sea and an eastern coastline on The Persian Gulf. It is clearly important for Saudi Arabia to move naval vessels between these two operational areas but the route is some 2,000nm long and passes through two choke points

(Rab-al-Mandah and the Straits of Hormuz), neither of which are under Saudi control. The 8,000-man navy played an active role in the recent Gulf War and some Saudi units took part in maritime combat operations against Iraq alongside USN and RN forces.

Naval HQ is at Riyadh and there are two fleets: Western Fleet with its HQ at Jeddah and a second base at Yanbu, and Eastern Fleet with its HQ at Jubayl, with subsidiary bases at Al Dammam, Ras-al-Mishab and Ras-al-Gar.

The pride of the fleet are the four Al Madinah class frigates. These 2,250ton ships are comprehensively armed and equipped, and are said by some to be over-complicated. They have eight Otomat SSM launchers, a Crotale SAM system, a French 3.9in (100mm) DP Compact gun, four 1.6in (40mm) AA guns and four ASW torpedo tubes. They also have a flight-deck and hangar facilities aft for a Dauphin ASW helicopter. They have a very sophisticated electronics fit, much of it using new and untried component systems. These four frigates will be reinforced by three air-defence frigates of a new design which will probably be based on the Cassard class destroyers now joining the French fleet.

The balance of the surface fleet consists of much smaller and older vessels. It includes four Badr class guided-missile corvettes (ex-USN PCG class), nine As Siddiq class guided-missile patrol boats (ex-USN PGC class) and three Dammam class torpedo boats (German Jaguar class).

The menace posed by naval mines has been demonstrated to the Saudi Navy in both fleet areas and the original minesweeper purchase consisted of four Addiriyah class ships obtained from the USA in 1978 (Bluebird class). A new order has been placed recently for six British Sandown class minehunters (Al Jafw class), the first of which was commissioned in 1991.

**Above:** In 1980 the Saudi Arabian government signed the massive naval Sawari Contract with France. The frigate *Al Madinah* was the first vessel to result from that order.

**Below:** *Al Jouf*, with her sister *Turaif* inboard, fitting out at the Blohm und Voss yard in Hamburg. Four are serving, two based at Jeddah and two at Al Dammam.

Surprisingly, considering the long coastline and the poor landward communications, there is only a small amphibious warfare component which comprises 16 craft of limited capacity: four German LCMs and 12 ex-USN vessels, the Afif class (LCU 1646) and eight LCM (6). As befits the Saudi Navy's bluewater ambitions, however, there are two large and sophisticated underway replenishment ships, both re-works of the French Durance class. The *Boraida* and *Yunbou* displace 10,500tons and have refuelling stations on either beam and astern. They mount two twin 1.6in (40mm) turrets and have a flight-deck and hangarage for two Dauphin helicopters. They have also been designed for use as training ships.

The Saudi Navy has firm plans to create an underwater force of up to 10 modern submarines. A variety of designs of various sizes, ranging from 1,000tons to 2,500tons displacement, have been examined but no firm order has yet been announced.

Naval aviation operates only helicopters with 20 ASW role SA.365. F/SA Dauphin 2, four SA.365.N Dauphin 2 search-and-rescue types and 30 Aerospatial e AS.332 Super Pumas with cannon and Exocets.

### EQUIPMENT

**Frigates:**
Al Madinah class
**Patrol Boats:**
As Siddiq (US PGG) class
Dammam (German Jaguar) class
**Corvettes:**
Badr (US PCG) class
**Mine Warfare:**
Al Jawf (British Sandown) class
Addiriyah (US *Bluebird*) class
**Naval Aircraft:**
Aerospatiale SA.365 Dauphin 2
Aerospatiale AS.332 Super Puma

## SUDAN

SUDAN has two naval tasks: the first covers some 500 miles (805km) of coastline on the Red Sea from a base at Bur Sudan, the second is a riverine commitment on the extensive Nile River, with the main base and naval HQ at El Khartum. The small navy of some 500 men is starved of resources and the few ships it has are now in a poor condition. There were eight patrol craft, including four Sewart type 40ft (12m) boats, which were made surplus by the Iranian coastguard in 1975, and four El Gihad class which were a gift from the Yugoslav government. Most are now inoperable.

## SYRIA

SYRIA has become one of the most important states in the Middle East and has assumed a leading role in trying to sort out the problems in Lebanon. Syria itself covers a large area, but has only a relatively short coastline on the Mediterranean; as a result, while the army numbers some 300,000 there are just several thousand men in the navy. The navy is reasonably equipped with relatively modern ships, all of them of either Soviet or Polish origin.

The largest vessels are two Soviet Petya class frigates (1,150tons), with two twin 3in (76mm) guns. One Soviet Natya class corvette was delivered in 1985; this type is outfitted as a minesweeper in the Soviet Navy but the Syrian vessel has neither sweeping gear nor ASW rocket-launchers, leaving an armament of just four 1.12in (30mm) CIWS and four 1in (25mm) cannon.

There are the inevitable patrol boats consisting of eight Osa-II class, six Osa-Is and nine Zhuks. There is also a small minesweeping capability with one T-43 ocean-goer, one Sonya and two Vanya class coastal boats, plus five Yevgenya inshore ships. There is a limited amphibious capability provided by three Polish-built Polnocny-B class landing ships.

There is an underwater fleet too and it has three Soviet-built Romeo class diesel-electric submarines which have been operated since 1985-86. Rumours of the delivery of one or more Kilo class submarines have not so far been substantiated.

The Syrian Navy operates three Kamov Ka-25 Hormone and 20 Mil Mi-14 Haze ASW helicopters. It is also responsible for coastal defence, for which it is equipped with truck-mounted SSC-1B Shaddock and SSC-3 Styx missiles.

### EQUIPMENT

**Submarines**
Soviet Romeo class
**Frigates:**
Soviet Petya-II class
**Patrol Boats:**
Soviet Osa-I & II class
**Corvettes:**
Soviet Natya class
**Amphibious Warfare:**
Soviet Polnocny class
**Mine Warfare:**
Soviet T-43 class
Soviet Sonya class
Soviet Vanya class
Soviet Yevgenya class
**Naval Aircraft:**
Kamov Ka-25 Hormone
Mil Mi-14 Haze

## TUNISIA

THE Republic of Tunisia is another of the former French territories on the North African littoral, sandwiched between Libya and Algeria. It maintains a small, 2,500-man navy with its principal bases at Bizerta, Sfax, Kelibia and Tunis.

The navy itself consists of an ex-USN frigate, *Inkadh*, of 1,850tons displacement armed with two 3in (76mm) DP guns and a 12.7in (324mm) ASW system. The remainder of the fleet is 30 patrol boats of various sizes and capabilities. The largest are three French Combattante-III class vessels (La Galite class) with eight Exocet launchers, an OTO Melara 3in (76mm) DP gun, two 1.6in (40mm) and four 1.12in (30mm) cannon. Three Bizerte class (French P-48) boats purchased in the early 1970s are armed with two 1.16in (40mm) and two 0.8in (20mm) cannon plus eight SS-12 guided-missile launchers whose effectiveness is marginal. There are two Vosper Thornycroft boats (103ft/31m types) purchased in 1977, which are armed with just two 0.8in (20mm) cannon, and two Chinese Shanghai-II gunboats of the Gafsa class. In addition there are several French boats of the 82ft (25m) and 105ft (32m) class and the fleet is completed by Hannibal class coastal minesweepers (ex-USN Adjutant class). There is at least one Aerospatiale AS.365 Dauphin helicopter which is used for search and rescue, and possibly to attack surface ships.

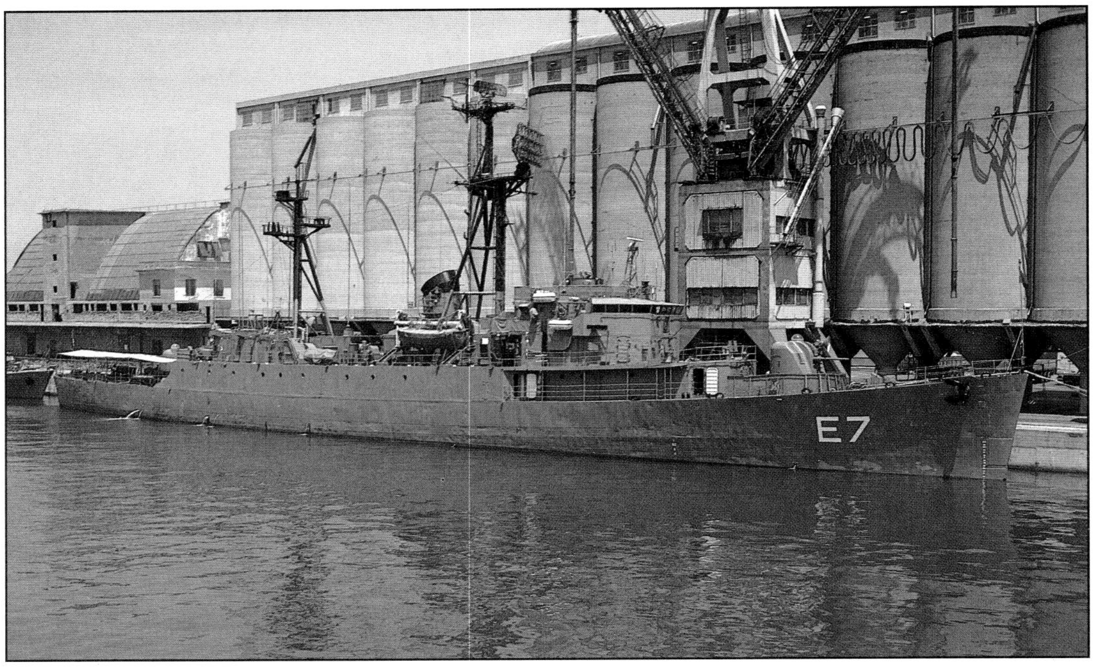


**Above:** The Savage class frigate USS *Thomas J. Gary*, commissioned in 1943, was transferred to Tunisia in 1973, named *President Bourguiba*, then renamed *Inkadh*.

**Right:** *Tunis*, a Combattante-III class fast attack craft in Toulon harbour in June 1987. Note the heavy armament. Electronically sophisticated, these boats also have four powerful engines which give a speed of nearly 40kts and a range of 700miles at 33kts.

## UNITED ARAB EMIRATES (UAE)

THE navy was formed on 1 February 1978 and is responsible for the maritime defence of Abu Dhabi, Ajman, Dubai, Fujairah, Ras el Khaimah, Sharjah and Umm al Qaiwan. It is the smallest of the three defence services and numbers only some 1,500 officers and ratings. Some Sheikdoms also retain boats for independent use; Dubai has two 65ft (19.8m) Commercial Cruiser class Swiftships.

The backbone of the navy is provided by eight guided-missile patrol boats, all built by the firm of Lürssen at Vegesack in Germany. The oldest in service are six Baniyas class (TNC-45) boats which displace 259tons and are armed with four Exocets, one of the widely used OTO Melara 3in (76mm) Compact DP guns, a twin 1.16in (40mm) Breda installation in a turret on the stern and two 7.62mm MGs. These are being supplemented by a new class of two boats, also armed with four Exocets and an OTO Melara 3in (76mm) gun (in a new "super-rapid" version) but with a French Sadral SAM system added. These are developments of Lürssen's FPB-38 design. There are 12 other boats: three Swedish, the others from the UK and designated Ardhana and Kawkab.

Two larger Lürssen Type 62 corvettes were delivered in 1990/91 which displace 630tons and are armed with eight Exocets, one 3in (76mm) DP gun, two Sadral SAM point-defence systems and, possibly, a Dutch 1.12in (30mm) Goalkeeper CIWS as well. These vessels have four engines, four propellers and a top speed of 35kts, making them very effective units indeed. There is a coastguard which reports to the Ministry of the Interior; it operates 40-plus armed patrol craft.

Naval aviation consists of two Britten-Norman BN.42 Maritime Defenders, which are used for maritime patrol, and eight Super Puma helicopters armed with Exocet anti-ship missiles.

### EQUIPMENT

**Patrol Boats:**
P 4401 (Lürssen Mod FPB-38) class
Baniyas (Lürssen TNC-45) class
**Corvettes:**
P 6201 (Lürssen Type 62) class
**Naval Aircraft:**
Aerospatiale AS.332M Super Puma
Britten-Norman BN.42 Maritime Defender

**Below:** The first Lürssen Type 62 guided missile corvette (630tons) for the UAE Navy sails along the Kiel Canal under the German flag prior to delivery. The flight-deck accepts a small helicopter.

## YEMEN

ON 22 May 1990 the two states of the Yemen Arab Republic (North Yemen) and The People's Democratic Republic of Yemen (South Yemen) combined to form the Republic of the Yemen. The armed forces of the two once separate states are in the process of integrating and it is assumed here that the two navies have now completed that process. Both used mainly Soviet equipment so it should not have been too difficult.

The main units in the 1,500-man navy are patrol boats. The largest are six Soviet-supplied Osa-II class guided-missile boats and three smaller (90tons) boats of US construction (ex-USN Broadsword class) armed with Soviet machine-guns. In addition there are nine Zhuk and two Mol class.

There are five Soviet Yevgenya class minesweepers and a single Ropucha class LST which, with its 3,200tons displacement, is by far the largest vessel in the navy. There are also three Polnocny-B LCTs, a fourth having been destroyed by fire during a coup in 1986, and two Ondatra class.

There is no naval aviation and there are no marines.

### EQUIPMENT

**Patrol Boats:**
Soviet Osa-II class
25 September (US Broadsword) class
**Amphibious Warfare:**
Soviet Ropucha class
Soviet Polnocny class
Soviet Ondatra class
**Mine Warfare:**
Soviet Yevgenya class

# SUB-SAHARAN AFRICA

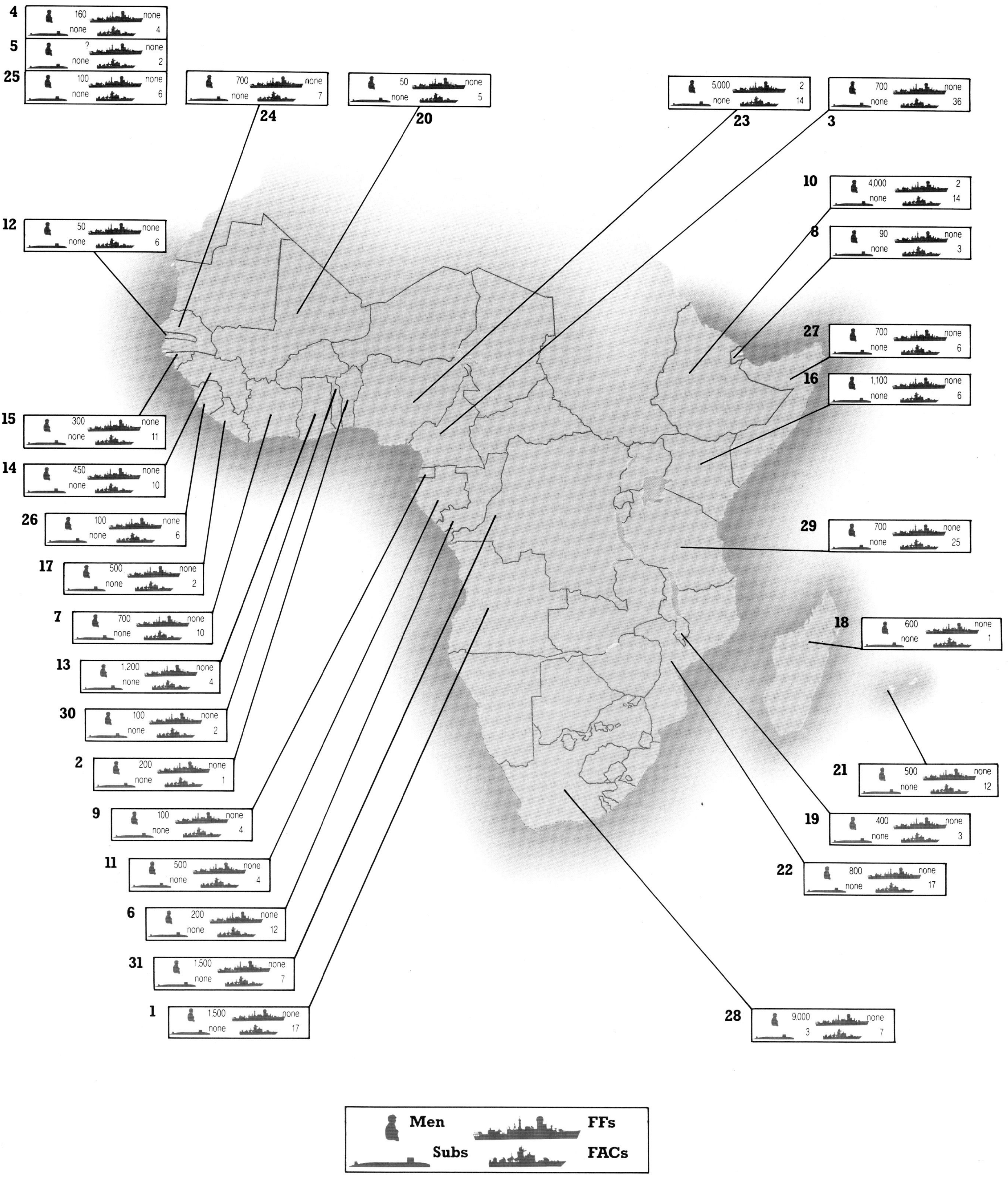
4 160 none none 4
5 ? none none 2
25 100 none none 6
24 700 none none 7
20 50 none none 5
23 5,000 2 none 14
3 700 none none 36
10 4,000 2 none 14
8 90 none none 3
12 50 none none 6
27 700 none none 6
16 1,100 none none 6
15 300 none none 11
14 450 none none 10
26 100 none none 6
29 700 none none 25
17 500 none none 2
7 700 none none 10
18 600 none none 1
13 1,200 none none 4
30 100 none none 2
2 200 none none 1
21 500 none none 12
9 100 none none 4
19 400 none none 3
11 500 none none 4
22 800 none none 17
6 200 none none 12
31 1,500 none none 7
1 1,500 none none 17
28 9,000 none 3 7
Men
FFs
Subs
FACs

## ANGOLA

THE former Portuguese territory of Angola on the Atlantic coast achieved independence in 1975 and virtually all its naval and military equipment since then has come from the USSR. The navy, some 1,500 strong, has its HQ at Luanda with other bases at Lobito and Namibe.

The largest vessels in the navy are five landing craft: three Soviet Polnocny-B (800tons) and two Dutch-built commercial landing craft (850tons). There are 13 Soviet-built patrol boats: five Osa-II, four Shershen, two Zhuk and two Poluchat-I, of which only the SS-N-2 Styx-armed Osa-IIs have any significant offensive capability. In addition, there are four patrol craft which formerly belonged to the Portuguese (Argos class).

The most recent vessels are two small Yevgenya class (90tons) inshore minehunters delivered in 1987. The mine threat to Angolan waters seem limited and they are most likely to be used for patrol tasks. It remains a possibility that a number of patrol boats and landing craft may be bought from Bazan in Spain.

### EQUIPMENT

**Patrol Boats:**
Soviet Osa-II class
Soviet Shershen class
**Amphibious Warfare:**
Soviet Polnocny-B class
**Mine Warfare:**
Soviet Yevgenya class

## CAMEROUN

SITUATED on the Gulf of Guinea, Cameroun has some 250 miles (402km) of coastline and like most former French territories in the area it has a small navy tasked with a patrol mission. Consisting of some 700 men the navy has its HQ at Douala.

There are several LCVP landing craft and the remainder is composed of a variety of fast attack or patrol craft. The main units are two French P-48 boats. The older of these, *L'Audacieux* (250tons), is armed with two 1.6in (40mm) Bofors and was supplied in 1976; the newer boat, *Bakassi* (308tons), was delivered in 1983 and is armed with eight MM-40 Exocet SSMs as well as two Bofors. In addition there are two Chinese boats, one elderly French craft and several dozen 38ft (11.6m) patrol craft from the USA.

### EQUIPMENT

**Patrol Boats:**
French P-48 type
Chinese Shanghai-II class
US Swiftship type

**Below:** A small French-built patrol boat, one of a number used by the Cameroun gendarmerie. They are employed on patrol and general duties on the Chad River, based at Doula.

## BENIN

BENIN is on the southern coast of Africa on the Gulf of Guinea. The Benin Navy is a coastal patrol force of some 200 men, with its HQ at Cotonou. The largest and newest vessel is the *Patriote* (70tons), a French 125ft (38m) patrol boat armed with a 0.8in (20mm) cannon and two machine-guns. The remaining vessels are four Soviet Zhuk class patrol boats (60tons) and two Soviet-designed P-4 hydroplanes which were supplied by North Korea without their torpedo tubes. Maintenance is believed to be very poor and it is possible that only *Patriote* is operational.

### EQUIPMENT

**Patrol Boats:**
French Patriote class
Soviet Zhuk class

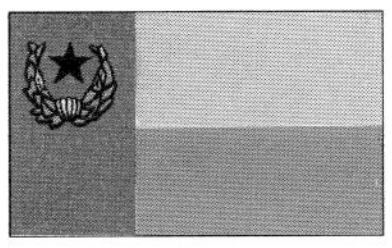

## CAPE VERDE ISLANDS

THIS Atlantic Ocean Island group is 385miles (620km) off the west coast of Africa but despite its setting it has a tiny navy of only 160 men. There are four Soviet-supplied patrol boats armed with machine-guns: two Shershen class (170tons) and two Zhuk class (60tons). There are also a few auxiliaries, including an oceanographic survey vessel supplied under the Icelandic foreign aid programme.

### EQUIPMENT

**Patrol Boats:**
Soviet Shershen class
Soviet Zhuk class

**Below:** The two Shershen class patrol boats operated by the naval force of the Cape Verde Island. Supplied by the USSR in 1979 they have had their torpedo tubes removed.

## COMORES

**S**ITUATED in the Indian Ocean off the east coast of Africa, the island state of Comores possesses two armed Japanese Yamayuri class patrol craft (40ton) and two transport ships.

## CONGO

**O**N the Atlantic coast of Central Africa, the People's Republic of Congo divides its 200-man navy into two elements: the coastal force and the riverene force. The main units of the coastal force are three Marien Ngouabi class (Spanish Pirana class) patrol boats (125ton) which were delivered in 1982-83. There are also six Soviet Zhuk class patrol boats, a Soviet Shersen class torpedo boat (less its torpedo tubes) and three Chinese Shanghai II class patrol boats.

Maintenance standards appear to be poor as the three Ngouabi class boats were inoperable within a year of delivery and had to be returned to the builders for a complete rebuild in 1985. Despite this experience all were again inoperable by late 1989, and it can be assumed that the same problems exist with the other boats.

The riverene force is equipped with four French-supplied patrol boats and a number of locally-produced light craft.

### EQUIPMENT

**Patrol Boats:**
Marien Ngouabi (Spanish Pirana) class
Soviet Zhuk class
Soviet Shershen class
Chinese Shanghai-IIclass

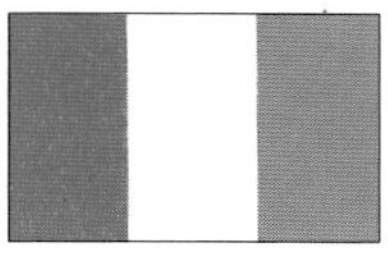

## COTE D'IVOIRE

**T**HE 700 strong navy has its main base at Abidjan (Locodjo) with several subsidiary ones elsewhere. Principal combatants are two L'Ardent fast-attack craft (French Patra class), two PR-48 patrol boats (Vigilant class) and six Rotork coastal craft. The largest single unit is *Elephant* (1,330tons), a BATRAL-E landing ship.

## DJIBOUTI

**D**JIBOUTI occupies a strategic position in the Horn of Africa on the Gulf of Aden and, although independent, still has a sizeable French garrison of over 3,000 men. Djibouti thus maintains only nominal forces of its own and its tiny navy (90 men) comprises three French-supplied patrol boats which are used for coastal surveillance: *Moussa Ali* and *Mont Arreh* of the Plascoa class; and *Zena* of the Tecimar class.

## EQUATORIAL GUINEA

**E**QUATORIAL Guinea consists of Rio Muni on the Atlantic coast of West Africa and the two offshore islands of Annobon and Bioko. It maintains a naval force of some 100 men and two coastal patrol boats. The *Isla de Bioko* of the Lantana type was a gift from the USA, while *Riowele*, a Dutch P-20 type, was a gift from Nigeria. It seems likely there are a couple of Chinese Shantou class armed with four 1.45in (37mm) guns and two MGs.

## ETHIOPIA

**E**THIOPIA is situated in the Horn of Africa on the Red Sea and with the victory of seccessionist rebels in the civil war — guerrillas from the provinces which provide the access to the sea — it remains to be seen what will become of the Ethiopian Navy.

Most vessels have been supplied by the USSR. The largest are two Zerai Deres class (1,160tons) frigates, which are standard Soviet Petya-IIs armed with four 3in (76mm) DP guns, two RBU-6000 ASW rocket launchers, 10 torpedo tubes and depth-charges. These are supplemented by four Osa-II class guided-missile boats with four SS-N-2 Styx missiles.

For inshore work there are 10 patrol boats. The largest are two Soviet Turya class semi-hydrofoils which mount two 2.25in (57mm) DP guns, two 1in (25mm) cannon and four torpedo tubes. They displace 250tons and have a top speed of 38kts. Somewhat slower are two Mol class (220tons) and two Zhuk class (60tons). Three US-supplied, 118ton Swiftships and a former Dutch minesweeper (Dokkum class) complete the inventory.

The amphibious warfare shipping is a curious mixture, with six similarly sized LCTs (6-800tons) of which two come from the USSR, two from Germany and two from France.

At one time the navy operated two DHC Twin Otters, some Bell UH-1 helicopters and a number of Soviet Mi-14 Haze ASW helicopters. Whether any of these are still in service is not clear.

### EQUIPMENT

**Frigates:**
Zerai Deres (Soviet Petya-II) class
**Patrol Boats:**
Soviet Osa-II class
Soviet Mol class
Soviet Turya class
**Amphibious Warfare:**
LTC 1037 (Soviet Polnocny-B) class
Chamo (German Schichau) class
LTC 1035 (French EDIC) class

**Below:** Soviet-supplied Petya-II class frigate of the Ethiopian Navy. This navy uses mainly Soviet equipment, although some US, German and French ships are serving.

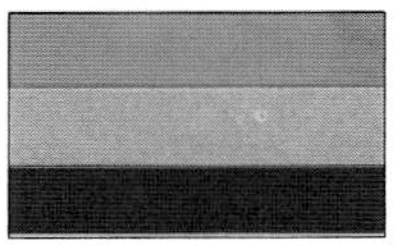

## GABON

SITUATED on the Atlantic Ocean, Gabon is a poor country with many tribes. The 500 strong navy operates predominantly French equipment and has a base at Libreville with the HQ at Port Gentil. The major combat vessel is *General d'Armee Ba Oumar*, a 446tons Super PATRA class vessel constructed by CMN Cherbourg. She is armed with a single 2.25in (57mm) Bofors gun and two 0.8in (20mm) Oerlikon cannon. A second vessel of this type is on order. There are also three other much smaller patrol craft, including a P400 type. The largest ship is a French Champlain class landing ship, *President el Hadj Omar Bongo*.

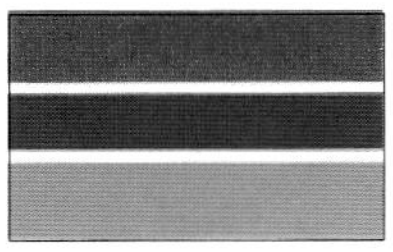

## GAMBIA

GAMBIA is a state founded around the lower reaches of the Gambia River and surrounded by the state of Senegal. Their army includes a 50-man marine unit based at Banjul. It operates four small British-supplied patrol craft (three Tracker types and a Lance boat) and two Chinese-supplied Shanghai class.

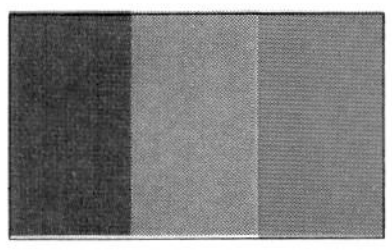

## GUINEA

THE 450-man Guinean Navy is officially a coastguard. It has its HQ at the capital, Conakry. The majority of the fleet consists of patrol boats but there is also a Soviet T-58 minesweeper without its gear which has four 2.25in (57mm) guns and four 1in (25mm) guns. Of the patrol boats there are two US-supplied Swiftships, one 77ft (23.5m) and one 65ft (19.8m) overall, two Soviet Zhuk class boats, two French P400 92ft (28m) type boats, and two Stinger class. All are armed with MG. There is also a Bogomal class FAC with a 3in (76mm) gun.

## GUINEA-BISSAU

THE West African navy of Guinea-Bissau has some 300 men and a mixture of vessels from five different sources. Most are patrol boats but the USSR has also supplied two Matka class hydrofoils; there are several Spanish LVC-1 landing craft too. Other boats are four Soviet Bogomol class (245tons) and two Poluchat class (90tons), two Chinese Shantou class (80tons), two French Plascoa 1900 class (30tons) and one Dutch PT 1903 MkIII class (33tons). All of these are armed with machine-guns, but the Shantou class boats also have four 1.7in (37mm) guns each.

There is a dispute with Senegal over territorial waters and in 1990 three Guinea-Bissau ships were arrested as the issue continued to smoulder.

## GHANA

GHANA, the former British colony of the Gold Coast, lies on the Gulf of Guinea in West Africa. It has a small navy of some 1,200 men and operates from two bases at Sekondi and Tema. At one time it operated several frigates, but due to lack of maintenance funds these have become virtually useless and are unlikely to be restored to service. The present naval force consists of a variety of fast, well-armed patrol boats purchased from Lürssen in Germany; the two FPB-57s, the Achimota class (410tons), were delivered in 1981 and are armed with one 3in (76mm) DP gun and one 1.6in (40mm) Bofors AA; the two FPB-45s, Dzata class (252tons), are slightly smaller and armed with two 1.6in (40mm) guns. Naval aviation is provided by the air force which operates two Fokker F-27-400M on maritime surveillance duties. There is no force of Marines.

**Below:** *Yogaga* is one of two Lürssen FPB-57 class patrol boats in the Ghanian navy. Delivered in 1981 she was completely refitted by Swan Hunter in the UK in 1988-89. Main gun armament is a 3in (76mm) OTO Melara DP.

## KENYA

A FORMER British colony, Kenya has proved to be one of the most stable countries in Africa with efficient and effective military forces. The navy has a strength of some 1,100 men and its main base is at Mombassa. All current naval ships have been purchased in the UK, although the weapons come from a variety of sources, including Italy and Israel.

There are six large patrol boats: the two Nyayo class (363tons) fast-attack craft were delivered in 1987 with a heavy armament for their size which consists of four Otomat SSM launchers, a 3in (76mm) Otomat DP gun, two 1.12in (30mm) and two 0.8in (20mm) AA cannon; the three Madaraka class (145ton) and one Mamba class patrol boats are armed with four Israeli Gabriel SSMs and two 1.12in (30mm) AA cannon. Three Simba class craft are now deleted. All these boats are well maintained and are refitted and updated regularly.

**Below:** Kenyan Navy patrol boat *Umoja* on maker's trials prior to delivery in 1988. Her four diesels give 40kts and she also has two 100hp electric motors for patrolling.

**Bottom:** Kenyan patrol boat *Mamba* in 1990 on completion of a long refit. The mount on the foredeck is a newly-installed BMARC twin 1.12in (30mm) Oerlikon cannon.

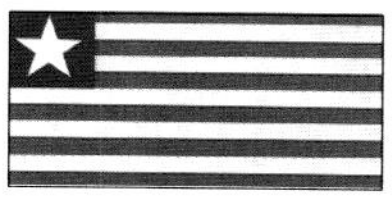

## LIBERIA

THE West African state of Liberia has a small coastguard at Monrovia which operates one Swedish patrol boat, a Korean Tacoma craft and a Cessna 337 Skymaster aircraft for coastal reconnaissance.

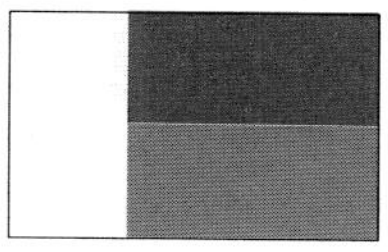

## MADAGASCAR

A LARGE island in the Indian Ocean off the south-east coast of Africa, the republic of Madagascar was once a French colonial territory. Its 600-man naval force operates from Diego Suarez and Nossi-Be. It has just one medium-sized patrol boat of the Malaika class (P48) and two rather larger landing-ships, one built with French aid at Diego Suarez. Six small craft complete the fleet, a surprisingly small navy considering its island status and strategic position. The navy also has a company of marines in its ranks.

## MALAWI

THE 400 strong marine police have several boats for use on Lake Nyasa: *Chikala* is a 36ton French SFCN design armed with a light machine-gun; P702 is a 4ton Fairey Marine Spear class; *Namacurra* is a South African-supplied vessel; and there are two launches.

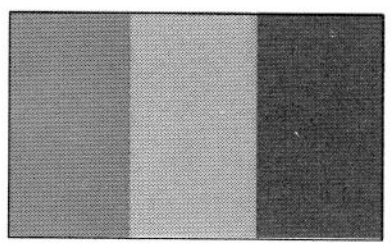

## MALI

IT received two Yugoslav patrol boats from Libya in 1974 and has three smaller ones. All are for the 50-man navy to undertake patrols on the Niger River from a variety of bases at the headwaters.

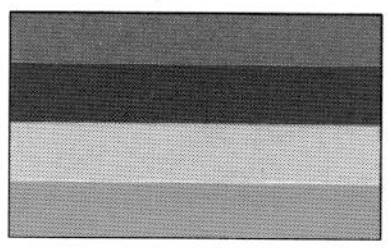

## MAURITIUS

THE former British colony of Mauritius is a densely populated (nearly one million) island republic in the Indian Ocean some 500miles (800km) east of Madagascar. It has a small coastguard which is equipped with nine patrol craft. Two Zhuk class were supplied by the USSR in 1989, the others by India. There is a deep-water harbour at Port Louis.

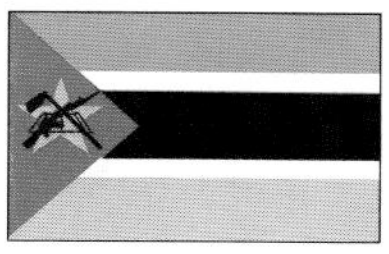

## MOZAMBIQUE

LOCATED in eastern Africa on the Indian Ocean, Mozambique has a very small navy of some 800 men operating mostly Soviet vessels. The main base is at Maputo on the coast, but there are also some units operating on Lake Nyasa. The USSR has supplied two SO1 class (215tons) and three Zhuk class (60tons) patrol boats, as well as two Yevgenya class minehunters which are almost certainly used only as patrol boats. In addition there are as many as 10 Indian-built patrol boats.

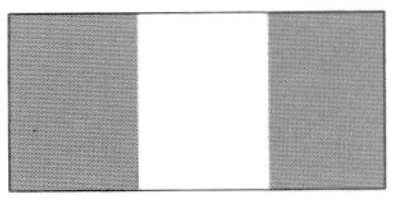

## NIGERIA

FORMERLY a British territory, Nigeria has the largest and most important navy in black Africa with 5,000 men. It is organized into two commands: Western Command at Lagos and Eastern Command at Calabar. There is also a large coastguard which operates at sea under naval command with its craft manned by naval personnel; a marine police force patrols the Niger River and Lake Chad.

The largest ship in the navy is *Aradu* (3,680tons), a German MEKO 360 frigate. She is armed with eight Otomat SSMs and a single Albatros SAM launcher, together with one 5in (127mm) main gun and eight 1.6in (40mm) AA guns. Anti-submarine armament includes six torpedo tubes and a Westland Lynx helicopter. This large and sophisticated ship seems to have suffered some bad luck in service, having not only collided at sea but run aground in the Congo River in 1987 and then struck a pier on her return to Lagos a month later.

A second frigate is the training ship *Obuma* (2,000tons), a "one-off" design from The Netherlands whose armament of two 4in (102mm) guns and four 1.6in (40mm) cannon would enable her to be used operationally, if required. In addition there are three corvettes; two Vosper Mk9 class (850tons) entered service in 1980 as the Erin'mi class. They have a heavy armament for their size, with a 3in (76mm) gun, Sea Cat SAM launcher, one 1.6in (40mm) and two 0.8in (20mm) AA cannon, and an ASW rocket launcher. These two ships are reported to be in poor repair and in urgent need of a refit. There were also two Vosper Mk3 corvettes, but one of these sank at her moorings in 1987 and the other — *Otobo* (650tons) — was allowed to deteriorate very badly after fumigation treatment had caused serious corrosion. She is now in Italy being refitted and converted to an offshore patrol vessel.

There are 14 patrol boats, six of which are armed with guided missiles. The two classes of these boats are very similar to each other, the three Siri class having been constructed in France (Combattante-IIIB) and the three Ekpe class in Germany (Lürssen FPB 57). Both are armed with one 3in (76mm) DP gun, two 1.6in (40mm) Breda-Bofors AA cannon and four Emerlec AA guns, the main difference is that the French boats are fitted with four MM40 Exocet while the German boats have four Otomat SSMs. The two have identical power units but the Lürssen boats are slightly faster, having achieved the remarkable speed of 42kts in trials. The other patrol boats are the Makurdi class (four boats of the British Brooke Marine type) and four German

**Left:** Nigeria's *Aradu*. There is a single 5in (127mm) gun forward, a twin 1.6in (40mm) AA at each corner of the super-structure and an Aspide SAM launcher forward of the hangar. No Otomats are fitted.

**Below:** *Erin'mi*, a Vosper Mk 9 corvette. The gun is an OTO Melara 3in (76mm) DP and the weapon immediately before the bridge is a Bofors twin-barrel 14.75in (375mm) ASW rocket launcher.

**Left:** Three Westland Lynx Mk 89s are operated for use aboard the *Aradu*. There are also two Bo-105 light helicopters which are used for shore liaison duties.

boats designated the Argundu class. The marine police have an additional six Tiger class craft and the coastguard 35 medium-sized and 50 small patrol craft.

There are two mine countermeasure ships — the popular Italian Lerici class — and two landing ships constructed in Germany to round out the fleet.

The naval air component operates three Westland Lynx ASW helicopters for use aboard the frigate *Aradu*. Other aircraft are operated by the air force.

**EQUIPMENT**

**Frigates:**
Aradu (German MEKO 360H) class
Obuma class
**Patrol Boats:**
Siri (French Combattante-IIIB) class
Ekpe (German Lurssen FPB 57) class
**Corvettes:**
Erin'mi (British Vosper Mk9) class
Dorina (British Vosper Mk3) class
**Amphibious Warfare:**
Ambe (German Type 502) class
**Mine Warfare:**
Ohue (Italian Lerici) class
**Naval Aircraft:**
Westland Lynx Mk89

## SENEGAL

THE Senegalese Navy is 700 strong and has its HQ at Dakar. The largest ship is the recently-acquired Fouta (500tons), one of the Thorneycroft Giles wide-beam designs being produced by Danyard A/S in Frederikshavn, Denmark, as the *Osprey* 55 type. She is armed with two 1.12in (30mm) cannon and a machine-gun, and is used for economic zone patrols and fishery protection.

There are six other patrol boats: *Njambuur* is of the French PR 72 MS type, the three Saint-Louis class are of the French P48 class, and there are two of the Chinese Shanghai-II class. Like most former French territories she also operates a French EDIC 700 type landing ship and two ex-USN landing craft.

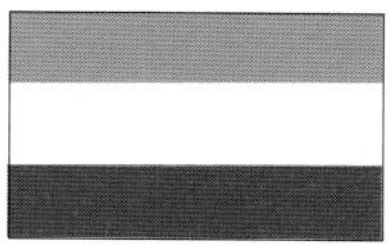

## SIERRA LEONE

SIERRA LEONE, on the West African coast, operates two Chinese Shanghai II patrol boats, four smaller types and three small Japanese-built landing-craft with its small, 100-man navy.

## SOMALIA

SOMALIA is in the Horn of Africa and lies on the Gulf of Aden and the Indian Ocean. It is a large country with extensive coastlines and there are three main naval bases for the 700-man navy: Berbera, Kismayu and Mogadishu, the capital.

All Somalia's boats are of Soviet origin and many are in poor condition. There are two Osa-II guided-missile boats, four Mol class boats and four T-4 light landing-craft.

**Below:** A Zhuk class patrol boat and *Topaz*, the former French minesweeper *Croix de Sud*, of the Seychelles Navy. The Zhuk's two twin 14.5mm MGs are visible fore and aft.

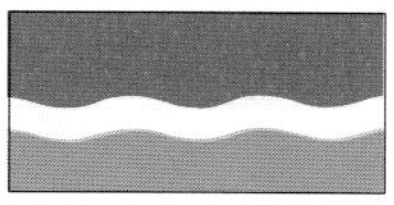

## SEYCHELLES

THE island republic of the Seychelles consists of some 100 islands in the Indian Ocean but despite the size has a very small naval force (100 men) based in Port Victoria. There is a French medium tank landing ship, *Cinq Juin*, and the remainder are patrol boats. There are several Soviet vessels: one Turya class (but without hydrofoils) and two Zhuk class. There are also two other boats, one ex-Italian FPB42, *Andromache*, and one ex-French Sirius class minesweeper, *Croix du Sud*. Most are fairly well armed

**Above:** The Seychelles Navy uses one Pilatus Britten-Norman Maritime Defender for coastal surveillance and surface search. It has search radar and can be armed.

## SOUTH AFRICA

THE Republic of South Africa occupies a most important strategic position at the southern tip of Africa with the Atlantic Ocean to the west and the Indian Ocean to the east, and even today a large amount of maritime trade still goes round the Cape of Good Hope.

South Africa's navy is the smallest of its three military services and, like the others, its equipment policy has been seriously affected by the lengthy international arms embargo. This has not only meant that new ships have been difficult to obtain, but also that, despite very high maintenance standards, existing ships have become increasingly difficult to keep in service due to a shortage of spare parts.

The navy has some 9,000 personnel, approximately half of them conscripts, and its marines force has been disbanded. There are a number of well-equipped operational bases, notably Port Elizabeth and Simonstown, as well as an enclave in Namibia called Walvis Bay which has been retained because of its strategic value. Organizationally, the navy has two commands: Western Command with its HQ in Cape Town; Eastern Command with its HQ in Durban.

The fleet did have two British Leander class frigates, but due to the embargo one had to be put into reserve in 1981 and is now a hulk, and the second was put in reserve in 1986; it is highly improbable that she will again be put into commission. The major surface combatants are therefore the seven remaining (out of 12) Minister class guided-missile patrol boats. These are direct copies of the Israeli Reshev class; the first was constructed in Israel and the remainder in South Africa. They are armed with six Skorpioen SSMs, a South African-produced copy of the Israeli Gabriel II missile. They also have two 3in (76mm) DP guns, two 0.8in (20mm) AA guns and four 0.5in (12.7mm) AA machine-guns. Other patrol boats are four FL9 type.

There are four Umkomaas class minesweepers (380tons) built in Germany in the mid-1980s as "fishing boats" which, upon their arrival in South Africa, were armed and fitted with minesweeping gear. Four elderly British Ton type mine warfare vessels also remain in service but are being retired progressively.

The capability of the South African shipbuilding industry has been demonstrated by the completion of the 12,500ton fleet replenishment ship *Drakensburg*, which was commissioned in 1987. However, with the retirement of the frigates there is little use for her in her primary role and she is now used as a patrol ship.

**Above:** *Drakensburg*, a fleet replenishment ship, was built in South Africa but there is now no surface fleet requiring her services so she is used as a patrol and SAR ship.

**Left:** The South African navy bought 10 British Ton class minesweepers in the 1950s. Four of these vessels are left in service, supplemented by four German minehunters.

Three French Daphne class submarines entered service in 1970-71 and have given many years of service. It was decided to give them all a major refit in South Africa; one completed in 1988, the second is halfway through and the third will follow in its turn. Two French Agosta class submarines were ordered in 1975, but were embargoed and sold to Pakistan instead. The navy very much wants new submarines and there have been repeated rumours of attempts to obtain plans of the Type 209 from IKL.

There is no naval air arm, but a section of the air force is permanently assigned to maritime duties. This is equipped with Piaggio Albatross aircraft and Wasp, Super Frelon and Puma helicopters. So severe is the pressure imposed by the embargo that two ancient C-47 Dakotas have been fitted with radars for maritime patrol!

### EQUIPMENT

**Submarines:**
Maria van Riebeck (French Daphne) class
**Patrol Boats:**
Minister (Israeli Reshev) class
**Mine Warfare:**
Umkomaas class
Kimberley (British Ton) class
**Naval Aircraft:**
Piaggio P-166S Albatros
Westland Wasp HAS.1
Aerospatiale Alouette SA.330 Puma
**Marines:**
One battalion

**Above:** *Hendrik Mentz*, an Israeli Reshev class patrol boat in service with the South African Navy. In 1991 three of this class and (opposite) *Drakensburg* visited Taiwan to show the flag.

**Below:** *Maria van Riebeck* is one of three French Daphne class submarines supplied to South Africa in 1970/71. They are old, but the arms embargo makes spares hard to obtain.

## TANZANIA

TANZANIA is composed of Tanganyika on Africa's eastern coast together with the Indian Ocean islands of Zanzibar, Pemba and other smaller islets. The 700-man navy is responsible for coastal patrols from its bases at Dar es Salaam and Zanzibar, and for the policing of Lake Victoria from Mwanza. Like many other African navies it is equipped primarily with patrol boats obtained from a variety of Communist countries, although it also has some Chinese landing craft of the Yu Chai class and two East German Schwalbe class minesweepers.

The principal patrol boat supplier is China with 15 (seven Shanghai-IIs, four Huchuans and four Yu Lins), then North Korea which has supplied five Kimjin patrol craft. The condition of all these boats is generally poor. Autonomous Zanzibar has four armed patrol craft.

**Below:** *JW 9864*, a Chinese Shanghai-II patrolboat, is one of seven transferred to the Tanzanian Navy in 1970-71. Beyond are a second Shanghai-II, a Huchuan class torpedo boat and a German-built survey craft.

## TOGO

TOGO is located on the Bight of Benin and its small, 100-man navy, based in Lome, operates just two wooden-hulled inshore patrol boats supplied by France in 1976.They are of the Esterel 105ft (32m) type and are designated Kara class.

## ZAIRE

ZAIRE has a very short Atlantic Ocean coastline of just 23 miles (37km). Its navy is some 900 strong and has an additional force of 600 marines. The navy operates five Chinese Shanghai-II patrol boats and two North Korean Sin Hung class patrol craft. There are also a number of small patrol craft deployed on Lake Tanganyika and the many rivers; most of these are from France and the USA.

# Index

**Illustrations are indexed in italics.**

## List of abbreviations

| | |
|---|---|
| AA | Anti-Aircraft |
| AAW | Anti-Air Warfare |
| AEW | Airborne Early Warning |
| APC | Armoured Personnel Carrier |
| ASROC | Anti-Submarine Rockets |
| ASW | Anti-Submarine Warfare |
| CG | Guided-missile Cruiser |
| CGN | Nuclear-powered Guided-missile Cruiser |
| CIC | Combat Information Center |
| CIWS | Close-In Weapons System |
| COD | Carrier On-board Delivery |
| CODOG | Combined Diesel Or Gas turbine |
| CTOL | Conventional Take-Off and Landing |
| CV | Aircraft carrier |
| CVBG | Carrier Battle Group |
| CVN | Nuclear-powered aircraft carrier |
| DMZ | De-Militarized Zone |
| DP | Dual Purpose |
| ELINT | Electronic Intelligence |
| ECM | Electronic Counter-Measures |
| EW | Electronic Warfare |
| FAC | Fast Attack Aircraft |
| FF | Frigate |
| FFG | Guided-missile Frigate |
| FPB | Fast Patrol Boat |
| FRAM | Fleet Refit and Modernization |
| GP | General Purpose |
| GRP | Glass-Reinforced Plastic |
| LCAC | Landing Craft Air-Cushioned |
| LCC | Amphibious command ship |
| LCM | Landing Craft Medium |
| LCT | Landing Craft Tank |
| LCU | Landing Craft Utility |
| LCVP | Landing Craft Vehicle Personnel |
| LDM | Landing Dock Medium |
| LHA | Amphibious assault ship |
| LHD | Multi-purpose amphibious assault ship |
| LKA | Amphibious cargo ship |
| LPD | Landing Platform Dock |
| LSD | Landing Ship Dock |
| LSL | Landing Ship Logistic |
| LSM | Landing Ship Medium |
| LST | Landing Ship Tank |
| MCMV | Mine Counter-Measure Vessels |
| MR | Maritime Reconnaissance |
| MTB | Motor Torpedo Boat |
| NATO | North Atlantic Treat Organization |
| OTH | Over The Horizon |
| PHM | Patrol Hydrofoils |
| RAM | Radar Absorbent Material |
| SAG | Surface Action Group |
| SAM | Surface-to-Air Missile |
| SAR | Search-and-Rescue |
| SCS | Sea Control Ship |
| SEAL | Sea-Air-Land |
| SEATO | South-East Asia Treaty Organization |
| SLBM | Submarine-Launched Ballistic Missile |
| SLCM | Submarine-Launched Cruise Missile |
| SLEP | Service Life Extension Progam |
| SNLE-NG | Nuclear-powered ballistic missile submarine (French) |
| SRMH | Single-Role Mine-Hunters |
| SS | Diesel-electric patrol submarines |
| SSK | Diesel attack submarine |
| SSBN | Ballistic missile submarine |
| SSGN | Guided missile submarine |
| SSM | Ship-to-Ship Missile |
| SSN | Nuclear powered attack submarine |
| VLF | Very Low Frequency |
| V/STOL | Vertical/Short Take Off and Landing |